More Praise for *Healthy Living at the L*

"With enthusiasm, generosity, and a formidable knowledge base, Noah Lenstra makes the case for library promotion of public health and provides librarians much inspiration and practical advice. Health, wellness, nutrition, and movement programming and related activities, from serving summer meals to lending bikes, aren't mission-stretching add-ons; rather, they are intrinsic to the purpose of the library and tremendously beneficial to participants. A wide array of examples from libraries around the United States and worldwide demonstrate that library involvement makes healthy living practices accessible and inclusive while enhancing the library's role in the community."

—Janet Ingraham Dwyer, Library Consultant, State Library of Ohio

"*Healthy Living at the Library* provides a wealth of examples helpful for any size library to start or add to their healthy living initiatives. What sets this book apart is the perspective provided for each example. Readers are not told what should be done; rather, they are given a variety of perspectives from librarians around the world who have been doing the work for years now of integrating healthy living into their library's programming efforts. Librarians can then take the ideas and adapt them to suit their community's needs. As someone who has integrated a variety of health-related programming at a joint-use library (serving public patrons as well as college students), I found myself agreeing with the approaches offered on how to get started as well as jotting down additional ideas of how to move forward strategically with future efforts. This book will be invaluable for any librarian wishing to increase the health education opportunities of their community through library programming."

—Kendra Auberry, Librarian/Assistant Professor,
Indian River State College

"Libraries are natural partners in encouraging healthy living for our communities. Based on my positive experiences with Let's Move Museums and Gardens promoting healthy practices in cultural spaces, I am thrilled to see similar success in this exciting compilation of health-related activities in our libraries."

—Susan Hildreth, Former Director,
Institute of Museum and Library Services

"Implementing physical health and wellness programs at the library allow it to be a one-stop shop to meet the needs of the community; patron services can be enhanced by increasing literacy and health and wellness activities for patrons."

—Michelle Bennett-Copeland, Youth Services Manager/
Central Fulton County Library System

Healthy Living at the Library

Programs for All Ages

Noah Lenstra

LIBRARIES
UNLIMITED®
An Imprint of ABC-CLIO, LLC
Santa Barbara, California • Denver, Colorado

Copyright © 2020 by Noah Lenstra

Library of Congress Cataloging-in-Publication Data

Library of Congress Cataloging in Publication Control Number: 2020933791

ISBN: 978-1-4408-6314-1 (paperback)
        978-1-4408-6315-8 (ebook)

24 23 22 21 20   1 2 3 4 5

This book is also available as an eBook.

Libraries Unlimited
An Imprint of ABC-CLIO, LLC

ABC-CLIO, LLC
147 Castilian Drive
Santa Barbara, California 93117
www.abc-clio.com

This book is printed on acid-free paper ∞

Manufactured in the United States of America

Contents

Part I

Setting the Stage for Healthy Living at the Library

1

Introduction to Healthy Living at the Library

What factors cause one person to be healthier than another over time? Some things—genetics, for instance—are beyond our personal control, but little things we do throughout our daily lives can, over time, have huge impacts. This book gives you the tools you need to support healthy living at your library by developing programs and partnerships that will improve the choices, habits, and environments that together contribute to our overall health.

Since health is such a big—and frequently misunderstood—topic, let's start with a definition. According to public health researchers, "health means physical and mental health status and well-being, distinguished from health care" (Braveman et al. 2017, 3). This definition has since been incorporated into the planning framework for *Developing Healthy People 2030*, the action plan for the U.S. Office of Disease Prevention and Health Promotion. Why is this important? Because this book does not, for the most part, focus on the formal health-care sector. That is indeed an important topic, but here we are instead focused on healthy living practices and not on engagement with health care.

Medical professionals and policy makers urge us to make healthy living a conscious and deliberate part of our lives. That means making conscious and deliberate choices about how we move and how we eat. As we'll see below, eating and moving are educational acts. Librarians of all types answer this call to support the lifelong learning of healthy living habits by offering everything from StoryWalk® to cooking programs, and even Zumba breaks during academic finals. There is no **one way** to practice healthy living. There is no **one way** to promote healthy living at your library. This book will help you discover, develop, and implement **your** library's path.

How you support healthy living at your library will look at least slightly different from what every other library does. This heterogeneity is in fact what policy makers recommend. *Physical Activity Guidelines for Americans*, released by the Centers for Disease Control and Prevention (CDC) in September 2018 focuses on the idea that you should *Move Your Way*:

> Walk. Run. Dance. Play. What's your move?
> Everyone needs physical activity to stay healthy. But it can be hard to find the time in your busy routine. No matter who you are, you can find safe, fun ways to get active—to move your way. (U.S. HHS 2018, para. 1)

National recommendations for healthy eating are remarkably similar. The *Choose My Plate* initiative launched as part of the *Dietary Guidelines for Americans, 2015–2020*, focuses on the simple idea that healthful meals have a balance of vegetables, fruits, grains, protein, and dairy. This simple message replaces more complicated food pyramids and other eating restrictions. Instead, the idea is that the path to healthy eating is paved by "finding *your* healthy eating style and building it throughout your lifetime" (USDA 2019).

Move *your* way. Find *your* healthy eating style. Those who spend a lot of time thinking about healthy living and how to support it find that they need to make it *theirs*. Start now. Today. Yes, you. If you want to do healthy living programs at your library, you need to start with yourself (and your library, more generally—more on that later!).

I've been studying this topic during the vast majority of my waking hours since September 2016. In this work, I look for patterns in library programs oriented toward healthy living. I ask, How did this tiny library with no programming budget develop such an impactful healthy living program? And why is this library doing so much, while the library down the road is barely doing anything at all? This book is about those patterns. These findings have been field-tested at public health conferences and in dozens of presentations at state and national library conferences, in continuing education webinars, in blog posts written for the American Library Association, and in peer-reviewed academic articles, all of which can be accessed online if you'd like to dig deeper into anything covered in this book. Or just email me with questions: lenstra@uncg.edu! I'd love to hear from you. Consider this book as an invitation to join an ongoing conversation. Indeed, in chapter 7 we'll go over how to get involved in these discussions.

What I've found is that the librarians who are passionate about healthy living are the librarians who are championing and developing this programming area. After you've found *your* way to practice healthy living, you'll become passionate about helping your community members find *their* way. It's all about lifelong learning and providing access to experiences that have the power to change people's lives.

What Is Healthy Living? Some Key Definitions

The Free Library of Philadelphia (2017, 3) states that "cooking and eating are educational acts." Moving, sitting, and the methods by which we procure our food are also educational acts. What does this mean? Every day we decide, consciously or unconsciously, how to eat and how to move. Making changes in these habits is not easy, nor is it a trivial matter. Given our focus on supporting lifelong learning and literacy, librarians have a unique and critical role to play in the ecosystem of actors and institutions focused on creating a healthier society.

Let's back up, though. What exactly are we talking about when we talk about healthy living? The cornerstones are food and physical activity. According to the North Carolina Division of Public Health,

> **What Is Eating Smart?** The food we eat affects our physical and mental well-being. It is the fuel that keeps our bodies going. A healthy eating pattern can help prevent chronic diseases and conditions including obesity, heart disease, stroke, some cancers, diabetes, high blood pressure, arthritis, osteoporosis, and depression. Also, a balanced diet combined with physical activity helps achieve and maintain a healthy weight. Making healthy food choices does not need to be hard!
>
> **What Is Moving More?** Physical activity helps enhance the quality of life for people of all ages and abilities. People who participate in moderate physical activity on most days of the week are at a reduced risk of heart disease, diabetes, osteoporosis, and colon cancer. Physical activity also reduces heart disease risk factors such as high cholesterol, high blood pressure, and obesity and overweight. Physical activity can also protect against stroke. It helps build a healthier body by strengthening bones, muscles and joints, aids in reducing depression and anxiety, enhances the response of the immune system, and reduces falls among older adults. Physical activity doesn't need to be hard! People of all ages can benefit from participating in regular, moderate-intensity physical activity. (NCDPH 2011, 7)

For decades, it has been known that physical activity is "good for you." Historically, physical activity occurred as part of daily living, such as household chores and walking rather than driving. Furthermore, food tended to be scarce, and as such we could, more or less, eat what we wanted when we wanted because we didn't always know when the next meal would come.

Times have certainly changed. New technologies have replaced a more active way of living. We eat out more, and our food systems often exacerbate our worst tendencies by encouraging us to make unhealthy food choices for ourselves and for our families. Many of us now live in food deserts, where fresh produce is hard to access, as well as in food swamps, where fast and junk food (in abundant portion sizes) is ubiquitous. Healthy living can be a daily challenge.

The science is in, and most of us need to do a better job eating smart and moving more. According to the U.S. Centers for Disease Control and Prevention (2019),

> Poor nutrition and inadequate physical activity are significant risk factors for obesity and other chronic diseases, such as type 2 diabetes, heart disease, stroke, certain cancers, and *depression*. Fewer than 1 in 10 children and adults eat the recommended daily amount of vegetables. Only half of adults get the physical activity they need to help reduce and prevent chronic diseases, and more than 93 million have obesity. During 1999–2016, obesity prevalence increased from 31% to 40% for adults and from 13.9% to 18.5% for children. (NCCDPHP, CDC 2019, n.p., emphasis added)

I emphasize the word "depression" in the paragraph above, because I think this word is crucial. I want to hammer this point home: **programs focused on food and physical activity *are* mental health programs.** One of the biggest mistakes we make is thinking that our bodies are separate from our minds. How we move and how we eat have enormous consequences on our mental health, so if you're interested in providing mental health programs, this book will help you develop them.

We need to HEAL our communities through **H**ealthy **E**ating and **A**ctive **L**iving. Studies have consistently demonstrated that maintaining healthy eating and physical activity habits reduces risks for cardiovascular disease and improves mental health. Plus, if we're doing it right, **it's fun**! The World Health Organization (2019) estimates that unhealthy diet, physical inactivity, and tobacco use are responsible for 80 percent of all heart disease, stroke, and type-2 diabetes and for more than 40 percent of cancer cases. WHO goes on to state that although tobacco use has decreased in the Western world, **our unhealthy eating and moving habits have barely budged.** *These are the public health challenges of today.*

Wellness: A Key Concept

The idea of libraries supporting the health of the body directly challenges a lot of stereotypical ideas that people both inside and outside librarianship have about what libraries do. One of my biggest pet peeves is the idea that you go to the library to exercise your mind and you go to the gym to exercise your body. I can't tell you the number of times I've seen this old canard show up on social media over the last five years, and more often than not it is a librarian who is sharing it!

Can we please once and for all put this antiquated idea into the dustbin, where it belongs? Since the 1970s, "wellness," and related ideas like the "whole person," "integrative health," and "well-being," have become common in society, in medicine, and in librarianship (cf. National Center for Complementary and Integrative Health 2019). Prior to the emergence of these concepts, the dominant model was one in which different institutions addressed different facets of personhood: you go to the gym to exercise your body, to the library to exercise your mind, to counseling for mental therapy, and to home economics to learn about cooking, gardening, and meal planning. Due to the more recent concepts, however, boundaries blur and disintegrate. There is now more of an expectation that *all* institutions will do *something* to support all dimensions of wellness, even as some institutions specialize more in some dimensions than in others. There is, further, increased expectation for cross-sector collaboration to support healthy living and wellness.

At a policy level, this new conceptualization of health and wellness can be vividly seen in the World Health Organization's (2018a) *More Active People for a Healthier World: Global Action Plan on Physical Activity 2018–2030*, which challenges us to "be active: Everyone, everywhere, everyday." The key word here is "**everywhere**"!

A sign of the arrival of this idea into librarianship was Lisa J. Hinchliffe and Melissa M. Wong's 2010 article, "From Services-Centered to Student-Centered: A 'Wellness Wheel' Approach to Developing the Library as an Integrative Learning Commons," published in *College & Undergraduate Libraries*. They discuss how academic librarians can (and do) support the six dimensions of wellness—spiritual, intellectual, emotional, occupational, social, and physical—through programs that include yoga study breaks and walking challenges, among others.

In the context of wellness, or whole-person librarianship, the idea that you go one place to exercise your mind and another place to exercise your body is gobbledy-gook. We *all* have roles to play supporting *all* the dimensions of wellness. To truly create healthy communities, *we all need to work together*.

I want to close out this section by sharing some definitions developed by public health researchers, which I find especially useful for organizing our thoughts on this topic:

What is health? Health means physical and mental health status and well-being, distinguished from health care.

What is health equity? Health equity means that everyone has a fair and just opportunity to be as healthy as possible.

What is a healthy community? A healthy community is *a community where **all** individuals have access to the resources they need to live healthy lives.*

How do we achieve health equity, and thus healthy communities? Health equity can be viewed both as a process (the process of reducing disparities in health) and as an outcome (the ultimate goal: the elimination of social disparities in health).

What are the consequences of these definitions? Supporting healthy living at the library cannot be accomplished through a one-off program in which a doctor lectures about eating right. As anyone who has tried to make a life change (diet, exercise, etc.) knows, personal transformations do not take place overnight. Think of how much more complicated community transformations are. This book invites you to get your library into a healthy living ecosystem and then stay there. Join those fighting the good fight to support health equity. Few issues are more important.

Passion and Partnerships Lead to Healthy Living at the Library

How do librarians step up to support healthy living? What I've found can be boiled down to two concepts: passion and partnerships.

Personal passion for healthy living drives most of the programs I've observed over the years. More often than not, it all comes down to a librarian who's passionate about health and gung ho to share that passion with others. Passion also helps libraries over hurdles. As this programming area develops, challenges arise. The early adopters get past these growing pains by drawing upon reserves of personal passion. These gritty librarians solve the problems associated with this type of library programming.

Libraries participate in the Walk [Your City] Campaign by posting signs that indicate how far it is to the nearest library. Learn more at https://walkyourcity.org/.

A quick story illustrates this phenomenon. A librarian I know (whose name is not included out of respect for her personal privacy) is passionate about gardening, healthy eating, and healthy living more generally. Based on her passion for healthy living, she connected with other passionate people in her small town of five thousand, and one of those individuals offered to teach tai chi for free at the library. Later, another volunteer stepped up to offer free yoga classes. And a group of gardeners decided to work with the librarian to install a community garden in front of the library. These programs, which didn't cost the library a dime, were going well, inspiring healthy life changes, and building community. But then a risk manager from the county government caught wind of what was going on and went apoplectic. All he could see was lawsuits, and he shut down the classes.

But the librarian did not give up. After fighting internally in her system and doing more research, she developed waiver of liability forms and procedures that appeased the risk manager while still enabling her to offer these healthy living programs at no cost to her community. If she did not have this passion, this grit, it is unlikely she would have persevered. Her library became a community hub for healthy living, and it has been one for years now. Small children and their caregivers move and groove in weekly music and movement programs, individuals of all ages participate in the community garden on the library's lawn, adults join the library's walking and yoga clubs, and older adults practice tai chi and learn how to prevent falls in classes led by the area agency on aging.

These programs cost the library next to nothing. And that brings me to the second pillar of *Healthy Living at the Library*: partnerships. Supporting healthy living at the library is not about mission creep. It isn't about taking over for someone else. It *is* about being a valued, trusted member of your community or campus. It's about forming and sustaining community partnerships. In her book *Sustainable Thinking: Ensuring Your Library's Future in an Uncertain World*, Rebekkah Smith Aldrich, the director of New York's Mid-Hudson Library System states,

> There are dozens of beacons out there, libraries "doing it right," who are hardwired into their communities, truly working hand-in-hand with their neighbors to create a better world through library services, but not enough of them. . . . Our strength is in our understanding of how things work, who needs to work together to make things better, and the fact that our library is a platform for others to make good things happen. (Aldrich 2018, 5, 40)

This book shows you how to become that platform for healthy living. Too often I hear librarians tell me they wish they could partner with x, y, or z, to develop something innovative, but they just don't have the time. We need to turn that attitude inside-out to see the big picture. From that vantage point, we'll see that up-front investments in time will have enormous returns on investment for our libraries and for our communities. It is time to reach out.

Don't worry. You are not going to be thrown into the deep end. Through detailed examples of libraries "doing it right," as well as examples of the types of documents they use to scaffold this process (e.g., memorandums of understanding, assessment surveys, waivers of liability, strategic plans), you will be given the tools to make healthy living a core and integral dimension not only of your library's programming but of your library.

Book Overview

In this book we'll go over, step-by-step, how to start, run, and sustain healthy living programs. Part I highlights *why* and *how* libraries offer these programs, including a short history of this trend. Part II outlines steps librarians should take when starting programs. We'll highlight the **critical role of community partnerships**: you want to work with others who are as passionate about healthy living as you are about creating these programs. The section also articulates specific challenges or roadblocks that may arise and offers tips on how to overcome these difficulties.

The middle, and largest, section, Part III, includes detailed instructions for running different types of programs, beginning with adding healthy living to programs your library already offers. The instructions are simple enough to be used by everyone considering making these additions.

In Part IV, we'll wrap things up by going over how to sustain programs: How do you keep the momentum going and assess and communicate impacts? An appendix contains tried-and-true exemplars that you can use at your library to get programs off the ground, including waivers of liability and a memorandum of understanding.

Exercises

Think of the community your library serves, however you define it.

1. What obstacles to health equity do you see in this community?
2. Who is working in your community to make it a healthier place?
3. How does your library support healthy living?

Why Libraries? *Everyone* Has a Role to Play

In October 2018, the director-general of the World Health Organization issued a press release to all corners of the world. In it, Dr. Tedros Adhanom Ghebreyesus spoke in no uncertain terms about the importance of **all sectors of society** stepping up to increase physical activity:

> We must get the world moving. Increasing physical activity is not an issue that can be solved solely by the education sector, or the transport sector: actions are needed by all sectors. Our job is to create a world that will help our children to be active and make cities easier for people to walk and cycle. (WHO 2018b)

In my work, I talk a lot both with librarians and with folks who have not set foot in a library in decades. The latter often ask me, "Why libraries?" My typical response (depending on my level of surliness on a given day) goes something like this: "**Communities need help learning to live healthily, and libraries are trusted institutions open to all dedicated to lifelong learning.**" This statement **does not mean** you need to fix all your community's problems by yourself. What it **does mean** is that you need to get yourself and your library into the mix of institutions and individuals focused on increasing healthy living in your community. It does mean forming partnerships and leveraging those partnerships to bring healthy living programs to your library.

A lot of the mechanics of how to do this work have actually already been worked out. All we have to do is look at what has been going on in the faith-based sector for decades to see how trusted community institutions created for one purpose (in this case, spirituality) branch out to support other dimensions of personhood (i.e., healthy living). The late Thomas A. Droege, former director of the Interfaith Health Program at the Emory University School of Public Health, asked,

Why this interest in churches on the part of national health leaders? Because improvements in health, especially among at-risk populations, depend heavily on lifestyle changes and volunteer caregiving that can be promoted more readily by churches than by hospitals. People go to hospitals when they are sick, but when they are well, they congregate in churches. (1995, 117)

Now consider this section of the recent book *Palaces of the People: How Social Infrastructure Can Help Fight Inequality, Polarization, and the Decline of Civic Life*, written by sociologist Eric Klinenberg:

Libraries are not the kinds of institutions that most social scientists, policy-makers, and community leaders usually bring up when they discuss social capital and how to build it. But they offer something for everyone . . . and all of it for free. Doing research in New York City, I learned that . . . everyday life in libraries is a democratic experiment, and people cram into libraries to participate in it whenever the doors are open. (2018, 35)

See the similarities? Consider, further, how former first lady Michelle Obama described "faith-based and neighborhood organizations" in her Let's Move! campaign to raise a healthier generation of kids. Do you think the following passage mostly makes sense if we replace "faith-based and neighborhood organizations" with "libraries"? I do.

Leaders in faith communities and neighborhood organizations have a unique and critical role to play in ending childhood obesity and hunger. These organizations are trusted in their communities and can motivate people to take action. The neighborhoods we live in teach us about healthy behavior and shape many of the ways we see health and success. **Trusted** leaders and members of faith communities and neighborhood-based organizations can contribute valuable resources, including people, buildings, kitchens, and land, to projects that encourage children and their families to live healthier lifestyles. Leaders and members of congregations and community organizations—people like you—know their communities well and can communicate important health and nutrition information in motivating and effective ways. Solving the challenge of childhood obesity will take all of us—parents, faith-based and neighborhood organizations, state, local and tribal governments, schools and child care centers, health care facilities and businesses—working together. (U.S. HHS 2010, 9)

Just as health leaders have collaborated with church congregations to support healthy living for more than thirty years, so, too, are we beginning to see similar trends in librarianship today.

Consider this: The American Public Health Association (2019) states that the fourth–most read public health news story in their newsletter during 2018 was the article "Libraries, Public Health Work Together on Community Health."

Or this: the Robert Wood Johnson Foundation and RAND Health now see the presence of a public library as a measure of a community's health (Miller and Chandra 2018).

Or this: public health scholars from New York's Columbia University frame public libraries as "a community-level resource to advance population health" (Philbin et al. 2019), while faculty from the University of Pennsylvania's Family Medicine and Community Health program have, since 2015, worked on developing what they call the "Healthy Library Initiative," an evidence-based campaign "to establish the feasibility of partnering with public libraries to improve population health" (Whiteman et al. 2018).

In case you need them, here are five more reasons why libraries are the perfect places to promote healthy living through public programs:

1. **All institutions share responsibility for promoting healthy living**.
   We see this idea in initiatives like the World Health Organization's Let's Be Active! Everyone, Everywhere, Everyday; in former first lady Michelle Obama's Let's Move! campaign, and in the U.S. National Physical Activity Plan, which has sections on how everyone, from faith-based institutions to workplaces, needs to step up to promote healthy living. We *all* have a role to play.
2. **Libraries are the perfect partners in healthy living initiatives.**
   Regardless of size, budget, or type, libraries are trusted community institutions that provide access to relevant and reliable information, have community-convening capacity, and transform lives through learning. Our libraries are the perfect partners for healthy living initiatives. Working intentionally with local partners, libraries can connect patrons to the inspiration, information, and expertise needed to change lives and communities. Mutually beneficial relationships advance both the unique mission of the library and the health-specific missions of our partners.
3. **Cross-sector collaboration levels the playing field by extending access to all.**
   Not everyone has equal access to healthy living inspiration, information, and expertise. Partnerships between libraries and others address these disparities by providing inclusive access to healthy living programs. Intentional collaboration and shared understanding of needs and opportunities between community organizations mean a stronger, more responsive network to address the health of all community members. The perfect example is summer meals at the library. Here we see public libraries and public schools doing a handoff when the school year ends. Youth who depend upon free meals at school

during the year can now count on continuing to receive those meals (and great educational programming!) all summer long at the library.

4. **Libraries respond to the evolving needs of their communities.**
   Libraries will continue to be relevant and essential to their communities by proactively addressing the evolving needs of their communities. The long-term success and sustainability of public libraries rely on their active participation in community development, and community development is not possible in the context of ill health.

5. **Library programming is taking off, and health programming is part of it.**
   Not only is supporting healthy living at libraries through programs something that makes sense from a theoretical perspective but it is also something that our communities increasingly expect of us. The American Library Association states that "as US libraries transform . . . public programming is rising to the forefront of daily operations" (2017, 1). A 2018 systematic study of voter perceptions of public libraries finds "significantly more voters today (43%) describe the library as a place that 'offers activities and entertainment you can't find anywhere else in the community,' than did in 2008 (34%), and more believe this is an important role for a library (48% in 2018 vs. 38% in 2008)" (American Library Association 2018, 8). To support the growing prevalence of health programming, in April 2019, the Public Library Association released a new Project Outcome toolkit focused on assessing health programs in public libraries. Immediately, the survey was taken up and used by public librarians to measure the impacts of everything from exercise to healthy cooking classes.

My research also shows these programs have big impacts (Lenstra 2017). Based on a survey of 1,157 public libraries in the United States and Canada, libraries that offer these programs report:

- These programs bring new users to the library.
- These programs attract media attention.
- These programs build community.

This last outcome is particularly important. Healthy living programs have *more than* just individual impacts. Perhaps even more important are their community-building aspects. That outcome, too, contributes to increasing and sustaining healthy living.

Today, we in libraries are increasingly being asked to join local, regional, national, and international coalitions to support healthy living. It's time to roll up our sleeves and get to work alongside our partners. These public health leaders are turning to libraries for the same reasons they turned to church congregations thirty years ago: because they are the spaces where people (of all ages and backgrounds) go. This is true not only in public libraries but also in schools and universities, where we see our libraries becoming "learning commons," or spaces rich in learning opportunities and collaboration potentials.

Will it be easy? Not always. But if we embrace this trend, we can make a huge difference in community health. Discussing the development of fitness programming in British public libraries, Anne Goulding quotes a library director who, over a decade ago, said,

> When we began to provide [exercise classes] some of our residents did not approve of the noise and bustle they created. . . . But at the end of the day people came round to these ideas and they accepted them. I think you do have to take a bit of risk. (2009, 41–42)

More and more librarians are taking these risks, and they are reaping the results. Are you ready?

Making the Case for Healthy Living at the Library: The Philadelphia Story

This sidebar about how the Free Library of Philadelphia advocates for its Culinary Literacy Center, the first commercial-grade teaching kitchen located in a library in the world, illustrates how to explain why libraries support healthy living. The language used here to discuss food could easily be applied to physical activity. Think of the mathematics involved in counting steps, weight-lifting repetitions, and the geometry of motion and dance, as well as the cultural learning that takes place through engagement in different forms of sports, dance, and movement. Access the full toolkit from which these excerpts come at https://libwww.freelibrary.org/assets/pdf/programs /culinary/free-library-culinary-literacy-toolkit.pdf.

Advocacy: Making the Case for Culinary Literacy

Cooking is a vehicle for strengthening math skills. A plant-based diet can improve health. Using data to support the preceding statements can strengthen your proposal and help you get the support you need from your library's administration and board. To help make the case for how culinary literacy programming can advance literacy, improve community health, and support your library's mission, please consider the following benefits. By focusing on the multiple benefits of using food as a topic in programming, and how it connects to community health priorities, this library has successfully advocated for the creation and sustenance of this program for years.

Advancing Multiple Literacies

At the Culinary Literacy Center, we advance multiple literacies through cooking. In our Edible Alphabet class, students learn English in our kitchen classroom. Library users can read nutrition labels, mix math and cooking, and explore the science of cooking. There is also the importance of a community-based understanding of food literacy. Your program can guide learning about the hands that feed us, cultural foodways, environmentally sustainable eating, and food insecurity in your community. What will your visitors learn in your library's culinary literacy program?

Improving Community Health

The Pew Research Center's report, "Libraries at the Crossroads," found that library users "view public libraries as important resources for finding health information" and that "73% of all those ages 16 and over say libraries contribute to people finding the health information they need" (Horrigan 2015, 8). Find information about your community's health needs and let what you learn guide your programming. Look for government resources like the Centers for Disease Control and Prevention's *Nutrition, Physical Activity, and Obesity: Data, Trends and Maps*, which provides information about the health status and behaviors of Americans, state-by-state, via clickable maps, charts, and tables; and Eurostat's *Health in the European Union, Facts and Figures* that provide recent statistics on health in the European Union, focusing on areas like health status, health determinants, and health care. For a global perspective, explore the World Health Organization's *Nutrition Landscape Information System: The Global Nutrition Report* or the Institute for Health Metrics and Evaluation's website. Zoom in, if data is available, to look for local information about your community (Free Library of Philadelphia 2017).

Repurposing a card catalog for a seed library at the Richland Library in Columbia, South Carolina: an example of a library extending its mission to support healthy living in new ways.

Exercises

Imagine you are presenting to funders or administrators about healthy living at your library.

1. What language would you use to make the case for healthy living programs and partnerships?
2. What would you like to know more about, to feel comfortable making this case?
    a. Community demographics and health statistics?
    b. Things that other institutions and individuals are doing to support healthy living?
    c. The objections that your funders may have to this idea?
3. What steps can you take to address these issues?

History: It's Longer Than You Think!

A secret hidden in plain sight is the fact that public libraries were conceived as spaces to exercise both the body and the mind. Sue Halpern observes in the *New York Review of Books* that the mission of the very first Carnegie library "was to exercise both mind and body" (Halpern 2019, para. 12). To do so, the Braddock Library, in Pennsylvania, included a basketball court and a swimming pool. Around the dawn of the twentieth century, there were statewide movements to create hybrid library-gymnasiums in Utah, Illinois, and Ohio (Stauffer 2016). It's important to remember that in the early days of public librarianship, no one knew what these institutions would become. For instance, something as taken for granted as storytime would be completely foreign to the first generation of public librarians. Wayne Wiegand, the foremost living historian of U.S. public libraries, points out that "there is no Holy Book in which God tells us what libraries should be. Over the centuries, the contours of library services and collections have instead been mediated by humans, including founders, funders, managers and—surprise, surprise—users" (2017, 39).

Wiegand discovered that early public libraries included bowling lanes, among other recreational accoutrements. Similar tendencies are evident in the United Kingdom. There, historian Robert Snape (1995) convincingly argues that these recreational tendencies were snuffed out by library leaders who wished to convey a more noble (read: mind-focused) idea of the library.

But the body never went away, and libraries never stopped supporting healthy bodies. In his book, *Planning Public Library Buildings: Concepts and Issues for the Librarian*, British scholar Michael Dewe notes that "the linking of libraries with some unlikely companions . . . has continued in the last 50 years or so, with libraries—usually branch libraries—built in conjunction with, for example, sports facilities, a swimming pool, health centres or clinics" (2016, 112).

In the United States, libraries have had various forms of community gardens on their properties for decades. This trend accelerated during World

Healthy living at the Roanoke Library in Virginia: a slide in the middle of the main library.

War II, when libraries across the country started growing victory gardens on their lawns. A San Bernardino County librarian recalled that at her library, they grew a large selection of herbs and salad vegetables. Those who worked in the garden got to take home produce for free. Others could buy surplus. Another librarian told scholar Cindy Mediavilla, "It was a fairly common sight . . . to see librarians in Levis and other suitable garb at work on their spring garden in the library's back yard" (Banks and Mediavilla 2019, 4). In addition to supporting community-based agriculture, during World War II librarians offered a variety of "programs on how to grow and preserve food" (Banks and Mediavilla 2019, 4). Although many of these gardens and programs ended after the war ended, some continued on, creating a precedent for the profusion of library-based community-gardens now popping up across the United States and beyond.

Collaborations between public libraries and health professionals have also occurred for decades. Ellen L. Rubenstein (2012) found in her research that during the 1940s, a bookmobile traveled throughout rural, Appalachian Georgia, with a nurse onboard who provided communities with vital health-care services to which these communities would not otherwise have had access.

Across the decades, active living programming has also been a mainstay in libraries. In Newark, New Jersey, in the 1950s one of the stated learning outcomes of the library's story hour was "learning dances" (Albright, Delecki, and Hinkle 2009, 14). And it wasn't just children dancing in the library. In 1971 the Copperas Cove Public Library outside of Waco, Texas, started hosting the Double C's Square Dance Club. Every week from 1971 to the present, this club has hosted free weekly dance classes at the library, as well as free monthly square dances (Ferraro 2018).

The very first handbook on *Library Programs: How to Select, Plan and Produce Them*, published by New York public librarians John S. Robotham and Lydia LaFleur, in 1976, features an entire section on "dance" programs. The authors note that

> sometimes a program demonstrating dances will end with the audience being urged to participate. And dances are held in libraries just to have a dance. That most frequently happens with young adult programs, and it seems to be worldwide. A library in Sweden held a dance as part of a Sunday evening youth program. A German library had "dancing among the bookshelves." . . . The Plainfield (N.J.) Public Library held a square dance for children and their parents, and a library in New York City presented a "Funky House Review," at which the audience was invited to dance to the music of a number of local groups. . . . Belly dancing demonstrations have been big in recent years. At this writing, disco dancing is the "thing" and libraries are having workshops on the subject. (1976, 72)

Later in the book they note that "participants probably had fun at a tap dancing workshop that a library held one Friday evening. It was taught by a professional dancer from a local dance school. Registration was limited to 60 persons over 16, and they were advised to wear comfortable clothes and leather soled shoes" (Robotham and LaFleur 1976, 113).

They go on to note that "to celebrate anniversaries, or other events, or for no reason at all, libraries sometimes have a kind of carnival, that is, a number of activities going on at the same time, usually throughout the library. The Port Washington (N.Y.) Public Library, for example, has a yearly 'Happening.' The idea is to have a 'summer party,' with a 'very festive atmosphere,' so that everybody can just have a good time. . . . The evening wound up with disco dancing. . . . A branch of the Milwaukee (Wisc.) Public Library celebrated its 25th anniversary by looking back to the 1950's. . . . At the library they could listen to the music of the fifties, ride unicycles or pogo sticks" (207–8). As we'll see, embracing the power of play in this way is one of the most effective ways to promote healthy living in library programs, and this idea has a *long* history.

Around the same time, D. W. Davies argued, in 1974's *Public Libraries as Culture and Social Centers: The Origin of the Concept*, that "though libraries are seldom equipped with gymnasium equipment . . . perhaps they should be, for judo and karate exhibitions have become common . . . and in some instances libraries offer judo lessons" (1974, 108).

Robotham and LaFleur also highlighted the growing tendency for libraries to offer food and nutrition programs in the 1970s. Their handbook includes a section on health programs and notes that "good health is essential . . . and library workshops are covering this ground, too." They highlight programs focused on "nutrition, including food preparation and storage" (1976, 108) and the fact that the Prince George's County Library in Maryland offered in the 1970s "a cooking contest," in which "the judges and prizes came from restaurants, 4-H clubs, Campfire Girls and Boy and Girl Scouts" (1976, 205).

My own research has revealed that the history of these programs is much deeper than most realize. When I first started digging into this trend, I did what scholars do and conducted a literature review. I found in the *Wilson Library Quarterly* an article from March 1994 titled "Sweat and Self- Esteem: A Public Library Supports Young Women" (Quatrella and Blosveren 1994) about how and why the Stratford Library in Connecticut started a hybrid healthy living support group/aerobics class at the library. From then to now, this trend has only accelerated. As my research continued, I kept finding more and more examples like this one. In Spring 2019 I invited public librarians who offered physical activity programs for older adults to tell me for how long they had offered such programs. One librarian responded that they have been offering yoga at their library for over thirty years.

Propelling this trend forward has been increasing interest over the last fifty years in the public health and consumer health roles of libraries. This interest dates back to the late nineteenth century (Rubenstein 2012), but has accelerated in recent years. Today, health librarians provide more than reference services. They work with partners to offer immersive health classes and programs for all ages. These programs include everything from cooking and healthy eating classes to Zumba to storytimes that incorporate physical activity (Flaherty 2018). The common trend in these health programs is a focus on increasing healthy living practices and knowledge among participants.

Too many of us have internalized that most egregious and inaccurate stereotypes about libraries and librarians, namely, that we are exclusively quiet, bookish places or people focused only on the mind. We need to see our true history for what it is and recognize that although the healthy living at the library trend may be accelerating in the present, it is certainly nothing outside of our historical wheelhouse.

Academic and School Libraries Step Up to Support Healthy Living

We've talked a lot about public libraries, but what about academic and school libraries? In fact, support for healthy living has been growing in academic libraries since at least the early 2000s. On the vanguard was Goucher College in Towson, Maryland, where administrative documents reveal that as early as 2002, librarians discussed including a yoga /stretch/dance/contemplation space in their new library. When it finally opened in 2009, the library included a cardio room for students, with ellipticals, exercise bikes, and rowing machines. Asked why he thought the library needed such a space, Goucher president Sanford J. Ungar said, "I think that if we are going to have a place where you can do everything, exercise should be part of it" (Carlson 2009). In her study on the evolution of this new library, Cunningham interviewed a user services librarian who stated that "the idea was to give students a reason to be in the library a long time" (2012, 45) and that is precisely what happened. More students have spent more time in the library since the renovations occurred.

In law libraries, there is some evidence that the trend goes back at least to the 1930s. Aiken, Cadmus, and Shapiro (2018) found that "Lewis Morse, a Cornell Law Librarian, introduced a squash court to the law library in the 1930s. An avid squash player, he believed a squash court to be as important to legal education as a moot court room. He considered the physical fitness of the students essential for their mental alertness and acuity. Due to this unique library asset, the Circulation Desk at one time provided students with both treatises and towels" (19). The squash court in the Cornell Law Library continues to be used to this day.

In school libraries, a lot of the same trends seen in youth services in public libraries can be observed—for example, dancing programs in an elementary school library. More recently, growing numbers of school libraries have started offering yoga programs and, like Goucher College, active study spaces. The history of this trend has yet to be written.

Recent Trends

The past decade has only seen this trend expand. A few signposts of this expansion include the following national initiatives:

- 2007: The American Library Association's focus on workplace wellness
- 2010: The Urban Libraries Council's awards for health and wellness in public libraries
- 2013: OCLC/WebJunction's Health Happens in Libraries, funded by the IMLS
- 2014: Surveying health programs in the Digital Inclusion Survey
- 2017: The Public Library Association's collaboration with the National Network of Libraries of Medicine

ALA Embraces Workplace Wellness

During the presidency of Loriene Roy (2007–2008), the American Library Association focused on promoting wellness among librarians. Through this and subsequent initiatives, such as the 2012 Workplace Wellness@Your Library Symposium, the ALA has helped bring awareness of wellness and its importance to the discourse of librarianship. More recently, during the presidency of Loida Garcia-Febo (2018–2019), the ALA launched the Presidential Citation for Wellness in the Workplace, with the inaugural award going to the Richland Library, in Columbia, South Carolina. Learn more at: http://ala-apa .org/wellness.

Urban Libraries Council

Susan Benton, president and CEO of the Urban Libraries Council, has attributed the growth of healthy living programming in public libraries since 2005 to the fact that "there are some communities where childhood or adult obesity is a real issue" (Mulholland 2011). Under her leadership, the Urban Libraries Council has recognized libraries that have developed healthy living programming in annual awards distributed since 2010. The ULC has given its top health innovator award to

- The Biblio Bistro, at San Francisco Public Library, "a mobile, librarian-staffed cooking cart, [which] offers demonstrations and classes to makes the connection between self-prepared meals and wellness, and offers lifelong skills to the community" (San Francisco Public Library 2016).
- BCLFit Wellness Centers, at Broward County Library, in Florida, "to provide access to a more active lifestyle. BCLFit provides nutrition/fitness counseling and free workout equipment/classes for all ages designed to improve health and wellness" (Broward County Library 2018).
- Bikes, Buildings and Broccoli, at the Arlington, Virginia, Public Library, which fosters healthy living "through programming, art, gardens, bikes, LEED certification, energy upgrades, collections, classes and partnerships" (Arlington Public Library 2012).
- A teen nutrition program at San Antonio Public Library: by partnering with the San Antonio Food Bank, the library "received the guidance and resources to develop a nutrition program for teens within the Library itself" (San Antonio Public Library 2012).
- Healthy L.I.F.E. (Literacy Initiative for Everyone), at the Houston Public Library, "an innovative health-based library literacy initiative designed to educate low-income youth and their families about the benefits of healthy eating and physical activity" (Houston Public Library 2014).
- Salt Lake County Library Services' Sustainability Initiative, which includes "piloting an employee gardening space. The project kicked off with an

open-house and almost 30 percent of the staff members expressed an interest to participate" (Salt Lake County Library Services 2014).

- A refugee health fair, at the Pima County Public Library, in Tucson, Arizona.
- A Read and Feed Garden and Seed Library, at the Sacramento Public Library.

Learn more about these and more than one hundred other healthy living innovators in libraries at https://www.urbanlibraries.org/innovations.

Health Happens in Libraries

In 2013, OCLC/WebJunction received funding from the U.S. Institute of Museum and Library Services (IMLS) to develop Health Happens in Libraries. The project initially focused on preparing public libraries to help patrons navigate the Affordable Care Act. Over time its focus widened to promote fitness, nutrition, health fairs, and other healthy living programming. One product of the initiative was the "Library Heroes Make Health Happen" infographic, which highlights the many ways libraries support healthy living. WebJunction continues to support the initiative, particularly around food insecurity and the library response to the opioid crisis. Learn more at https://www.webjunction.org/explore-topics/ehealth.html.

Surveying Health Programs in the Digital Inclusion Survey

A turning point in our understanding of the trend came in 2014, when researchers from the University of Maryland, in partnership with ALA, asked, for the first time ever, What types of health programs do American public libraries offer? They found that 22.7 percent, or 3,784 public libraries, had offered fitness classes, such as Zumba, yoga, or tai chi; 18.1 percent had brought in health-care providers to offer limited health-care screenings, such as weigh-ins and blood pressure tests; and 48.1 percent had offered programs focused on understanding specific health or wellness topics, such as how to develop a healthy lifestyle or manage a health condition or disease. For the first time, we had unambiguous proof that libraries support healthy living through new and innovative programming. Learn more at: https://digitalinclusion.umd.edu/content/2014-survey-results-and-reports.

The Public Library Association's Collaboration with the National Network of Libraries of Medicine

In 2016 ALA staff convened a focus group on health services in public libraries at the biennial meeting of the Public Library Association. They asked public librarians, What is your library doing to improve health in the community? and the responses they received included "Zumba for kids ages four to twelve run by library staff," "pilates services for the public once a week," "meeting room set up for staff to do yoga and a walking exercise program," "exercise equipment can be checked out," and "library provides physically active story-times at Head Start locations" (Public Library Association 2016, 4). Based on these trends, in October 2017, the ALA Libraries Transform initiative released a Health Literacy Toolkit that featured ideas for how to incorporate healthy living into health programs. The toolkit advocated for yoga, walking, gardening, and general exercise classes in public libraries. These efforts morphed into the PLA Promoting Healthy Communities initiative, a collaboration with the National Network of Libraries of Medicine (NNLM). I am honored to serve in the initiative's advisory group. This unprecedented effort has led to numerous initiatives and continuing education sessions, including modules focused on helping libraries develop healthy living programs. The collaboration culminated in April 2019 with the release of the first national toolkit to assess the outcomes of healthy living programming in public libraries. Learn more at http://www.ala.org/pla/initiatives/healthliteracy.

Healthy Ireland at Your Library

This is by no means an American (or even North American) trend. For definitive proof, just look across the pond to Ireland, where, a few years ago, the national library started Healthy Ireland at Your Library. Imagine the U.S. Department of Health teaming up with the IMLS. That is essentially what is happening in Ireland, and it is amazing! The initiative focuses on "improving the health, wellbeing, and overall quality of life of communities and individuals at all life stages." Through this effort, libraries across Ireland have been able to launch health fairs, do programs on cyberbullying, bring in personal trainers to help people make and implement exercise and nutrition goals, organize walking clubs, teach yoga, have cooking classes focused on diabetes prevention, and so much more. I can't recommend this effort enough. Learn more at https://www.librariesireland.ie/services/healthy-ireland-at-your-library.

All these national efforts only begin to scratch the surface. The real innovation, in my humble opinion, takes place first in the local community. If you think these initiatives are innovative, wait until we drill down into what is happening in specific places. Just to whet your appetite, at least *two* public libraries now have climbing walls for children (Nashville Public Library and the Free Library of Philadelphia), and things only get more exciting from there. Buckle up and get ready to go on a journey you'll never forget!

Exercises

1. What is the history of healthy living programming, if any, at your library?
2. Have you learned about this topic in library school or later, in continuing education?
3. How do you conceptualize healthy living within the history of librarianship?
4. Write down three or more reflections about how the information presented in this chapter alters your understanding of the roles and responsibilities of librarians in the promotion of healthy living.

4

How Do We Do This? Partnerships Extend Access to Healthy Living Opportunities

One of the most remarkable aspects of my work has been discovering that librarians have organized programs around virtually every form of healthy living activity you can imagine. I've found libraries that have offered introductions to CrossFit, Parkour, Capoeira, Jazzercise, ballet, skateboarding, snowshoeing, and countless other forms of moving, plus cooking programs on everything from making healthy albóndigas to getting started with juicing to learning how to cut meat. Nora Armstrong, of the Cumberland County Public Library, in Fayetteville, North Carolina, told me she is willing to try almost anything once. You don't know what is going to resonate with your community until you've given it a shot.

How are librarians doing all of this? By and large, we're not leading all these programs by ourselves. Instead, we are teaming up with partners to extend access to learning opportunities focused on healthy living.

Based on everything I've learned, here are my . . .

Ten Steps to Healthy Living at the Library

1. **Talk about the importance of healthy living to anyone who will listen.** That includes your colleagues, your funders, and your patrons. Use what you've read in chapters 1 through 3 as a guide.

2. **Identify a Healthy Living program coordinator at your library.** Some libraries (e.g., Kansas City, Missouri; Nashville, Tennessee; Harker Heights, Texas) have designated staff responsible for healthy living programs. Most libraries do not have that luxury, so think about who will be the point person (probably you!) for healthy living at your library.

3. **Start a Healthy Living at the Library campaign.** By branding this initiative, you let potential partners know your library is ready to get involved. Some libraries already do this by using things like WebJunction's Health Happens in Libraries logo on their flyers or by using the health literacy toolkit developed by the American Library Association. Some have even started using the Let's Move in Libraries logo that I developed. The main thing is to make sure potential partners and patrons know you're making healthy living a priority at your library.

4. **Build financial support.** Do you have any money you can use? A great starting point is your Friends of the Library group. Many libraries turn to their Friends for help starting new programming initiatives. Could you work with your Friends to develop funding for your programs? Think about organizing a special fundraiser, such as a Bookin' It 5K, to fund your healthy living programs.

5. **Assess your community and its members.** A great way to test the waters is to actually offer a specific type of program, perhaps a health or how-to fair that consists of a smorgasbord of healthy living opportunities. You can use these events as opportunities to build partnerships, build your coalition, and see what really pulls in your community.

6. **Develop a program/partnership plan.** You can't do it all. No library could possibly do *all* the programs covered in this book. Think about what you're passionate about, what your partners are passionate about, and what your community is interested in, and start there. Your plan could focus on a particular program you want to offer *or* it could focus on a particular partner. This is a chicken-versus-egg situation; both approaches are valid and have proven to work.

7. **Implement your plan.** As we'll see below, expect challenges. The good news is that a lot of early adopters have worked out many of the kinks. Nonetheless, the goal is *not* for everything to work perfectly the first time but instead to embrace the idea of failing fast. Quickly identify when something isn't working, learn from it, and then rapidly move on to something better.

8. **Evaluate your programs.** There have never been more tools to assess healthy living programs in libraries. Learn what these tools include, and start to apply them to document and communicate the impacts of your programs.

9. **Celebrate!** Make sure to rejoice over wins both big and small. Make sure those in positions of power know about the differences you are making!

10. **Plan future programs.** Don't stop, keep things going, expand. We have a lot of work to do before we achieve the goal of equitable, healthy communities, and libraries have a big opportunity to make a huge difference.

The Let's Move in Libraries Collection at the public library in Gorham, Maine. An example of a library tying its efforts to promote healthy living to national and international initiatives.

Here are a few inspiring stories to help carry you along your path.

In the small town of Crandon, Wisconsin (pop. 1,920), library director Michelle Gobert was invited in 2011 to participate in her county health department's five-year strategic planning process. As a result of that initial partnership, all kinds of things started taking place. The library actually organized a community fun run to support healthy living, and then it did an Iron Chef: Healthy Fruits and Vegetables Edition program that involved teaching cooking skills and a fun competition to see which families could make the best-tasting dishes using fresh produce.

Gobert said, "Partnering with our local health department on specific initiatives has made a huge impact within our community. The library is now seen as a community partner. It has allowed us to be part of the conversation and therefore part of the solution" (Monaghan 2016).

This is what our libraries are becoming: part of the public health conversation and therefore part of the solution. In the urban United States, perhaps no one has adopted this ethos so thoroughly as the Nashville Public Library. Since 2015, the library has had a Be Well at NPL campaign managed by a public health professional. The yoga, Zumba, nutrition, meditation, and other programs offered through this campaign have been particularly impactful in the lives of older adults. For eighty-nine-year-old Dean Stevens, the free yoga class she attends weekly at the library has given her a newfound stability she says her peers are often lacking: "So many of my friends are falling," she explains. "I almost fell in the strawberry patch the other day, but because I have better flexibility and control over my body, I was able to recover. And that's because of yoga" (Brantley 2017).

As in Wisconsin, this library's ability to offer health programs depends upon a robust array of local, regional, and national partnerships. Locally, the library teamed up with a yoga studio, among many other community partners. Regionally, the library teamed up with Blue Cross Blue Shield of Tennessee, whose foundation was thrilled to support healthy living at the library as part of its commitment to preventive health. Nationally, the library partnered with the National Institutes of Health and their All of Us campaign, which seeks to establish and confirm the reputation of public libraries as sites that support health literacy for all through engaging community programs.

Libraries across the country have jumped on the healthy living bandwagon, with at least twenty-five now checking out bicycles from the library (Lenstra 2018a). The most recent library to join this national movement, as of this writing, is the Lorain Public Library System (2019), whose bike share launched May 18, 2019, in partnership with Lorain County Public Health, Lorain County Metro Parks, and the Lorain County Community Action Agency. Libraries are similarly stepping up to ensure that food-insecure children have access to meals throughout the summer. In fact, approximately 10 percent of the Ohio and California sites that participate in the U.S. Department of Agriculture's Summer Food Program are public libraries (Team Vittles 2018).

We offer things like bicycles, summer meals, yoga, and cooking classes because we recognize that many in our community would not otherwise have *access* to these lifelong learning opportunities. Our partners in these endeavors include everyone from public health departments to yoga studios to bike shops and more. I would be remiss not to recommend to any U.S. library a membership in the National Network of Libraries of Medicine (NNLM). It is free to join, and you get access to continuing-education resources and funding opportunities that you can use to improve health in your community.

What this book gives you is the tools, resources, networks, and templates you need to work with partners in your community to increase healthy living through fun, engaging programs and initiatives. *Now* is the time to take action to support community health.

By working with partners, you'll be able to introduce your community to numerous and diverse opportunities to practice healthy living in day-to-day life. There is no *one way* to practice healthy living. Offering a variety of programs—from exercise classes to demonstrations on healthy meal preparation—will ensure that audiences with different interests are reached. Libraries support healthy living by varying program formats (e.g., workshops, exercises, stories/performances, etc.) to accommodate diverse health needs and to endorse the library's role as an advocate for healthy lifestyles.

Inclusive programming is vital, to ensure the health needs of different ethnic and age groups are well considered and covered. Don't just offer one type of health program over and over again. Mix it up, and try something new. The health programming offered at San Jose Public Library includes everything from nutrition workshops to vision screenings to an annual bike tour of the branches to yoga classes. Different things appeal to different audiences. To have a big impact, you need to know your community, and your partners can help you do that. You may find that there are groups and organizations in your community that spend all day thinking about health needs in the local community. They can help you develop programming tailored to the unique needs of your area. The San Jose Public Library strives to tailor health programming to the unique cultures of the local community, and "one of the most frequently offered programs was Mexican Folkloric Dancing Class, which corresponds with the high percentage of Hispanic population in the community served by" (Luo 2018, 242) the library.

By offering partnership-based, community-driven healthy living programming, we change perceptions of libraries in a good way. We can embrace our role as "Health Heroes," as WebJunction puts it, connecting the trusted library image with the global movement toward building equitable, healthy communities. By becoming team players, we increase our value and thus our sustainability in the communities we serve.

By showing up when our partners call on us, we demonstrate our value. In addition to partnering with other groups to develop programs offered at the library, librarians also actively participate in local health initiatives. The "San Jose Public Library not only engaged community partners in providing workshops, leading exercises and offering services at the library, but also actively participated as a partner in community-wide health initiatives such as supporting Bike to Work day in the Bay Area (the library invited people to pick up a free Bike to Work bag on that day, and encouraged the public to read more about bicycles and biking by noting relevant library resources in the program announcement)" (Luo 2018, 242).

In other words, to strengthen partnerships, *we need to give as well as get*. Remember this in your work: it isn't only about what programs you can get out of your partners; it's also about how the library can be a good partner in regional health campaigns and initiatives. This, too, is part of how libraries support healthy living.

Exercises

1. Have you or your library undertaken any new initiatives within the last decade? How have those gone?
2. What lessons learned, if any, can you apply to support healthy living at the library?
3. What has been your experience working with external partners around programming or around other initiatives at your library?

Part II

Starting Programs

5

Look Inward:
Healthy Libraries Create
Healthy Programs

Part II focuses on the steps you need to take to get healthy living programs going at your library. This programming area requires a bit of internal development before it is ready for prime time.

To get started, you'll have the opportunity to make changes that will improve healthy living at your workplace, form new community partnerships, and connect with librarians as passionate about healthy living as you are. In this chapter, we'll go over how internal actions lead to external programs: Learn how to work with your library team (including staff, volunteers, board, Friends, and others) to get your library ready to offer healthy living programs. In chapter 6, we'll focus on doing this process with external partners. In chapter 7, we'll expand to the broader library community. We're all in this together, so let's figure it out together! Part II concludes, in chapter 8, with a brief description of common challenges associated with this type of programming, focusing on logistical challenges, safety concerns, theoretical issues (e.g., Why is the library doing this?), and how to make your programs as accessible as possible.

If you're reading this book, you are probably excited about healthy living. People like you tend to be the people driving this programming trend. We are not necessarily all the healthiest people, but we are the people who have decided to make healthy living a priority in our lives, in our family's lives, and in our communities. In conversations with librarians across North America, I found over and over that library staff who develop healthy living programs are library staff with deep personal interests in nutrition, fitness, and healthy living more generally.

When I reached out to the Durham County Library in North Carolina in 2016 to ask about their health and wellness programming, director Tammy Baggett referred me to Stephanie Fennell, then an adult services manager and now a branch manager. I asked Stephanie how she got started with this programming, and this was her response:

> I started working part-time in the library in 2007, full-time in 2008. It was explained to me by my manager that it was a requirement to do programming. My manager suggested doing programming based on your interests, so I have always done active-related programming. One of the first programs that I did was . . . ballroom dancing. It initially focused on seniors and then opened up to everyone. The library is [also] the perfect place for yoga because everything is free and open. It's a great way to introduce people to something new. (Lenstra 2018e, 151)

Over the years, Stephanie has developed cooking classes, aromatherapy, dancing, yoga, Zumba, tai chi, fitness games, music and movement, bike rodeos, free fitness days, and so much more. Her latest project involves creating a fitness class for amputees, whom she discovered find it difficult to exercise in more conventional fitness and recreation centers. She's developing these classes with funding from the National Institutes of Health. Being able to develop programs around her passion for healthy living enabled Stephanie to focus her library career, at least in part, around this passion.

I heard similar stories from nearly everyone I interviewed. A librarian who started an annual 5K fun run told me, "We have some runners here on staff, and I am a runner myself, so we thought it would be fun." A librarian with expertise in agriculture started a community garden and a seed exchange at her library. Librarians who love to cook start cooking classes. There are so many of us that we've started to band together in online communities. There are online groups dedicated to librarians who run, librarians who lift, and biking librarians. I don't know of a librarians who garden or librarians who cook group, but those would definitely fill an important niche. We need to nurture our healthy living passions, support and grow them through continuing education, and then share what we've learned within our communities. You don't need to be the expert. Research shows that peer coaches can be *more effective* educators than experts. So dive in and learn with and alongside your coworkers and community members.

A Shared Journey to Better Health at the Dee Brown Library

Note: Harlem Wilson is the assistant branch manager of the Dee Brown Library in Little Rock, Arkansas. This article was written by Rosslyn Elliott about how Harlem's journey to healthy living intersected and overlapped with his library's and his community's journey. Throughout *Healthy Living at the Library*, you'll see references to an online supplement to this monograph. Go to http://letsmovelibraries.org/healthy-living-at-the-library to access additional photographs associated with this story, including pictures of librarian Harlem Wilson leading free fitness classes at the Dee Brown Library, a branch of the Central Arkansas Library System.

"C'mon! You ain't gonna get this at Big Fitness! They're gonna charge you fifty dollars!"

Harlem, our library fitness coach, sounds like a pro. He yells encouragement and funny comments to keep the class moving and happy. It's working. Everybody is smiling, sassy, out of breath, or all three.

We follow him across the yard outside the Dee Brown Library to start some simple strength and cardio moves. Some of us are faster, some slower. Our class is diverse, including a ten-year-old girl, young adults, and middle aged folks. All are welcome. Harlem will help everybody take the exercises at the right pace.

"I do it my way, you do it your way, but we're gonna get it done!" When he says it, we believe him. We step a little faster.

A Fitness Success Story Leads to a Passion for Helping Others

To look at Harlem Wilson, no one would ever know that he had once struggled with health issues.

Now, he looks like a weightlifter, with huge biceps and the kind of healthy glow that only comes from regular exercise. When he teaches "Harlem's Boot Camp," he lifts 30 pounds for curls while the rest of us lift our one- or two-pound weights.

The Dee Brown Library of the Central Arkansas Library System also offers immersive cooking and walking programs as part of its commitment to supporting healthy living both among library staff and library patrons. Used with permission from Rosslyn Elliott, Central Arkansas Library System.

A Saturday morning fitness class is a unique contribution from a man who also happens to be the Assistant Branch Manager of the library, but Harlem's personal history motivates him to help.

"I started working out five years ago when I weighed 364," Harlem says. "I knew I had to do something different. I didn't want the health problems that were coming. So I started my own workouts for 30 minutes, 3 times a week. About a year and a half in, I had dropped 130 pounds."

Harlem's dedication to helping others is energizing, and it comes through in every minute of his class. "I want to share what I've learned," he says. "It's just something to help you feel better."

Like all the other health and fitness offerings at the Dee Brown Library, Harlem's class is free. And we get to do it together, for mutual support.

In a world where many of us spend hours sitting at desks, health and fitness are more important than ever. It can be hard to find the time to work out, and gyms with trainers are expensive. In what can feel like an uphill battle to stay healthy, support from other people helps us stay motivated.

Those encouraging people are on staff at the Dee Brown Library. This CALS branch offers a number of health-oriented classes free of charge to the community, including Harlem's Boot Camp, cooking and nutrition classes, and a walking group.

Cooking and Nutrition Class from an Expert, Served with a Side of Hospitality

This Saturday, the cooking class begins one hour after we finish Harlem's Boot Camp. Samantha Toro, our instructor, has years of experience in nutrition and cooking education, having worked for several major organizations that offer similar community programs. Her expertise shows when she teaches the "Jams and Jellies" class. Her instructions are lucid, and when a class member asks whether a recipe can be altered for a diabetic diet, she knows exactly how to answer to ensure food safety.

Samantha's class shows the polish and depth brought by a true professional in the field. All the ingredients are set out neatly. She explains how the canning process works. With her knowledge and poise, combined with the well-equipped teaching kitchen in the library, we might as well have walked into a cooking show.

Attendees will often get to take home samples of their own work. The previous class in this series was about pickling, and there is a mouth-watering jar of pickles waiting for one of our class members.

Class is interactive. We gather around the steaming pots, pouring in the colorful ingredients, having fun slicing and mashing things up. There is a feeling of togetherness in the air. It's the magic of food, the ancient ritual of coming together to make something delicious that also sustains life. We all need this kind of community, but many of us don't experience it often, either because we are too busy to cook with others or because we live alone. But here it is, the gift of group hospitality, an unexpected and welcome benefit of cooking class.

Walking Group Takes Pleasant Steps toward More Energy and Well-Being

Walking has been popular as a gentle route to fitness for years. Many people who have other physical limitations can still walk. With some company and conversation, a walking club makes exercise feel a lot easier.

Karen Guthrie, Adult Programmer, started the Dee Brown Library's Walking Group, which currently walks at 6:00 p.m. three times a week.

"Dee Brown Library is fortunate to have a lovely park right here as part of our SWLR community center complex," Karen says. "Amazingly, walkers often tell me they didn't know it was here until they joined our walking group."

The sidewalk winds through trees, surprisingly private and peaceful here only yards from the library. Karen's three dogs trundle around on the ends of their leashes, sniffing the edges of the path. The walkers share stories, talk about mutual interests, and exchange information about new local discoveries. Before long, we've finished our trails and covered three miles at a rate everyone could handle.

"My goal is to enhance the lives of our community members," Karen says. "And the walking group is one way to do that."

We can see as we walk that Karen's community knows and loves her. A young teen bikes by, gripping the handlebars with one hand and holding a book in the other. "Ms. Karen!" he says. "Is the library open?"

She calls him by name and stops to talk. It's clear that Karen has spent time with people at the library, as an invested and caring friend. This is part of what the library has to offer. It's not just an institution but an integral part of the community where the staff knows its patrons and reaches out to be a supportive part of their lives.

We finish our walk. The dogs are content and ready to jump back in the car. Feeling post-exercise good, with better circulation and freer breathing, we make our good-byes and drive away from the Dee Brown Library.

Summer twilight is just stealing over the park. Thanks to the library, its dedicated staff, and these free programs to help and encourage the community, the world seems like a more caring and hopeful place tonight. We're all in this together.

Getting Folks on Board: Talking Up Healthy Living in the Library

How do you get your library team, including volunteers, board members, trustees, Friends, security staff, and others on the healthy living at the library train? Here's how:

1. Inform
2. Update
3. Coordinate
4. Collaborate

Inform everyone even remotely connected to your library that you are setting out to support healthy living; include staff, volunteers, trustees, boards, Friends, and foundations, among others.

Update everyone on your progress tell them your library has taken the Healthy Meeting pledge, started a weekly all-library Instant Recess program, participated in the town's pedometer challenge. Whatever it is, share the news within your library team.

Coordinate with your library team to build a culture of resource sharing around healthy living in your library. Link to the talents of others; maybe a member of your Friends group is also a member of a cooking club.

Collaborate, to encourage participation and expertise sharing. Maybe you have some Master Gardeners among your volunteers who are ready and eager to bring their passion for gardening to the library by building a community garden on the library lawn. Exercise your resources!

Your library team is bigger than you think! It includes staff members at your location, potentially staff at other libraries in your system, volunteers, board members, trustees, security staff, student workers, facilities staff, and anyone else who plays a role in making your library the jewel it is. When starting healthy living programs, it is good to get everyone on board or at the very least informed. All these individuals influence your library's programmatic and strategic priorities and are critical to the success of your healthy living initiative.

Key questions to ask include:

- How does your team like to receive updates about new initiatives?
- How does your team like to provide feedback on new library initiatives?
- What concerns do you think your team will have with healthy living at the library?

In talking with your team, the key message should be that the library cares about healthy living and is excited to join others in making the community a healthier place.

Your messaging should also take your team members' stances into consideration and include themes of leadership and responsiveness. If your team has not thought about the library in this way before, they may raise concerns. These concerns may be especially common among library board members, in

my experience, for whom this topic may seem new and potentially threaten-
ing to their idea of the proper role of the library. Listen, reflect, and respond
thoughtfully and empathically. **Illustrate** how playing an active role in healthy
living positions the library as a community leader. **Reinforce** the idea that
aligning library programming with community goals is both forward-looking
and sustainable. Your team members are in the position to be your biggest
advocates for this endeavor, and as such, it is critical to be thoughtful about
how you engage them. Your goal is not to start arguments but to build an
enduring coalition.

Where to begin? A good starting point is a healthy living pledge. A pledge is
different than a policy. It's OK if you don't always achieve your goals. But do make
an aspirational statement that articulates your values and your library's values.
Just beginning to talk about nutrition and physical activity within your library
puts the idea into people's heads. Plant a seed that may bear fruit down the road.

You don't need to start from scratch. Guidelines exist, and I recommend the
National Alliance for Nutrition and Activity (NANA) Healthy Meeting Pledge
(and related resources) at http://healthymeeting.org. The pledge includes a
commitment to support nutrition in the food served in the workplace and to
embrace physical activity wherever possible.

Some libraries have already signed on. In December 2018 the public library
in Johnson City, New York, passed a resolution to adopt the NANA guidelines. They even successfully received a $500 award from the Broome County
Health Department's Creating Healthy Schools and Communities initiative to
support this work. Library director Ben Lainhart says this is a way to promote healthy lifestyles both internally and in the area: "Our staff is the most
important resource we have here. Anything we can do to make sure the staff
is healthy, they're not out sick or susceptible to chronic illness it's good for the
library and the community. The other thing we do, too, is educate the community on a whole variety of issues and one of them is how to live a healthy
lifestyle" (Binghamton.com 2018).

See what he did there? He moved from supporting healthy living among
staff to supporting healthy living in the community. In fact, that is what I've
seen happen over and over again. More on that in a minute.

For now, just remember there are all kinds of fun ways to support healthy
living within your library team. One of the most creative examples I've seen
comes from Richland Library, in Columbia, South Carolina. To support
employee wellness and active transportation, the library purchased bicycles
for staff to use for meetings in the downtown area. Maybe you can't bike to
work every day, but you'd like the option to bike to your meeting at town hall.
This library made bikes available so staff can do just that, *and* they put a small
bike rack in the staff area so that the bikes are protected and secure. The library
also gives each of its units discretionary funds for what it calls Project Play,

which enables departments to invest in playtime activities like bowling, karaoke, or a healthy lunch together.

Other libraries empower staff to take walks on breaks or even just get up and jump around. Some libraries in the southwestern United States have embraced the instant recess credo. Instant recess is all about building a culture and society that make activity the easy choice. Rather than shaming someone for getting up and dancing around or stretching out their calves, this model makes physical activity the **norm**. To get started, you could create some designated times for instant recess at your library. Say, "Every day at 2:30 p.m., we're going to get up and move around for ten minutes." At first, people may look at you like you just landed from Mars, but people are malleable and if you stick with it, folks will join you. This model has become routine in many corporate cultures and could be applied to libraries as well. And by doing the activity together, even the most sedentary individuals are attracted to the social aspect—it's fun! Learn more at https://infopeople.org/civicrm/event/info?reset=1&id=77.

Youth services librarians *already* do this in their programs. Think of asking kids to get out their wiggles after sitting for a storytime. In fact, *we all need to get out our wiggles*. Making movement a part of your library culture also shows your community that the library cares about health—that it is a priority. Seeing all the library staff get up and move around for ten minutes at 2:30 p.m. creates a strong and tangible message and invites partners to think of the library as a potential partner for healthy living programming. Invite your patrons to join you!

Here's a word to the wise: when trying to encourage healthy living, it is best to make it an option and not a requirement. At the library in Harker Heights, Texas, Destinee Barton, the library's youth health and program coordinator found that giving teens the option of choosing between healthy snacks and the junk food the library had served in past programs led more teens to experiment with healthier options. Rome wasn't built in a day, and a healthier society won't be either. Don't be afraid to take it slow. It's not a competition, it's a community.

Asset Mapping

A communication plan is one thing; an action plan is another. Let's get ready to program by mapping our assets. Rather than start with the negative, start with the positive! I cannot emphasize enough the importance of staying positive when doing healthy living programming. This is true both for personal journeys and for institutional and community transformations. We are bombarded with images in the media of idealized bodies and diets, and they frequently lead us to feel shame and despair. Sometimes just talking about physical activity in libraries can generate concerns that we're pushing an ableist, fat-shaming agenda. **We need to counteract these harmful messages and create more positive images of healthy living in our libraries**. We can change the national conversation about what it means (and what it looks like) to practice healthy living in everyday life.

Think about what assets you *already* have within your library that could be used to develop healthy living programs. Assets include not only money but also relationships, programming skills, previous programs you've offered, spaces, volunteers, staff, and more.

Use these prompts to get started.

1. What resources does my library *already* invest in that I could use for healthy living programs? (Following are examples.)
   a. Meeting rooms
   b. Green spaces around the library
   c. Technology (e.g., a projector)
   d. Other types of tangible resources
2. What activities does my library currently offer to promote healthy living, both among staff and for patrons?
3. What audiences does my library reach (or not reach) through these efforts?
4. What healthy living expertise already exists in my library team?
5. What healthy living advocates already exist on my library team?

When Elizabeth Roth became the coordinator of the Be Well at Nashville Public Library initiative (Be Well at NPL), one of the first things she did was to see what assets were already in the library system. She was pleasantly surprised to find numerous library staff members who *already* had advanced training in everything from food handling and preparation to gardening and Zumba. You may have such hidden gems in your own library, especially if you think broadly and include not only staff, but also volunteers, Friends of the library, and others.

Build your healthy living programs around these assets! Here are two more examples to inspire you. In Detroit, Michigan, a clerk at the main library's Technology, Literacy, and Career Center is also a certified yoga instructor. When the head librarian found out the clerk had this expertise, the librarian asked the clerk to start teaching "Yoga for Job Seekers" at the library, which has since become a regular, ongoing program. An Ohio librarian told me that Zumba classes are taught by someone whose official job title is "technology educator" but who also has a background in Zumba instruction. When library staff learned of their colleague's training, they invited the staff member to utilize it by teaching Zumba at the library. Use your assets!

Support Staff through Continuing Education

In my research I found countless examples of library staff seeking continuing education around healthy living practices. In 2005 the Rural Hall Public Library in North Carolina started weekly chair-based exercise classes, through a partnership with the county public health department, which supplied the instructor. In 2014 the instructor began to lose her eyesight, and by April 2015 she was no longer able to lead it. At that point, the adult services librarian realized that the library had to find a way to continue offering the class, since it had become a popular and expected part of the library's recurring programs. To fill the void, the librarian took classes to become a certified fitness instructor. She told me that she had never taught an exercise class in her life before this point. She said, "Exercising for its own sake was not a big thing for me: I jumped into this because it was a need, a practical logistical need someone needed to step in" (Lenstra 2018e, 153). As a result of going through the training, she said that fitness and physical activity are now bigger parts of her life. In addition to teaching the weekly exercise class, she has become a health and wellness ambassador for the county government.

In Port Angeles, Washington, and in Wilmington, North Carolina, the library paid for youth services librarians to learn yoga so that it could be incorporated into youth programming. In Stillwater, Oklahoma, the library paid for staff to learn tai chi to extend the number of popular tai chi programs the library could provide. In Indiana, Jesse Lewis at the Brownsburg Public Library decided to get her Zumba license a few years ago. She now offers four free classes a week at the library, including a preschool "Kids Jr. Zumba," a seated chair class, a low-impact version, and the original Zumba. The classes have become so popular that librarians from the region go to the Brownsburg Library for the classes. Librarian Katie Scherrer has even developed a structured training program for youth services librarians interested in incorporating yoga and movement into Pre-K storytimes: "Stories, Songs, and Stretches." Learn more at: https://www.storiessongsand stretches.com.

Others have sought out food preparation certificates or have gone through master gardening programs run by extension agents. Continuing education opportunities abound, and more and more librarians are seeking them out. Support your staff who want to better prepare themselves to offer healthy living programs at your library by encouraging them to take advantage of these resources, which will contribute both to improved staff wellness and to improved capacity for healthy living programming.

As this type of work becomes more common, librarians report expecting (or at least hoping for) different things from their staff. A librarian in a medium-sized city in Oregon said,

We found that the biggest challenge with movement programs, especially for children, is finding someone who has the right combination of skills, training and stamina to present them. Our Toddlerobics program is run by the most energetic person in the world, with a background in education and an MLS. She pioneered the program, has trained other staff and wears a tutu during each session. We were [also] very lucky to have a staff member with Tai Chi training and certification who loves working with older patrons. (Lenstra 2018k, 197)

Here we see a librarian who values staff who have the requisite skills to lead physically active programs in libraries, with high energy being seen as a key skill for youth services, and with training in a specialized type of movement (e.g., tai chi) seen as valuable for working with adults.

Other libraries have embraced gardening and cooking and have hired staff with this training. The Pottsboro Library in Texas hired a part-time garden manager to run its expanding community garden initiative. The libraries in Philadelphia and in Columbia, South Carolina, have full-time culinary-literacy librarians who are trained to do cooking and nutrition programs. In Grand Rapids, Michigan, the library hired a volunteer coordinator from the local bike community. Calli Crow now administers the library's BikeKDL (Kent District Library) initiative, focused on increasing bicycling both among library staff and in the local community. If you don't already have these skills in your library, there is no harm in writing them into your staff continuing education or hiring plans.

There is also no harm in mixing the personal and professional. Find something that resonates with you, learn more about it, and share your passion with your patrons. Invite others to do the same. A great example of this occurs in Bellingham, Washington, where at their SkillShare space in the middle of the library, staff invites community members to share their skills, including, among others, yoga and tai chi. This is a model for what we want our libraries to become: incubators of lifelong learning in which everyone learns and everyone is empowered to teach. Have a skill? Share it! Start this message internally with your library team, and then open it up to the whole community. Learn more at https://www.bellinghampubliclibrary.org/skillshare.

From Internal Programs to Public Programs

A recurring pattern I notice in my research is that healthy living programs for staff morph into programs for patrons. Libraries that invest in staff wellness also invest in the health of the communities they serve. Here are a few examples that illustrate this finding.

At the University of California in San Diego, a hugely successful yoga program that has been offered to library staff weekly since 2008 has led, over the years, to a proliferation of yoga programs for all students, faculty, and staff, as well as to the purchase of FitDesks (stationary bikes with built-in platforms for laptops or books) to support healthy living among college students studying at the library.

At the High Point Public Library in North Carolina, the library had the best space, among all governmental facilities, to host city employee fitness programs. In 2015 the library became the official spot where the city's wellness coordinator leads lunchtime yoga and exercise programs for city staff. Over time, the library decided to open up the programs to the public. They had ample room for more participants, so why not? Now the library offers free yoga every Monday and free fitness on Fridays at noon for both staff and patrons.

In rural Athens County, Ohio, library staff found themselves in the fall of 2012 "struggling to implement a wellness plan for the staff, a challenge for seven far-flung branches with anywhere from 1 to 15 employees" (Hill 2017, 43). Library administrators put their heads together to think about what they could to develop something that would increase employee health across all their branches. The director came up with the idea of making bikes available, and the staff said, "Why keep them just for the staff? Why not let patrons borrow them?" And with that, the Book-A-Bike program was born. It is now possible to borrow a bicycle from multiple branches of this rural library system.

The more you can build up healthy living practices among your library team, the more capacity you will have for public programs.

Exercises

1. How can you get the conversation going about healthy living at your library?
2. How could resources like the Healthy Meeting Pledge help?
3. Thinking broadly about your library team, who are the individuals you'd like to reach out to in order to get healthy living at your library off the ground? Who are the likely champions that would support this work?

6

Exercise Your Resources and Don't Do It Alone

In Delaware, the Dover Public Library "is working hand-in-hand with parks and rec to offer a multitude of recreational and educational programs" during the summer months (Finney 2019). Their Tuesdays in the Park collaborative program emerged from a shared realization that both institutions—the library and the Parks and Recreation Department—needed to do more to extend access to their respective services beyond what they provided in their indoor facilities. Each program includes literacy components led by the library, physical activities led by Parks and Recreation, and free meals provided by the Delaware Department of Education. Each partner has clear responsibilities that play to their strengths, and assessment is incorporated into the project plan. During the first year, the partners discovered that families wanted to be able to check out books, so in the second year, the Kent County Public Library started bringing the bookmobile to the weekly programs. This is an example of a community coming together to support healthy living. This is what we want to see.

In this chapter, we'll go over how to form and sustain the relationships needed to offer healthy living programs like this one and many others at your library and in your community. Here's how to do it:

1. **Inform** potential partners of what the library is doing or planning to do.
2. **Update** them on the progress of a program or its planning.
3. **Coordinate** with them to cross-promote programs and initiatives.
4. **Collaborate** with them to develop healthy living programs.

You can't work together if you don't know each other. Start by informing potential partners of what the library is seeking to do (and ask them to inform you of their initiatives, in turn). Then keep the communication channels open. Update them on new programs you're offering or new strategic directions you're exploring. Move from information exchange to coordination.

In Greensboro, North Carolina, where I live, a few years ago the library started cross-promoting summer programs with the city's Parks and Recreation unit. Rather than compete for kids during the summer, they coordinate. The step after coordination is collaboration. A perfect example of a library reaching this final stage is the Tuesdays in the Park program described above.

Shared Use in the Library

The perfect way to think about this collaborative work is the concept of "shared use." This idea may be new to you, but it has been extensively developed and deployed in the public health sector for years. The concept refers to institutions like churches, schools, and other safe, trusted community spaces opening their doors to host healthy living programs like cooking classes, free fitness, and more. We already do this work in libraries we just haven't developed the vocabulary to describe it. A shared-use framework will give you a powerful way to describe and advocate for collaborative programming.

First, though, I want to introduce the concept of **community-led librarianship**. This concept refers to a deep commitment by librarians to truly and authentically collaborate with communities to identify, develop, and implement library programs and services. The process of engaging in community-led librarianship is, according to the Canadian librarians who developed it, "humbling . . . [as] it requires a shedding of the personas of the librarian as educator and expert, and adopting a new identity, librarian as facilitator" (Pateman and Williment 2016, 217). Based on this new identity, the librarian works with communities to decide what the library will do.

Community-led librarianship is the framework. Shared use is the process. Let's start with a definition:

> Shared use—also called joint use, community use, or open use—occurs when government entities or other organizations agree to open their facilities for use by the broader community. One common example is a school playground available for public use after school hours; however, shared use arrangements can allow new users for many types of spaces, such as gymnasiums, pools, playing fields, parks, walking trails, garden plots, kitchens, meeting and performance spaces, and pavilions. Shared use can take place on an informal basis (based on historical practice) or on a formal basis (based on a written legal document). A written agreement can help address concerns about resources, maintenance, security, and liability. (ChangeLab Solutions 2019)

Shared use arrangements have been empirically proven to increase access to healthy living.

A major part of former first lady Michelle Obama's Let's Move! campaign was to empower faith-based and neighborhood organizations to open their spaces. Let's Move Faith and Communities challenges you to

> **Open your Facility:** Provide open access to your organization's facilities, such as large open green spaces . . . or other meeting spaces. Allow after-school programs, clubs, or groups to use these spaces to increase opportunities for physical activity after school and on weekends. Concerned about the complications of opening your facilities to the community? Develop a joint-use agreement to facilitate a partnership between your organization and other nonprofit, private or governmental organizations in your community. This formal agreement can clarify and define shared responsibilities over maintenance, operations, ownership, liability, and cost of your facilities. (U.S. HHS 2010, 12–13)

Rather than keeping spaces locked and inaccessible, many schools, congregations, *and libraries* embrace shared use as a strategy to create more opportunities to exercise, play, grow food, cook, serve healthy meals, and engage in other healthy living activities. The possibilities are endless. In addition to those sketched above, some libraries host community gardens on the library lawn, bike rodeos in the parking lot, farmers markets, and much more. These programs are not developed by librarians working alone. They are developed by librarians working hand in hand with community partners. Promoting healthy living at the library is *all about community*, so *whatever you do, do not do it alone*.

Do you have a meeting room that isn't always being used? Do you have corners of your parking lot that could be blocked off? Do you have the capacity to serve meals, either inside or outdoors? Does your library have drinking fountains, restrooms, and the capacity to serve as the launchpad for walking or running groups?

If you answered yes to *any* of these questions, then shared use is something you can do. If you answered no, you can *still* apply these principles through outreach programming. For instance, Clancy Pool at Washington's Whitman County Library uses the principle of shared use to offer librarian-led cooking classes in the kitchen of a nearby church, since her rural library lacks any cooking facilities. By embracing the concept of shared use, we open up our libraries and also consider other spaces in our communities as potential program sites, including parks, churches, and other venues. Whether you use the principle for in-house or outreach programming, shared use is a powerful idea that *every librarian* should know about.

Even though we don't always use this language, **we already put these principles into practice**. Consider summer meals at the library. Across the United

States, more than one thousand public libraries serve as summer meal sites in the U.S. Department of Agriculture's summer feeding program. The meals are not prepared at the library. Instead, they are prepared by what the USDA calls "sponsors," institutions that already engage in meal preparation on a routine basis, such as schools, colleges, camps, nonprofit organizations, or senior centers. The meals are then brought to the library, where they are served to youth up to the age of eighteen. This is what **shared use** is all about: libraries, churches, schools, and other public spaces open themselves up to working with partners to extend their reach and to increase access to healthy living resources and opportunities.

The same principle is utilized by public libraries for physical activity initiatives. In New York City, libraries across the five boroughs participate in the Shape Up NYC initiative led by their Department of Parks and Recreation. The libraries have entered into joint use and shared space agreements with Parks and Recreation that enable the libraries to host (at no cost) aerobics, yoga, Pilates, and Zumba, all taught by expert fitness instructors. This program has dramatically increased the number and availability of affordable, accessible, and fun fitness options for New Yorkers. It has been a tremendous success, with over 550,000 visits to Shape Up classes since 2010. Learn more at https://www.nycgovparks.org/programs/recreation/shape-up-nyc.

Although the New York City program is the most formal and developed shared-use initiative I've seen that involves libraries, there are dozens of more informal shared-use arrangements taking place. In the small town of West Jefferson, North Carolina, a community in the Appalachian Mountains, the library hosts the town's yoga club, a community-driven group free and open to all. It operates as a hybrid yoga class/support group and is led by club members. Asked how the yoga club started meeting at the library, a librarian told me, "I knew they were having difficulties [at their former location]. I moved them to the library because we had room for it" (Lenstra 2018e, 151).

In Woodstock, New Brunswick, the library hosts the town's running club. Group runs begin and end at the library and, as a result, library staff and patrons have joined the group. In Walkertown, North Carolina, a local walking group meets in the morning at the library. They call themselves the Walkers of Walkertown, and they are self-managing, with the library helping to promote the group and offering them a meeting room in which to chat and have coffee after the walk. In other communities throughout North Carolina, public libraries participate in the Area Agency on Aging's Age Well programs, which involve trained volunteers coming to libraries to lead free classes on everything from how to improve your balance to how to use tai chi to cope with arthritis. In northwestern North Carolina, these programs have become so popular that library staff themselves have now become trained to lead the programs.

Dozens of libraries open up their outdoor spaces to support community gardens maintained independently by community groups and individuals. At Madison County Public Library in North Carolina, 2018's "Best Small Public Library in America," according to *Library Journal*, a local gardening club developed and maintains the library's garden. At the public library in Monterey Park, California, "Line dance leader Kit Cheung teaches her class in an unlikely place— the parking lot of a local library" (Robert Wood Johnson Foundation 2017). Library director Norma Arvizu says, "There was a concern for me in the beginning because they would interrupt the flow of folks coming through. Later on I realized that this would be a positive image for the library because these are residents, these are actual people that live here. Why are we not allowing them to use what their taxes pay for?" (Robert Wood Johnson Foundation 2017). In all of these cases, shared use of the library has benefited everyone involved.

Shared Use at the School Library

We've talked a lot about public libraries, but I want to introduce some examples of shared use in a school library. At the Belleville West High School in the St. Louis metro area, Alonzo Nelson Jr. is a mathematics teacher whose passion is to increase interest in yoga among African American men like himself. Every Monday he teaches free yoga to teachers and students at his high school library. Through these free classes at the library, he has increased access to yoga for individuals who otherwise would not consider it. Learn more at https://www.instagram.com/p/Bqa8PV5DUQL.

The school library is the perfect place to host yoga classes. And there is evidence that more and more school libraries are opening themselves up to host yoga classes taught by math teachers, guidance counselors, and librarians themselves. This point came through in a poignant way after the tragic mass shooting at Marjory Stoneman Douglas High School in February 2018. A month later, Chalkbeat, a news organization that covers K–12 schools, caught up with Diana Haneski, the school's librarian. Reporter Sarah Darville asked Haneski how the library was helping the school recover from the tragedy, and Haneski responded,

> Yes, teachers really need more material and different resources than they needed before. We do yoga in the library on Monday afternoons, and I was stretching and I looked up at a shelf and there was this book on display—"The Gun Fighter." That is not a book I want on display right now! (Darville 2018)

The school library helped people recover not only with books but also with free yoga, facilitated by a librarian willing to enter into a joint use agreement with someone eager to offer this program at her library.

The idea of shared use of public spaces for healthy living is now extremely well developed, with ample resources for everything from how to manage disagreements among partners to how to deal with perceptions of legal liability. In many respects, librarians are late to this game, with faith-based institutions, schools, and many other institutions already having embraced the idea of opening up their spaces to support initiatives focused on increasing healthy living. The good news is that many of the kinks have already been worked out. So what are you waiting for? Let's catch up and take a leading role in this movement to extend access to healthy living opportunities by sharing our spaces. Get started at https://www.changelabsolutions.org/healthy-neighborhoods/shared-use.

Showing Up: Get in the Game, Stay in the Game

Let's not get ahead of ourselves. Before you're ready to enter into a shared use agreement with your local gardening club, you first have to become known, and to know, the constellation of individuals and institutions passionate about supporting healthy living in the community. If you are lucky, folks will spontaneously approach you with the idea of hosting a free yoga or cooking class. But opportunity does not always knock. Shirley Chisholm, the first black woman elected to the U.S. Congress, famously said, "If they don't give you a seat at the table, bring a folding chair." Be ready to make the cold calls needed to jumpstart these relationships and to show up when opportunities arise.

The concept of **embedded librarianship** can help here. I first learned about embedded librarianship in public libraries at the Public Library Association conference in Indianapolis in 2014. At the program "Creative Community Connections," librarians from Colorado and Ohio shared stories of embedding library staff in community institutions outside of the library. The panelists defined embedded librarians as those who "attend meetings and events hosted by the organization, share library programs/services of interest to the group, and may take on a leadership role within the group" (Galston, White, and May 2014).

I was particularly impressed by the infrastructure the Akron-Summit County Public Library in Ohio developed to support this process, including a form that library staff (at all levels) can fill out to propose becoming an embedded librarian. The form includes the expected time commitment and asks, How will engagement with this organization benefit the library? Think about the staffing implications that emerge when library staff spends significant amounts of time working outside library facilities. Download the form here: https://cslinsession .cvlsites.org/files/2014/06/Proposed-Community-Engagement-Form.pdf.

The librarians in Jackson County, North Carolina, put this concept into practice in their long-term partnership with the Jackson County Health Department. A librarian goes to two monthly health department meetings: one on physical activity and nutrition and another on substance abuse. By being part of these conversations, the library has been able to work with the health department to become part of "the solution," which includes hosting programs at the library.

Smyrna Strong at the Library

In January 2018, the Smyrna Public Library in Georgia launched the Smyrna Strong Collection, which consists of fitness equipment, board games that require movement, and hiking backpacks. Mary Wallace Moore, the library director, said, "My city administrators love, love, love" the idea of the library supporting healthy living. The city loved the idea so much that they included the Smyrna Strong collection in the strategic vision for the entire community, making it one of the city's strategic initiatives to pursue and develop between 2017 and 2027. The strategic plan includes this message: "Do you want to improve your health and well-being but find it a little overwhelming? Where do you start? Joining a gym and buying fitness equipment costs money. How do you know what type of exercise or what equipment will work for you? Then come to Smyrna Library. Yes, really, come to the library."

Mary Wallace Moore shared the story of how this initiative came to fruition:

> Smyrna Public Library is an independent municipal library serving a city of approximately fifty-five thousand people in Cobb County, Georgia, which is in the metropolitan Atlanta area. Smyrna made national news a few years ago when the Atlanta Braves professional baseball team announced it would relocate to Cobb County, just across the street from Smyrna's city limits. Due to intentional and aggressive city planning, Smyrna had been growing steadily since the mid-1990s. But the construction of the stadium and the accompanying battery of shops, restaurants, hotels, and housing accelerated economic development.
>
> Smyrna Public Library is unique among Georgia public libraries. By state law, public libraries are organized into county and multicounty cooperatives. Since Smyrna's library retained its independence and did not join Cobb County Public Library, Smyrna Public

Smyrna Strong Collection at the Smyrna Public Library, Georgia. Reprinted with permission from Mary Wallace Moore.

Library does not receive any state or federal funding. Smyrna Library is fully funded by the city of Smyrna.

As a city department, Smyrna Library writes its goals and strategic plans to support city goals. In 2014 the city published a vision statement that provided a framework for all strategic initiatives. The library uses this document to prioritize spending and labor for programming, services, and collections. One of the desired outcomes under its "Quality of Place" pillar was to "elevate opportunities for recreation." The library carries books, magazines, and DVDs related to sports, fitness, and recreation, but I knew the average person did not usually think of the library as a partner in recreation.

After watching a Noah Lenstra webinar about fitness initiatives in other libraries, a lightbulb went off for me. We could create a collection that would help fulfill a portion of the vision statement but also create publicity for our existing collections. Using funds we had received from a community foundation, we created a health and fitness collection of circulating materials for all ages. The guiding principles for selecting materials were the following:

- price
- size
- weight
- durability
- appropriateness for novices, that is, can be used by individuals without any advanced training

There are 24 kits in the Smyrna Strong Collection, and these materials have checked out 289 times in a year and a half. The inspiration for the name of the collection came from a city-sponsored health initiative led by city employees. I liked the name. It was catchy. But I also thought that the name might resonate with city employees, spurring them to check out materials too.

In September 2018, the library partnered with Cobb County Public Library and Cobb Senior Services in their Falls Prevention programming. The visitors from Cobb Senior Services were blown away when I showed them our Smyrna Strong collection. They immediately asked if they could steal this idea for the Senior Center. I replied that I had stolen the idea from other public libraries, so steal away! I don't know if they have implemented the idea yet in their locations, but I hope to find out . . . when they visit again.

One lesson we have learned since developing nontraditional collections is that regular promotion is vital. Since these are not materials the public associates with libraries, they need a spotlight from time to time to remind the public of these amazing resources. As soon as you display them creatively, a new patron discovers them for the first time.

Putting Things Together in a Health or How-To Fair

A health or how-to fair could be described as a smorgasbord of lifelong learning opportunities. They are great, low-stakes programs around which you can build partnerships and communicate, in a big way, that the library is ready to step up to support community health. I have seen three different approaches, and all work well.

The **first** approach is the conventional health fair, which is exactly what it sounds like: an opportunity to expose your community to a variety of health institutions and information, as well as to offer quick introductions to healthy habits like exercise and nutrition. The **second** approach is the how-to fair, which has the advantage of being, typically, more engaging and participatory. Some how-to fairs have very successfully incorporated a variety of healthy living programs into them. The 2019 How-To Festival at the San Diego Public Library was "a celebration of experiential and peer-to-peer learning [featuring] community experts from all walks of life." The festival included opportunities to learn how to do chair yoga, traditional yoga, yoga for success, and yoga for children; how to prepare healthy turkey albondigas; how to maintain peace, health, and well-being with laughter; how to use essential oils; and how to start an exercise routine for youth and the young at heart. Even pets were included, with one session on how to make homemade dog treats "using healthy ingredients." Learn more at https://www.sandiego.gov/blog/how-festival-library.

A **third** alternative is to organize a community meeting to discuss how the library, in collaboration with others, could support healthy living. That is what the Athens County Public Library in Ohio did in November 2012 and again in January 2013. Library administrators were developing a proposal to check out bicycles from their branches, but first, they wanted to see what the community thought. So they invited "local hospitals, bike shops, schools, police departments, city officials, the health department, and other nonprofits" (Hill 2017, 44) to a community meeting. The meeting was a success, but reflecting on it years later, librarians noted that "even if the library decided not to pursue bicycles, the meeting brought together the right people and advanced the conversation about bikes and safety and the desire to get our community outside more" (Hill 2017, 44). The county and city planners both pointed out that the idea dovetailed perfectly with "their respective long-range comprehensive plans of improving alternative transportation access and increasing access to resources such as the paved bike path, rural parks, and preserves" (Hill 2017, 44). A local nurse was also instrumental in helping the library figure out the logistics of this program and how to get it off the ground successfully. These sorts of dialogues on issues relating to community health can be a great way to build relationships and to solicit ideas about how libraries and others can work together to address local issues.

If you'd like, you can focus these events around a theme. In Denton, Texas, the public library won an award from the Urban Libraries Council for its bike parade, an annual program focused on increasing physical activity and bike safety. In Durham, Connecticut, the library held a Holistic Health Fair that featured workshops and informational booths on wellness practices like meditation and mind-body practices like tai chi and acupuncture. In Lafayette, Louisiana, the library's summer reading program kickoff is organized around and in collaboration with an annual bike safety fair. Tailor your event to local needs and interests.

No matter what you do—a health fair, a how-to festival, or a community conversation—this should be the goal: bring together those who care about healthy living, to form the relationships you need to offer healthy living programs.

How can you get such programs started? Find partners and learn tactics that will work best when collaborating with them. Your library may already have existing partners with whom you work on a regular basis. Or you may be interested in exploring new opportunities. Some common partners I've found libraries work with include:

- Parks and recreation units
- Campus wellness and athletics units
- Public health departments
- Cooperative extension agencies
- Local schools
- Colleges and universities
- Health-care agencies
- Service agencies like the YMCA, YWCA, or Scouts
- Social service nonprofits, like food banks
- Faith-based institutions
- Local businesses
- K–12 schools
- Individual fitness and nutrition instructors and coaches
- Health libraries, including member organizations of the National Networks of Libraries of Medicine (NNLM)
- Many, many more

Other partners with which libraries have worked on health fairs include:

- Health insurance companies
- Grocery stores and nutritionists
- Master gardeners
- Breast cancer coalitions

- Chiropractors
- Massage therapists
- Nearby nursing colleges or medical schools
- Bike, running, and sports stores
- Outdoor equipment stores
- High school students (request help with programming outreach and legwork)

Whether working with established partners or developing new contacts, take the time to have conversations with key contacts to reaffirm old relationships and build new ones. Doing this can help raise awareness of what your library is doing (and/or hopes to do) to support healthy living, while also uncovering areas of common interest around which collaborations could develop and expand.

When reaching out to potential partners, take the time to research how they approach healthy living, and think about how their approach dovetails with yours. Engage all partners with the expectation that you will learn more about how to serve your community through conversations with them, since they have unique and invaluable perspectives on community concerns and needs. Be prepared to, in turn, share what you have seen from your library's perspective. Even if the conversation does not ultimately result in a program, it may still be beneficial in terms of building the library's reputation in the community and informing you of relevant initiatives.

Reaching out to partners around something tangible like a fair can help structure the conversation and give you and your new partners something to work toward together. Alternatively, or in addition, you can offer to send someone from the library to any fair/expo-type events a new partner may be organizing. Let partners know you're looking for a two-way relationship. One of the best ways to get to know people is by working with them.

It is important to know and understand that no two partnerships are identical. Each relationship is unique, and how you communicate with different partners should be tailored to them. One common theme, however, is to make sure to reference the **value** of partnering with the public library and the **leveraged impact** of cross-sector collaborations. **Highlight your library's position as a trusted institution and community convener** and showcase your strength as a hub for public programs and lifelong learning.

Examples of techniques you can use to form partnerships include:

- Pitching a project or idea (e.g., a health fair) to a potential partner
- Reporting on the outcomes and evaluation results of an existing program
- Requesting outreach to a partner's networks to disseminate information about library resources and services

Family Health and Safety Fair in Pennsylvania

In February 2019, the Bellwood-Antis Public Library, located in a small town in central Pennsylvania, held its 13th Annual Family Health and Safety Fair. Several hundred attendees turned out on a Saturday for a Run for Reading 5K, children's Zumba, a tai chi class, a demonstration by local firefighters, health screenings, and informational booths for health services like organ donation and kidney health.

Surprisingly, the library did not spend any money, beyond staff time, on this large event. Jessica Ford Cameron, the library's director, said they "could not have done this without the Tyrone Regional Health Network and the Northern Blair County Recreation Center" (Lenstra 2018d). This is the power of these types of events. By pulling in a bunch of partners around a tangible program, you don't have to spend a lot on supplies. Don't get me wrong, it certainly does take some time to get the ball rolling, and time has huge value, but if you frame this work as laying the groundwork for future relationships, you will be better able to justify the investment of time. Furthermore, every year it gets easier. I've seen that first-hand here in North Carolina, where an annual health fair organized by librarian Maxine Days at the High Point Public Library gets bigger and better (and easier to manage) with each passing year.

These events can even lead to recurring programs. That is exactly what happened at the Bellwood-Antis Public Library, where, during the thirteenth annual health fair, a tai chi class was so well received that the library decided to start offering it as a regular, recurring program at the library, beginning in summer 2019.

The Nuts and Bolts: From Idea to Reality

Answers to the questions posed in this section will help you bring your idea to life.

How do I get started? Forming partnerships starts with relationships. Do you or your staff already have informal or formal relationships with some of the potential partners suggested above? Start there! For example, do you go to a gym? Do you go to a doctor for an annual physical? Ask staff at such locations if they want to participate in a health or how-to fair.

How do I market it? Pitch a broad tent and you will be surprised at how many partners you will find wanting to participate—and most will be happy to invite their own clientele or supporters. Once you have the event details in place, get a press release out to the local media. The media tend to give good coverage to health fairs.

How do I run it? If your health fair has been well advertised, expect lots of people to come, including many first-time patrons. Make sure you have ample staffing; think about asking your Friends of the Library to have a table at the fair so they can help with crowd control and sign up new cardholders. Also, if you have any physical activity demonstrations, you may want to have participants sign waivers of liability in case of physical injury. Injury probably won't happen, but better safe than sorry!

The best location for a health fair is in your library's meeting room (space permitting), but depending on the season, you may want to have part of the fair outside on your library's lawn. In any case, be prepared for many attendees to also come inside the library and look around. You may want to set up book displays highlighting books and DVDs related to health and wellness. Or you could highlight how your library's downloadable collections could be listened to during exercise.

Be ready for people to come into the library looking for information and materials to help them live healthier lives. You may want to have a staff training day so that everyone knows what parts of the collection could be useful for particular health needs.

How do I assess it? Don't forget to do a post-event wrap-up. Thank everyone who came, and ask them what programming they would next like to develop with the library. More likely than not, at least one partner will be ready to work with you to develop more free healthy living programs.

Next Steps: From a Fair to a Relationship

OK, so you've brought together a bunch of folks for an expo at your library. Now how do you develop this one-off event into an ongoing programming relationship? We'll be answering this question in the rest of this book.

Check Out Colorado State Parks: Getting Families Outside via Their Library Cards

Note: This story was authored by Beth Crist, youth and family services consultant, Colorado State Library.

> I have been city-bound for way too long. I used to visit State Parks often. It has been so long (years) since I have been out in nature. Life has been tough lately, this [backpack] was an unexpected surprise that filled my heart with joy and hope. Thank You!
> —Patron comment

Overview

In 2015 the Colorado State Library (CSL) and Colorado Parks and Wildlife (CPW) joined together in an exceptional partnership to circulate state park passes in every public library in Colorado. The program, called

Check out Colorado State Parks backpacks.
Reprinted with permission from Beth Crist.

Check Out Colorado State Parks, quickly expanded to include putting those passes in a nature backpack filled with two field guides (one for Colorado wildlife and one for Colorado trees and wildflowers), binoculars, a list of suggested activities, a Leave No Trace outdoor ethics card, a state parks brochure, and an evaluation form. By 2017 it also spread to include the military libraries and most of the publicly funded academic libraries in Colorado, for a total of 297 participating libraries, with most libraries circulating two backpacks each. Since then, we've added a night sky field guide and an activity card explaining fishing basics, to each backpack.

Our goals for this program include increasing access to state parks and outdoor experiences for low-income residents, expanding residents' views of the services that libraries offer, providing a "try before you buy" option for residents to visit a state park or two before buying a pass, providing hands-on educational materials to increase learning in and enjoyment of nature, and, of course, encouraging residents and visitors to get outside to engage in healthy, educational activities in the best classroom of all—nature.

Patrons can borrow a backpack for a week at a time with their library card; during that week, they can visit any—and as many—of Colorado's 41 state parks as they like for free by using the hangtag park pass in the backpack. Some libraries allow holds on one or both of their backpacks; others use a "lucky day" approach to allow first-come, first-served access.

Along with the backpacks, CSL provides an online toolkit for the program (http://www.cde.state.co.us/cdelib/checkoutcostateparks) with display and PR materials, state park photos, list of contacts at individual state parks, item replacement information, and the cataloging files for the backpack.

Evaluation and Impact

We ask patrons to complete a simple paper evaluation form when they return the backpack at their local libraries; CSL compiles and enters these evaluations each year from all participating libraries. We also ask staff at participating libraries to complete an annual online survey. The data from both sets of evaluations goes into creating an annual infographic to share out about the program's success, and it also serves as the basis for CSL and CPW to evaluate the program, address challenges and suggestions, and consider future changes.

The program has been extremely popular with patrons, library staff, and CPW staff. In 2018 there were approximately 7,630 backpack checkouts statewide. Of the patrons responding to that survey, 98 percent would recommend a state park visit; 77 percent were likely to purchase a day pass; and 54 percent were likely to buy an annual pass. Also, 82 percent of these patrons reported that their park experience helped them learn more about nature, and a resounding 95 percent said that this program changed their view about what libraries have to offer.

A quote from a patron

In 2017 the program offered a fun social media contest inviting library patrons to check out a backpack and take a photo of themselves in a state park holding their library cards, and post them to Instagram or Twitter using the hashtag @CheckOut-Colorado. This clever entry beautifully blends libraries and parks to show the joy of reading outside. Reprinted with permission from Beth Crist.

sums up these results very well: "It's a great way for people to have a chance to go to a state park that otherwise might not be able to afford it. Thank you for having this program. It's also a great way for folks to discover just how much your local library has to offer."

Another benefit the program has had is in increasing partnerships between libraries and the state parks near them. Staff members at several parks are now providing nature programming at nearby libraries, and librarians at a few libraries are in turn offering occasional storytimes at nearby parks. In an example of a more extensive partnership, Barr Lake State Park provided nearby Anythink Libraries with bird feeders and offers regular programming at the libraries, and in 2018, Anythink Libraries purchased CPW gift certificates to give as summer program incentives and featured state parks prominently in their summer programming.

Because of this program's ongoing success, we expect it to continue indefinitely. With stories like these, how could it end? "Once upon a time there were two boys who loved to play Minecraft all day long. Then their grammie went to the library and got a state park pass and said, 'We are going on a hike!' The boys jumped up, ran, hiked, waded in the clear water, and caught crawdads. The grammie smiled and said, 'This is what makes good memories.'"

Exercises

1. Has your library ever hosted a fair, expo, or some other event in which you invite a number of presenters and organizations to participate?
2. Has your library ever been invited to participate in such a fair or expo?
3. What have your experiences been with this type of program?
4. How could you make "shared use" work at your library?
5. What obstacles do you anticipate needing to address prior to opening up your facility in this way?

7

Seek and Give Support in Communities of Librarians

The same principles we've applied to developing healthy living in our libraries and with our partners can also shape how we engage with the broader library profession to build this movement forward.

Here's how:

1. Inform other librarians about what you're doing.
2. Update them on how things went and lessons learned.
3. Coordinate with them around regional and national initiatives, like summer programming.
4. Collaborate with them around initiatives like sharing StoryWalk® titles or Charlie Carts within consortia.

There has never been more support for healthy living programming in libraries. Nonetheless, this trend is still not as developed as it could be, with a great deal of unevenness from place to place. For instance, in the state of Ohio, over 10 percent of the state's summer feeding sites, that is, sites where youths can go to get free meals during the summer through the USDA's Summer Feeding Program, are in public libraries. Nationwide, only 3 percent of such sites are in libraries (Lenstra and D'Arpa 2019). Why is Ohio so far ahead? A new report finds that "since the State Library became involved, the number of public library summer food service program sites has increased by 73 percent" (State Library of Ohio 2019).

The networks that knit together libraries matter. You can turn to them for support, and you can, in turn, support others through them. Don't overlook this topic when developing healthy living at your library. Share your enthusiasm in your region and online. Share the knowledge you acquire in your community. Many other librarians want to hear your experiences. Let's figure this out together!

I first learned about the importance of peer-to-peer support networks for the development of healthy living programming while interviewing public librarians in North Carolina. As they discussed their experiences, they contextualized their work in relation to national and regional trends heard about through their professional networks. Staff reported becoming inspired to develop healthy living programming because of discussions they had with other library staff, especially in the same region. One started a music and movement program because she heard another library was "doing what sounded like what we wanted to do" (Lenstra 2018e). Another said she started yoga programs because she had seen how successful they had been at the library where she formerly worked. A third said she engaged colleagues in the state library association in discussions about how to develop Zumba programming for adults.

I have since heard similar insights in all my conversations with librarians across North America. When I visited the Richland Library in Columbia, South Carolina, I asked Sarah Gough, programs and partnerships librarian, how it came to be that the library offered so many cooking classes. Sarah told me that the idea initially came from hearing about the Culinary Literacy Center, which opened in 2014 in a branch of the Free Library of Philadelphia, at a library conference. Richland Library staff were so impressed that a number decided to go to Philadelphia and take a tour. Now, a recently renovated branch of the library has a teaching kitchen in it with a full-time culinary literacy coordinator who does cooking and nutrition classes not only at this branch but throughout the Richland Library system. This is how ideas develop and spread. The successful example of culinary literacy at this library led the State Library of South Carolina, in turn, to purchase a Charlie Cart (think of it as a mobile kitchen about the size of a table with all you need tucked inside) that the library moves around the state to support culinary literacy programming statewide. This is how the diffusion of innovation happens.

This process can be seen playing out in the development of early literacy programming that focuses on physically active play. This trend has completely exploded over the last twenty years, with multiple handbooks focusing extensively on how and why to get small kids and their caregivers moving and learning in the library (e.g., McNeil 2012; Kaplan 2014; Prato 2014; Scherrer 2017). As a result of these resources, librarians frequently tell me they have numerous opportunities to learn how to develop these types of programs. One stated that "many staff members have explored new ideas and techniques through professional development opportunities." Another said that "the movement part of the programming was something that was beginning to happen more and more in libraries in the late '90s and early 2000s as recommendations began to come out from brain studies about the importance of using language and movement together in the development of the very young brain" (Lenstra 2018e, 149). Armed with these resources, librarians report feeling confident as they develop this active living programming, which one described as "story-time without the stories" and another described as venues in which "families get a workout" because they require so much physical activity from youth and caregivers (Lenstra 2018e, 149).

I've found that sometimes all that is needed for healthy living at the library to flourish is for someone to say that it's OK to do this work. It may seem new and far out initially, but we've done these programs in many places already. So when you speak up about the work you're doing in your library to support healthy living, you are validating and authorizing this work for other librarians who may feel hesitant or unsure of themselves.

Oklahoma's Efforts to Promote Healthy Living in Libraries

To illustrate the power of these networks, I want to share the story of health literacy in Oklahoma libraries. Since 2011 the Oklahoma Department of Libraries has made health literacy a strategic goal, and the state library has funneled thousands of dollars given to it by the Institute of Museum and Library Services to public libraries to develop everything from community gardens to cooking classes to StoryWalk® and yoga at the library programs. In 2017 the state library went even further. It started a small, closed online group for "for libraries and literacy programs to exchange ideas and resources for Oklahoma Health Literacy projects." Leslie Gelders, from the state library, let me join the group to see what was being discussed, and I was amazed! In this group, librarians share everything from success stories to program ideas to troubleshooting problems. This small little group, and the years of work in Oklahoma that lay behind, truly represents a model that others could follow. The Oklahoma Department of Libraries health literacy projects were made possible thanks to funding from the Institute of Museum and Libraries Services. Its story is provided here.

Note: Go to http://letsmovelibraries.org/healthy-living-at-the-library to access photographs associated with the story of health literacy promotion via the Oklahoma Department of Libraries.

> Health information is so important and so many people don't understand how to ask the right questions. It takes a lot of courage to tell someone you don't know something. As long as you treat us with respect and show the right attitude, we're not going to be offended by how many questions you have to ask us in order to help us find the information we're looking for.
> —Carol, adult learner from Tulsa

In 2018, twenty-ninth annual America's Health Rankings, produced by the United Health Foundation, listed Oklahoma as one of the five least healthy states. Contributing to the low score were high rates of obesity, diabetes, and heart disease, and low rates of physical inactivity, child immunizations, and consumption of fresh fruits and vegetables.

Oklahoma ranked forty-seventh overall. But more and more, there are opportunities for all types of organizations to collaborate to promote health and wellness in the community. Nationally and in Oklahoma, public libraries are resources for credible health information and sites for health-related programming directed toward children, teens, adults, and families.

Why libraries? A 2015 Pew Research Study indicated that 73 percent of people who visited a public library in the United States went there looking for answers about their health. Libraries are trusted community institutions that offer a nonthreatening environment, are staffed with information experts, and provide free access to a wide variety of resources.

For the past few years, the Oklahoma Department of Libraries has helped foster significant partnerships at state and local levels to promote health and wellness. Federal funding from the Institute of Museum and Library Services allowed ODL to offer health literacy grants to public libraries and adult literacy programs. As a result of this funding, grantees have targeted the specific health needs of their community and expanded resources and services to address these needs.

> I am proud to say that I learned so much from the presenters. I have a heart issue and when I applied what I learned to my everyday life, I lost weight and feel great!
> —Adult learner from the Opportunities Industrialization Center (OIC) of Oklahoma County

> This project gave our library a new focus based on a real community need. We have come away from this determined that providing for lifetime learning about ways to achieve healthy living will become one of our core programs.
> —Marcia Johnson, Miami Public Library

The Southern Oklahoma Library System hosted a number of health and wellness programs in public libraries throughout south-central Oklahoma. Classes included everything from healthy cooking demonstrations and tai chi to a hay bale garden and chair exercise classes at a Veteran's center.

Bartlesville Public Library Literacy Services offered forty-five classes, including Stress Management, Preventing Influenza, and Healthy Aging. Special health presentations provided basic health and wellness information to adult learners participating in the adult literacy program.

Beaver County Pioneer Library helped children understand the importance of eating fruit and vegetables during the Grow It, Try It, Like It program. During the four-week series, library staff shared books about fruits and vegetables, and community partners talked to parents and children about healthy eating. Tai Chi, yoga, and Pilates classes were also available, free of charge, to members of the community.

Moore Public Library reached more than 2,835 children, teens, and adults through more than 108 health and wellness classes. Their Argentine Tango class provided a fun and interesting way to get participants up and moving. A Back to School Health Fair was attended by more than 255 community members.

Seminole Public Library collaborated with a number of community partners to promote physical activity with Jump Rope Clubs in six schools throughout the county. By the end of the project, participating third- through eighth-grade students improved their jumps per minute and their body mass index. They also learned how to read food labels, why it is important to reduce sugar and salt consumption, and why exercise is good for heart health.

Western Oklahoma Learning Center, in Elk City, provided health and wellness information to English-language learners, seniors, and the community at large. Two family swim nights featuring water aerobics for all ages, and low-intensity exercise classes were available to seniors. Twenty-six community members participated in the American Public Health Association's Billion Step Challenge logging 12,960 steps.

> As a result of this grant, the Noble Public Library became a hub for community members, organizations, and nonprofits to create new partnerships. We were able to assist local residents with access to health information and tools. Several participants are eager for the next round of classes, frequently coming by the library to ask about upcoming dates.
>
> —Noble Public Library

If you're not lucky enough to live in Oklahoma, tell staff from your state library that *you're* interested in this topic and would love more support. Submit proposals to your state library association. Speak up, and support will follow. Since the pioneering efforts of the Oklahoma Department of Libraries, other state libraries, including those in North Carolina, Massachusetts, California, Montana, and Ohio. have also made funding available for health literacy programs.

At the national/international level, a lot of really wonderful support networks already exist. Here are some of my favorites:

- The Association for Rural and Small Libraries (ARSL) listserv. This list is only accessible to members of this association, but the cost of joining is worth it just for the listserv! I get the daily digest, and it seems like at least once a month, someone mentions a healthy living program they've done or want to do.

- The Programming Librarians interest group. Supported by the American Library Association's Public Programs Office, this is an online space where programming librarians share tips and inspire others. As in the ARSL list, pretty much every program discussed in this book has come up once or twice in this group.
- Storytime Underground on Facebook. *The* place for children's librarians— a great resource for StoryWalk®, Yoga Storytime, and other kid-focused programming.
- Libraries Are Champions of Healthy Communities. A newer online group administered by staff from the National Network of Libraries of Medicine and a great place to get advice, especially if you're looking for a venue with less traffic.
- Online communities formed around hashtags on Instagram and Twitter, such as #LibraryYoga, among others.

In these online spaces, you can get advice on everything from what to do when your Tai Chi instructor fails to show up to how to get a food preparation license to how to maintain your garden if interest wanes. This book will hopefully get you started, but to keep going your best bet is get connected to and to stay connected in these and other online networks.

I also want to make especially big plugs for OCLC/WebJunction, the Programming Librarian (an initiative of the ALA Public Programs Office), and the National Network of Libraries of Medicine. These three entities have invested an enormous amount of time and energy into supporting this type of programming, and their websites are chock-full of useful resources, some of which I authored. They also always seek stories of what is happening in libraries. So speak up and share with them. They can help you, in turn, to inspire others.

Here's a recap of the resources mentioned:

ARSL Listserv
   https://arsl.info/board/frequently-asked-questions
Programming Librarians Interest Group
   https://www.facebook.com/groups/ProgrammingLibrarianInterestGroup
Storytime Underground
   https://www.facebook.com/groups/storytimeunderground
Libraries are Champions of Healthy Communities
   https://www.facebook.com/groups/LibsChampionHealth
Health Happens in Libraries, at OCLC/WebJunction
   https://www.webjunction.org/explore-topics/ehealth.html
Programming Librarian (ALA Public Programs Office)
   http://www.programminglibrarian.org
ALA-PLA/NNLM Health Portal
   https://publiclibrary.health

Movement-Based Book Club at Tompkins County Public Library, Ithaca, New York

This story from Ithaca, New York, is a great example of librarians supporting librarians. Staff from the Durland Alternatives Library, a project of the Center for Transformative Action on the campus of Cornell University, teamed up with the local public library to develop and deliver this movement-based book club. Heidi Eckerson of the Durland Alternatives Library wrote the story of this collaborative program.

Flyer for Movement-Based Book Club at the Tompkins County Public Library, an example of a collaborative program. Courtesy Heidi Eckerson and the Tompkins County Public Library.

Our movement-based book club meets weekly to explore and experience the questions posed by Katy Bowman in her book *Move Your DNA: Restore Your Health through Natural Movement.* The book is meant to be a practical resource to help you move your body in new ways, which can sometimes be challenging without guided instruction. Our 1.5-hour meetings will combine discussion with movement in a safe and supportive environment, applying Katy's approach to "restore [-ing] our health through natural movement."

Melissa Miller, D.C., RN, has had extensive training with Katy Bowman and is a Nutritious Movement™ certified restorative exercise specialist. She is excited to offer her expertise to help participants feel confident with the exercises so they can start incorporating them in daily life activities.

Heidi Eckerson, MAT, MS-ILS, a librarian at the Durland Alternatives Library, is also a New York state–licensed massage therapist and believes that moving better is living well. This book club is being offered by Durland Alternatives Library and is cosponsored by Tompkins County Public Library.

Where It Came From

An idea hatched between friends almost a year earlier while on a walk grew into the announcement that went live in April 2018 on the Tompkins County Public Library (TCPL) website. Ideas are easy; it's their implementation that requires more thought. Fortunately, our field boasts professionals working in a variety of roles with rich, diverse backgrounds and skills. In the end, many hands made our movement-based book club not only possible but successful.

As a librarian I connect people, information, and ideas. Prior to getting my MS-ILS, I was an educator for nearly twenty years, most recently teaching kinesiology at a local vocational school for massage therapists, where I met Melissa Miller. Ultimately, we both moved out of the classroom and into new positions [Heidi at the Durland Alternatives Library and Melissa starting her practice, Nuravita]. But we knew we wanted to partner on a movement-based project. We had shared pieces of Bowman's work in our classroom, and students were intrigued. The idea of a book club based on her 2017 *Move Your DNA: Restore Your Health through Natural Movement* started to form when we realized the concepts she wrote about were accessible to laypeople and contained important health and wellness information for anyone to consider.

However, we didn't want to just talk about moving better. We wanted to move. The club would be experiential, combining the corrective exercises from the book with thoughtful discussion about the science. A key consideration was to create an inclusive program where participants did not need movement experience or a science background but only a curious mind.

A library was a perfect place to hold the club because it provided several degrees of access: people could borrow the book and there were no instructor fees to pay. Most importantly, it was not a fitness studio atmosphere, a setting that can feel intimidating to some folks.

Such a book club aligned with the Durland Alternatives Library's mission. Since 1974 the Alternatives Library has been creating a space through its collections and programming that nurtures dialogue and promotes an alternative approach to social change. As is true for many libraries, we operate with limited resources. Even with Melissa volunteering her time and expertise, funds to purchase the books were lacking. While space wasn't an insurmountable issue (our small library transforms into a music venue every Sunday night), getting to us was, for some folks. We are a public library and a project of the Center for Transformative Action located on the Cornell University campus, where parking is challenging.

Walking through the stacks at TCPL, inspiration struck. Noticing the book group kits on the shelves, I wondered, Who buys these? Dashing off an email to Jenny Shonk, continuing education and outreach librarian at the Finger Lakes Library System (FLLS), I explained our idea and asked her who made purchasing decisions. She responded that it was one of her jobs, and she was interested in our idea. In short order, ten copies of the book were ordered, and we began developing a book kit that would be available to patrons at all thirty-three member libraries.

Partners Involved

Reaching out to Jenny at FLLS, a cooperative library system to which TCPL and DAL belong, was key. In addition to purchasing the books and assembling the book kit, she introduced us to Teresa Vadakin, head of information and learning services at TCPL. This connection led to our libraries cosponsoring the book club.

TCPL already had a thriving wellness program that included well-attended yoga and midday mindfulness classes. The library also hosted several popular book clubs. When we pitched our movement-based book club to Teresa, she was on board and provided advice on the logistics of how we could turn our idea into an actual program.

> With numerous experiences hosting book clubs and cosponsored programs, the library was able to provide a space and promotion for the wellness program. Promotion included the website calendar with an online registration tool, and a press release that is sent all over the community. Book distribution is handled by reference and each participant was able to pick up the book ahead of the program.
>
> —Teresa Vadakin

How It Operates, and Its Impacts

While the Alternatives Library and Nurativa developed the program and marketing content, TCPL provided the physical space and marketing channels, and it coordinated program registration and the distribution of books. The ten slots filled quickly on the first day online registration opened. Meeting weekly over the course of a month, each of the four 1.5-hour sessions focused on a specific set of chapters and concepts discussed in the book. Held midweek between 6:30 and 8:00 p.m. to accommodate work schedules, the sessions roughly unfolded as follows:

- Opening discussion surrounding essential questions we had crafted, as well as space given to participants to bring up aspects of the week's reading they found interesting, insightful, problematic, and so forth (approximately 15–20 minutes)
- Guided movement, where discussion could continue (approximately 45–60 minutes)
- Closure piece and, time permitting, a brief mention of the topic for the upcoming meeting

Certainly, habits don't change in one month. Our intention was to get folks thinking about ways to bring more movement into their lives and to show them how to do it. And based on discussions, we felt that an awareness had been cultivated and curiosity had been stirred. One member checked out another book written by Katy Bowman from TCPL's stacks. Teresa observed some new faces among the members of the book club, reminding us of the importance of offering diverse programming opportunities in order to include all members of the community. Because it is a book kit, all patrons may borrow it and hold their own movement-based book clubs. Melissa and I are available to consult or assist in club implementation.

Other interesting impacts of our movement-based book club:

- The program was so successful that a second session was added. Eight people were on the waiting list from the spring program.
- Our libraries were able to help support a local businessperson. Essentially, Melissa's donation of time and expertise functioned as a marketing tool for her local business. She brought rack cards and flyers to the meetings and directed participants to her website for more information on her programming.

Exercises

1. Where do you currently turn to for support and continuing education as a librarian?
2. Have you heard any discussions about healthy living at the library in these spaces?
3. If you answered no, how could you get that conversation going?
4. If you answered yes, what have been the healthy living topics or programs discussed?

8

Watch Your Step: Key Challenges and Solutions

Reflecting on the development of the Culinary Literacy Center, staff from the Free Library of Philadelphia noted that

> the early days . . . involved a lot of throwing pasta at the wall to see if it stuck, which meant trying so many different things out. We knew what it meant to be librarians, but weren't so sure about how to open a cooking school or a restaurant, which was what it felt like we were doing some days. We were inventing what it meant to do culinary literacy programming in a library. It was exciting and a little terrifying. The biggest difference between now and then—besides the size of our staff—is that now we rely much less on our partners to determine what our programming looks like. **We found our voice. We defined our mission**. (Free Library of Philadelphia 2017, 4)

You'll need to go on this journey at your library as you develop healthy living programming. But unlike the Free Library of Philadelphia and the many other trailblazers highlighted in this book, you have the benefit of standing on the shoulders of all the librarians who have come before you.

In this chapter, we'll focus on some common obstacles and common solutions. The caveats should not discourage but should sensitize you to the fact that not everything may go smoothly the first time out. Rebekkah Smith Aldrich urges us to "fail fast" in library innovation:

> Failing fast is not encouraging failure but **shortening the cycle time** of admitting something isn't working. Rather than drag out a program for multiple years that two people sign up for, let's close that down, assess what is behind the low attendance, repackage the program, and either try again or drop it and use the resources that had been doing into it for something else. (2018, 143)

I encourage you to go into this process with your eyes open. That will enable you to fail fast and course-correct quickly, if and as needed (it will be needed).

Be on the lookout for these four types of challenges:

- Logistical challenges (e.g., space, funding)
- Participation challenges (too many, not enough)
- Theoretical challenges (why is this happening at the library?)
- Accessibility (how to make the programs as accessible as possible)

Logistics

Librarians have told me about **all kinds** of logistical challenges related to healthy living programs, including partners not showing up, struggling to purchase equipment (if needed), not enough time to promote programs, not enough space, noise complaints, and on and on. Let's break apart some of the more common challenges and address them.

Space is a frequent concern, but there are some common work-arounds I've seen librarians employ to make sure they have the space they need for their healthy living programs:

1. If you don't have a meeting room, do programs in the children's section of the library.
2. Book the space far, far in advance, and make healthy living programs (including shared-use programs) a priority for meeting-room use.
3. If your location isn't conducive—that is, you don't have enough space, or the space you have is so small that the noise generated by the program would distract other patrons—see about doing them at another branch of your library system or even off-site, in a church kitchen, school, or even outdoors (weather permitting), on the library lawn or in a nearby park.
4. Add additional sessions if you find too many people are coming to the program and your space is getting overtaxed.

Challenges with program leaders and supplies are also common. One thing that surprised me is that some libraries actually ask patrons to pay modest fees to make the programs financially sustainable. This is far, far from ideal, but it may be a temporary measure you have to take. In the long term, you'll want to think about fund-raising, which we'll cover in part IV of this book.

Other libraries develop policies, especially for programming that involves external instructors. Some make it a point to "try to find volunteers and an instructor who is reasonably priced." One librarian said, "Where possible [we] tried to find people willing to volunteer time." Still, others will use technology instead of live instructors. As one librarian said, "The only issue we had was that we didn't have a TV to show the Geri-Fit videos. We contacted one of our generous donors, and they purchased a large-screen TV, DVD player, and a cart to mount both so they are mobile" (Lenstra 2019b). If you don't ask, you can't receive!

If healthy living programming is new to you, you may find yourself struggling to get the word out and to build up an audience, at least initially. Your community may not expect such programming of you, so this is critical. Librarians stress using multiple messages in multiple formats: "Try multiple communication sources to best reach target audience"; "advertise in different places"; "be varied in our advertising of these types of programs"; "advertise at local medical centers, hospitals, grocery stores, and churches"; or simply, "get the word out about what is offered in every possible format."

Others emphasize the personal touch. One librarian told me that what has really worked for them was "personal encouragement of patrons by individual staff to 'enjoy with us' this healthy living program." This invitation to connect with others at the library really resonates, especially for individuals who may feel uncomfortable participating without this personal encouragement.

Finally, before you think about deploying your messages, consider whether you have particular patrons in mind for your programs (such as children's caregivers, senior citizens, or English-language learners), and if so, what their unique communication needs may be. Once you have clarified whether your audience is broad or targeted, talk directly to them and help them understand why they should participate. In this messaging, reinforce the view of the library as *their* trusted resource center. It should be clear in your messages that the library is committed to healthy communities and that health happens everywhere, including at the library.

If you're concerned about having too many participants (or too few!) you could ask people to indicate if they'll be coming. Some libraries now enable patrons to register online, and some enable patrons to sign waivers of liability online so that by the time they get to the program they're ready to go.

Although, in general, library staff report programs being very popular, some librarians did share challenges related to participation. One librarian found that she "hasn't been able to get [a yoga class] off the ground." Another said participation in programs has been "rather disappointing," with usually only two or three patrons participating. This individual did note, however, that "of course as soon as we say we won't do it anymore, then people come in and ask about the walking group," illustrating that it takes time for new programs to develop. Other participation challenges include people showing up to watch female participants and not to participate themselves, caregivers not wanting to participate in programs with their children, and the like. Some of these challenges are outside of your control, but in many cases, reminding people that these programs are safe spaces open to all may help.

Other staff mentioned struggling to encourage participation among certain populations. One librarian said that "one summer we did yoga for teens—but it was just not well attended, and those who did attend were, like, ten years old, so the following summer we did it for elementary school–aged." You may need to make similar tweaks in your programs as you learn what works and what doesn't work.

Safety and Legal Issues

Virtually every time I have given any talk about this topic, the first question people want to know about is safety. There are no magical solutions to the issue of safety in programs that involve the body. Anything you do beyond the mere dissemination of information, such as preparing food, eating food, or moving, will have risks. Even in the safest programs, there are always risks.

The good news is that now so many libraries are doing these programs that we've worked out most of the kinks. Here are the two most important things we should ask ourselves:

1. Should patrons sign a waiver of liability, indicating they are aware this program involves food or physical activity and that they waive the right to hold the library liable in case of any injury that may result from said food or physical activity?
2. Is this a conversation you should be having with your partners, who in many cases have extensive experience dealing with these questions?

You may also want to think about, and talk about within your library team, what risks you're willing to take in order to bring these learning experiences to your community.

In addition to waivers of liability, you may want to develop a boilerplate, one- or two-minute speech that is delivered at the start of all your healthy living programs, along these lines: "No one is, under any circumstances, to engage in anything that makes him or her feel uncomfortable. If you feel uncomfortable at any point, stop what you're doing, and speak up to let us know so we can address what is happening. If you have any allergies or mobility impairments, let us know."

There may also be municipal, regional, and national codes to which you need to adhere, especially around the topics of food preparation, food storage, and food serving. Your best bet is to engage your partners and your library administration on these topics. Related are concerns—which typically come from outside the library—that the library may be putting itself at legal risk by offering these programs. One librarian told me that a big challenge for them is city "lawyers worrying about the library being sued if participants hurt themselves." Being able to sit down with your library's or town's legal counsel and calmly and articulately explain why you are doing a particular program, ideally with examples from other places, can go a long way to assuage fears.

You may also need to talk with your insurance provider to make sure you have the appropriate coverage for these programs. Many libraries already do, but it doesn't hurt to check. It really depends on what coverage you have and also whether you are part of your city/county government. You also want to be mindful of the fire code. Sometimes these classes can be *very* popular. Just be safe and think ahead.

In any case, by the time these programs become more common, a lot of the public's fear has dissipated. The initial shock of seeing people cooking food and practicing yoga in the library has worn off. We now realize that these programs are actually a lot safer than some librarians and library administrators originally feared; for one thing, lawsuits never materialized. Nonetheless, you do want to start this programming on the right footing, cognizant of the risks involved, and with procedures in place to ensure that programs proceed with safety first.

Theoretical Issues

It may seem a bit abstract to talk about theoretical issues here, but trust me, these are very real issues. Don't just take my word for it. Here is the advice that Liz Fitzgerald, administrator of the Free Library of Philadelphia's Culinary Literacy Center, offers to **any** librarian who wants to start healthy living programming: "**Define the mission**: That is the best piece of advice I have to give when speaking with the people who contact us to learn about how to open a kitchen in their library" (Free Library of Philadelphia 2017, 4).

If you don't know *why* you're cooking or gardening or doing yoga at your library, you're unlikely to be successful. Your "why" should not be something you come up with on your own but should rather be the result of dialogue within your library team, with your community partners, and with your community members.

Librarians commonly relay to me struggles they experience positioning these programs within the overall mission of the library. A staff member who has led yoga storytimes for almost a decade at her library said, "There are two ways to approach this type of programming. One is to keep it focused on literacy and to make a strong connection with literacy and physical movement: what StoryWalks® do and what yoga storytime is about. It is all based on learning through movement and play. And the second is library as community centers. If you look at [it] this way, you don't need to justify the connection to literacy and learning" (Lenstra 2018e). This astute statement illustrates the two main approaches found in my data. Some librarians endeavor to ensure that literacy and reading are at the center of all library programs, including healthy living programs. Others have embraced the identity of the library as a multipurpose community center. Both are valid and legitimate, and you can do healthy living programs through either lens. The key thing is to define your library's approach to this topic.

Again, don't do this alone but in collaboration with your community. A librarian in western Kansas wrote that "[as] a rural library . . . we are working hard to promote fitness and movement without infringing on businesses who sell their services." Public librarians also report taking care to ensure that what they do is not only not competitive but also complementary. A librarian in rural Vermont wrote that "many of the summer reading programs are planned with the Recreation Department. Library and Recreation personnel work together with StoryWalk® as well." In other places, there are few other entities that provide free support for physical activity. A librarian from rural Ontario wrote that they provide these programs because "we are a small, low income town. We have no YMCA." Another librarian from rural Nova Scotia wrote that "we see the library as having a community development role, so we try to increase our small community's access to health and wellness opportunities." These quotes (Lenstra 2018k) illustrate public librarians' support for healthy living in the context of the unique needs of their particular communities. You'll need to figure out your own answer, your own path, your own healthy living mission. Use these resources as starting points, and then work out the details with your partners, colleagues, and communities.

Accessibility

One final, often-voiced concern relates to accessibility. There are two ways to approach this matter: On the one hand, there is a need to ensure that individuals of all abilities have access to these types of programs so as not to inadvertently reinforce health inequities. On the other hand, there is also evidence that programs focused on healthy living can, in fact, enable our libraries to become *more* accessible. Doris Gebel, a librarian in Virginia, found that adding physical activities to library programs for youth made those programs more accessible to individuals whose first language was not English: "When the second-graders attended the Wednesday session, it was at the end of a long school day and they were tired. Activities, such as Migration Hopscotch, energized them for the rest of the program. In addition, there was no language barrier during any of the activities using action and movement, and thus easier to enjoy for these second-graders" (Holmes 2016, 3). Nearly identical experiences were reported by librarians in Lethbridge, Alberta, who added physical activities into their programming mix (Weekes and Longair 2016).

Nevertheless, it is true that not everyone can participate equally in all healthy living programs. Thankfully, a number of creative librarians have developed some great advice on how to increase accessibility for these types of programs. What some are doing is detailed below.

The Andrew Heiskell Braille and Talking Book Library, a branch of the New York Public Library, is at the forefront of active living programs for differently abled populations. As part of its "Barrier Free Library" initiative, it works to ensure that the free fitness opportunities being offered throughout the New York Public Library system do not exclude anyone because of their abilities. One of the programs it has offered is "Accessible Personal Fitness: Tips, Tech and Resources: Exploring Fitness at the Heiskell Library." Nefertiti Matos, assistant trainer for assistive technology at NYPL, said,

> At the workshop, we first acknowledged our remote participants [those unable to physically attend], introducing ourselves and talking about the role that fitness plays in our lives. Responses included "I like to eat so I have to do it," "I hate getting up early to exercise or passing up fries, but I love the energy boost after a hard workout," and "how empowered I feel knowing that I chose to fuel my body, not just to fill it." Personally, I believe that true fitness goes beyond the physical: Fitness means an overall soundness of our whole self, involving emotional and mental wellness too. (Matos 2018)

We could not agree more, and we love how this library is working to build a supportive community so that individuals of all abilities, including those physically unable to visit the library, can take advantage of opportunities to move and be healthy. At the workshop, participants learned about technology like Eyes-Free Fitness, an app that offers nonvisual workouts with clear, detailed verbal descriptions, and also learned about the work that the NYC Parks Department is doing with libraries (and other partners) to extend access to active living for all.

In addition to active-living support groups that include information all can use to practice healthy living, other libraries endeavor to ensure that their programs are open to all. The word *adaptive* signals that programs have been adapted to meet the needs of all abilities. Turning yoga into chair yoga is an example of such an adaptation. Some libraries, like the San Diego County Library, also offer adaptive fitness programs. Tom Christensen of the County of San Diego Communications Office writes,

They come from a variety of backgrounds and each has different challenges, but for one hour a week in the Lemon Grove Library, a group of special needs adults all have one thing in common—their enthusiasm. Between 20 and 30 show up each week for an adaptive Zumba class that has them kicking, twirling, clapping and doing "the Stanky Leg." "They follow routines very well," said Lisabeth Garces, the certified Zumba instructor that leads the class. "I make it inclusive and simple and motivate them to do what they can do." For some, it's their primary exercise outlet. All participants are welcome including those in wheelchairs or those who need to sit in order to do the routines. "You get people with all levels of coordination, but you get that in any class," said Garces. "They can do the same work sitting or standing—it's the movement that's important." "The library is an inclusive space where everyone is welcomed," said Liz Vagani, Lemon Grove branch manager. "Programs like adaptive Zumba bring underserved populations into the library, and show the participants the value we place on their presence in our branches. Every week we have at least 20 special needs adults waiting at the door for the program to start." (Christensen 2016)

In Durham, North Carolina, branch manager Stephanie Fennell also found that the exercise needs of amputees were not being met, a discovery that inspired her to develop free fitness classes for these individuals at her library. She said that in addition to the benefits of exercise, the program builds community. The library can (and often is) a safe space for *all* individuals to increase healthy living in their lives.

There are other things that you can do to practice inclusion. In Michigan, the state library has made funding Braille-enhanced StoryWalks® a strategic priority. As of spring 2018, at least thirty-two Michigan libraries had these inclusive StoryWalks®. Learn more at https://www.michigan.gov/som/0,4669,7-192 -29939_34761-465892--,00.html.

You can also take inspiration from some of the cooking programs that the Free Library of Philadelphia has developed for groups that otherwise receive inadequate resources and services in their community. These include:

- Edible Alphabet, an English-as-a-second-language course for new Americans
- Cookability, a program for people who are visually impaired to learn and share about food and cooking
- Chow Down on Wellness, a plant-based cooking class for military veterans designed to promote healthy eating habits and team building in a relaxed social atmosphere
- Cooking with Confidence, a beginner cooking class designed for adults with disabilities

Not just in special programs but for any food programs you offer, you need to think about allergies. You may consider a blanket "no nuts" policy, given the prevalence of various nut allergies, especially among very young children. Or you may want to make sure alternatives are available for common allergies. The most important thing you can do is publicize, well in advance, the full ingredient list you plan to use, along with a note that anyone requiring adaptations, based on this list, should contact the library ahead of time. You'll want to know in advance, so no one feels excluded on the day of the program.

If you do any gardening or outdoor programs, there are also things that you can do to promote accessibility. At a minimum, you should ensure that any outdoor spaces maintained by the library meet or exceed Americans with Disabilities Act (ADA) standards (or related requirements in your nation). Have you made sure that your StoryWalk® or other walking paths in or around library gardens accommodate wheelchairs and strollers? If you have a garden at your library, think about having the garden beds at various heights, from ground level to about thirty-six inches (a best practice for purposes of inclusion).

If you're doing a movement program for small children in which caregivers are present, you should "leave modifications to programs up to the child's parent or caregiver," according to librarians Kristin Grabarek and Mary R. Lanni, who have extensive experience on this topic. They find that rather than assume you know what children can or cannot do, you should instead "simply welcome the child and family in the same way that each of the other children and families are welcomed and . . . offer any help or accommodation the caregiver might like. . . . The key is to create a space that is welcoming to all" (2019, 48). This approach is basically the one you should take with other ages as well: Assume that people know what they can or cannot do (they have to indicate as much when they sign the waiver of liability), and remind people not to do anything that feels uncomfortable. Let people make informed decisions for themselves.

Two final notes on accessibility:

1. Universal accessibility is a journey, not a destination. Rather than **not** offer a program because you aren't sure whether it is accessible for all, you should offer it in a way that opens up a dialogue. When working with your partners, your community members, and your staff, accessibility should always be in the back of your minds, but these concerns should not keep you from offering what could be a life-changing program.
2. Rely on your partners to help you out! In many cases, the partners with which you work to develop programs will have expertise in accessibility for healthy living programs. If you're not sure about something, ask them. Also, ask other librarians using the resources in the last chapter.

Checklist for Accessibility in Healthy Living Programs

For All Programs

1. Do I have a blurb in my advertisements that articulates our library's commitment to inclusion for all, requesting that patrons who require adaptations to contact library staff?
2. Do I have talking points ready at the beginning of the program that explain exactly what we will be doing, so people know what they are getting into?
3. Have I thought about the needs of differently abled individuals? Do I have a plan in case someone comes forward whose needs we had not considered before?
4. Is there any way I could offer all or part of this program to individuals physically unable to visit the library?

For Healthy Eating Programs

1. Have I thought about common food allergies and made alternative ingredients available?
2. Are my library gardens accessible? Could I raise one bed up higher, to increase inclusion?

For Active Living Programs

1. Is my StoryWalk® ADA accessible?
2. Have I worked with my partners to communicate the library's commitment to inclusion for all, ensuring that they are ready to make adaptations to active living programs as needed? For instance, could any part or all of a given activity be done from a seated position?

Exercises

1. Thinking about your library, what challenges do you envision arising (or have you seen arise) as you offer healthy living programming?
2. When challenges like those discussed in this chapter arise, to whom do you turn for help and support? Your staff colleagues? Your community partners? Other librarians? Family and friends?

Part III

Offering Programs

9

Healthy Living in All Programs

Part III covers how to offer healthy living programs at your library, using five different techniques:

1. Adding healthy living practices to existing programs
2. Embracing the power of play to change how people think about healthy living
3. Offering immersive cooking and exercise programs
4. Developing new collections and spaces to support your healthy living programs
5. Taking your programming outside

Before we get into these program models, let's do an exercise. Try doing it now and then again after you've read through this part III.

1. Reflect on your library's mission, vision, and current assets.
   Now identify and write out *three potential programs* that you might wish to provide to support healthy living in the community you serve.
2. Reflect on the constellation of individuals and institutions in your community.
   Now identify and write out *three potential partners* that you might wish to work with to bring these programs to fruition.

We'll end by putting the pieces together into a programming plan that you can implement at your library. And then there will be a little bonus: chapter 15, "Healthy Living across the Seasons: Programming Ideas for Year-Round Healthy Living," includes some ideas on what to offer at your library in winter, spring, summer, and fall.

In September 2018, the Stewart C. Meyer Public Library, in Harker Heights, Texas, hired a new employee, Destinee Barton. Destinee had recently earned a bachelor's degree in community health from Texas Woman's University and was hired for the new position of youth health and program coordinator. Library director Lisa Youngblood said, "Destinee provides advice so that all of our programs (including adult, children and outreach) can become healthier programs. How can we slip health in every program we do? For instance, Destinee is a big believer in physical activity, and we're working so that every single program we do includes physical activity for all age groups, if we can and if it's appropriate" (Lenstra 2019c). Destinee added, "For summer 2019, we're doing a lot of programs with physical activity, including Zumba, tai chi, cardio kickboxing, yoga and including healthy snacks as well in the programs. With teenagers, we've found that we need to make it feel like it isn't a program. The key is not making them do anything, but instead trying to get them interested and listening to them" (Lenstra 2019c).

In this chapter, we'll go over how you can think about healthy living programming as this library does. We'll focus on healthy living during summer programming, which can be adapted to school and academic libraries for finals time programming. Then we'll look at two specific types of programs: Active storytimes—including yoga storytimes—and walking book clubs. These are great examples of librarians infusing healthy living into existing programs in fun and impactful ways.

Summer Programming

This section focuses on things public libraries can do to infuse healthy living into summer programming. The strategies described could just as easily be applied to finals programming in a school or academic library. Whenever your library is full of people, such as spring break, that's the perfect time to think about how you can infuse healthy living into your programming.

Starting Summer Right

In the small town of Taylorsville, North Carolina (pop. 2,098), nestled in the foothills of the Appalachian Mountains, Melissa 'Miss Mel' Hager starts off summer at the library with a hike at Rocky Face Mountain Recreation Area: "Our hike at Rocky Face Mountain Recreational Area is an annual summer reading activity, usually done for the first or second program. Our county park is a treasure, and it is the library's way to encourage local families to use the park for hiking, picnics, and the like. After our hike, children are fed through the federal summer feeding program or are served watermelon [if they do not use the feeding program]. We will definitely do this hike again every year

for summer reading." Go to http://letsmovelibraries.org/healthy-living-at-the
-library to access photographs of this annual summer reading hike.

Starting your summer programming with a healthy event sets the tone
for the rest of the summer. Here are some ideas from other places. The
Corvallis-Benton Library, in Oregon, starts summer with a free family fun
run. The Lafayette Public Library, in Louisiana, starts with a bike safety festival. Many libraries start with carnivals that feature things like bounce houses,
sports (Quidditch on the lawn, anyone?), active games, and more. If you have
a big party, you could also invite vendors to do pop-up healthy cooking demos,
or, as they did in Taylorsville, think about partnering with a group to bring
healthy food to participants. Academic libraries do similar things at the start
of finals. Throw a party at the library on Reading Day; have some active games
and some healthy food to show your students you want them to thrive during
finals, and that includes staying healthy. You could adapt this to a school
library by offering some de-stressing activities in the lead-up to and during
testing times.

There is one program model in particular that I really want to recommend,
and that is the "play street" or "open street." This model, initially developed by
public health, parks and recreation, and urban planning people in the early
twentieth century (the first play street occurred in New York City in 1914)
focuses on opening streets up for play by closing them to traffic. Dr. Renee
Umstattd Meyer, of Baylor University's public health program, has worked
with public libraries (and others) in the small towns of Talihina, Oklahoma,
and Cameron, Texas, to bring play street programs to these rural communities. In Talihina, the library hosted a play street in collaboration with the
Choctaw Nation, a Native American territory and federally recognized Indian
tribe. According to Dr. Umstattd Meyer, during the play street program, there
was a constant flow of people in and out of the library, playing in the street
and then going into the library to relax, recharge, and read. In Cameron,
Texas, the library brought its bookmobile to the play street program held at
a local school. In Oklahoma, the partnership was so successful that in 2019
the library in nearby Purcell, Oklahoma, started a weekly play street program.
According to organizers, nearly 150 people come out every Wednesday for this
program (Purcell Register 2019). Dr. Umstattd Meyer is currently developing
a play streets toolkit and is very excited to share what she has learned with
librarians interested in trying out this program idea. Learn more at https://
paresearchcenter.org.

The play street program offers a low-cost way for neighborhoods and libraries to create more spaces for active recreation and lifelong learning. By creating
new outdoor play spaces, you also transform how people see their communities, including libraries, seeing them now as interconnected spaces for active
play and community and not just as disparate destinations only accessible

by automobile. You will literally build community by offering a play street program.

Before you even think about doing this program, you will want to do an environmental scan to see if these types of programs already take place in your community. If they do, get involved with them. Show up at planning meetings and offer the library's support. That's what the Fulton County Public Library System, based in Atlanta, Georgia, does. Staff set up a pop-up library at an open-streets celebration that took place in Roswell, Georgia, on Sunday, April 28, 2019, by, according to the library, bringing "Giant Chess, Giant Legos, Giant Connect 4, and regular size library cards" to the event. Learn more at https://www.instagram.com/p/BxN5bU1gnAb.

If you find these programs aren't already occurring in your community (or there isn't one happening around the time you want to start or end your summer programming), then take the leap and plan a play street at your library! The first step is figuring out a location. The traditional idea is literally on a street, but sometimes these closures can be logistically difficult to achieve, so alternatives include closing parking lots, or even using open greenspaces that are near to a library. Next, decide on a timeline. Typically, play streets run all day, from, say, 10:00 a.m. to 4:00 p.m., but you could also do something more focused on an early evening, if that makes more sense for your community. Make sure, in any case, you've given yourself and your partners enough time for setup and teardown.

After you've settled on the space and the time, partner with community groups to make sure there are ample supplies available for unstructured play, including things like jump ropes and hula hoops. If possible, see if you can also find volunteers to demo the play equipment throughout the day and to encourage people to try them out.

You can also have pop-up programs going throughout the event, including everything from running groups, to dance classes, to giant games, to yoga and soccer workshops (all of which have been offered in play streets in New York City). The more you can get community members involved in organizing and leading these programs, the better and more engaging the programs will be.

Participants will become progressively sweatier and hungrier as the day advances, so think about how you can infuse healthy eating into the play street. Many programs team up with summer meal programs to ensure youth get free meals. You could also work with local food banks to make sure free food is available for adults as well. Go a step further, and see if you can find some local chefs, nutritionists, or just plain cooking aficionados to do pop-up cooking classes throughout the day.

As the day winds down, everyone, including organizers and partners, will be exhausted. Hold off on the debriefing and evaluation. A few days later, touch base with everyone involved in planning the play street. It will be difficult to do this, as summer programming will be underway, so make sure to build this postevent follow-up into your program plan. You could draft your email follow-ups ahead of time and even schedule them to be sent out at a particular time in the future, so that you don't forget.

In any case, don't let the healthy living momentum end after the kickoff. Here are a few other ways I've seen libraries infuse healthy living into summer programming:

- Incentivize active transportation and physical activity. Award raffle tickets or extra points in your summer reading challenge for families or children who bike, walk, or roll to the library or who visit local parks, go on hikes, go swimming, and so forth. Here's an example from the Charlotte Mecklenburg Library, in North Carolina: The "play" category of their summer learning challenge incentivizes families and individuals to "visit a playground," "take a walk on a greenway," "play a sport," or "go swimming," among other activities. Learn more at https://summerbreak.cmlibrary.org/play.
- Give bikes or passes to the YMCA away as summer reading raffle rewards.
- Take walks to parks, orchards, and gardens, and do programs in parks, orchards, and gardens.
- Finish things off with a pool party at a local YMCA or municipal swimming pool, to celebrate those who completed the summer challenge.
- Serve free summer meals *and* offer healthy living programs around them.

Summer can also be a great time to develop off-site programs with partners. In Keokuk, Iowa, the library's collaboration with the local YMCA led the two partners to work together to organize a free fitness event. The Y and the library split the cost of a performer, who led the program at the YMCA's gym as a free event.

You can take things to the next level by having special, annual challenges focused entirely around healthy living. Every summer, the Akron-Summit County Public Library, in Ohio, offers Mind, Body & Sole. The library encourages you to "make reading and exercise a part of your day—every day. Both have the power to brighten your spirit, stimulate your imagination and improve your health" (Akron-Summit County Public

Logo for Mind, Body & Sole at Akron-Summit County Public Library. Reprinted with permission from Akron-Summit County Public Library.

Library 2019). Participants get a free pedometer and logs to track both reading and exercise. You get points for staying active however you wish: "running, walking, bicycling, yoga, gardening, outside play, physical therapy, and more. When you have reached 26 days of exercise AND 26 days of reading, you will receive a Mind, Body & Sole T-shirt and have the chance to be entered into our Grand Prize Drawing" (Akron-Summit County Public Library 2019). To help participants along their journey, the library curates a list of recommended books and magazines focused on healthy living. Like pretty much every program model described in this book, Mind, Body & Sole depends upon community partnerships, in this case, the local marathon, Cuyahoga Valley National Park, the public health department, and the parks department. Every year, more than eleven thousand people participate in this program. You could mix it up and add healthy eating into the challenge as well, giving people points for trying out a new recipe or a new ingredient or planning their meals for the week. Learn more at https://akronlibrary.org/273-events/mind-body -sole/437-mind-body-sole.

Some libraries have now made fitness part of summer at the library in other ways. In La Crosse, Wisconsin, library director Dawn Wacek said the library is now taking a different approach to summer reading. Summer at this library now means encouraging young patrons to branch out into volunteering, exercising, and creating. Its program rewards kids for doing these things throughout the summer.

Meanwhile, in San Francisco, California, summer at the library is now organized around three dimensions: (1) deepening reading enjoyment, (2) sparking STEM learning, and (3) connecting with mindful experiences in nature. The staff invites you to "expand your learning with nature through shuttles to local national parks and ranger talks" (San Francisco Public Library 2019). Since 2016, the library has progressively deepened its collaborations with local parks and with the National Park Service. Now, active engagement in nature is a routine part of their summer programming. Take the first step by reaching out to your local parks to talk about how you can work together this summer and beyond!

Healthy Living in the Collaborative Summer Library Program

A turning point in the development of healthy living in summer programming came in 2016, when the Collaborative Summer Library Program (CSLP) focused its program manual around the themes of sports, fitness, and exercise. This focus developed in response to problems of obesity among Americans and in response to the 2016 Summer Olympics (Lenstra 2018i).

Throughout the United States, public libraries used the theme as a launchpad for innovative fitness programming. Lawrence Public Library, in Kansas, offered "Fitness Fridays on the Library Lawn." Participants of all ages and skill levels could come to the library to learn yoga, tai chi, plyo, bodyflow, Pilates, POUND!, and even CrossFit. Examples abound of other public libraries that developed similar fitness programming during summer 2016 in response to the CSLP theme. Here is a sampling (Lenstra 2018i):

- Carrollton, Texas, held "Shape Up Saturdays" throughout the summer.
- Lima, Ohio, started its summer reading program with a kickoff walk and held "Shake It Saturdays" throughout the summer.
- Austin, Texas, used the theme, "My Library Inspires: Body, Food & Mind," to offer a variety of fitness, nutrition, and reading programs.
- Cranston, Rhode Island, offered Zumba Kids, a ping-pong smackdown, bike maintenance 101, and a Quidditch tournament.
- Portsmouth, Virginia, offered Zumba for adults and beginning line dancing classes.
- Lewistown, Montana, sponsored hikes, visits to parks, and walks on city trails.
- Danville, Kentucky, offered guided hikes in area parks for families, as well as a couch-to-5K program, and self-defense classes.
- Newport, Rhode Island, offered yoga, dance, tai chi, aerobics, and CrossFit programs.
- Nappanee, Indiana, featured images of weight lifting, running, biking, yoga, soccer, and dancing in its newsletter, and offered yoga, dancing, running, geocaching, self-defense classes, an inflatable obstacle course, cardio drumming, a couch-to-5K program, ping pong, and "piloxing," a fusion of standing Pilates, boxing, and dance.

These programs were so popular that many libraries started making healthy living an integral facet of summer at the library, going forward. The 2017 CSLP theme was "Build a Better World" and many libraries took this theme and did special programs around the idea of "Build a Better Body." One of my favorites comes from Muscatine, Iowa, where on June 16, 2017, the library offered "Build a Better Body: Warrior CrossFit with Kyle Jack" as part of their Teen Fridays programming. See https://musserpubliclibrary.org/event/teen-friday-2.

In 2018 the CSLP theme was "Libraries Rock," and dozens of libraries offered special rock-climbing programs. Some kicked off (or wrapped up) summer programming with a mobile rock-climbing wall at the library. Others took field trips to rock-climbing facilities. For instance, on June 28, 2018, the Forsyth County Public Library posted on Facebook that "Libraries ROCK! You can learn how to rock climb this Saturday at the Hampton Park Library!"

In 2019 the theme was "A Universe of Stories," and a bunch of libraries adopted the outer space theme to offer programs focused on how to train like an astronaut. At the Hays Public Library, in Kansas, "the children [were] exercising on Wednesdays during Astronaut Training, just as the astronauts have to do in space to keep up their muscle tone in low gravity" (Janney 2019). Some libraries also did nutrition programs focused on the rigors required to become healthy enough to go into outer space.

These examples show that *whatever* the theme, you can make healthy living an integral dimension of summer programming at your library.

Summer Meals (and More!)

Unfortunately, food insecurity is a major issue, especially in the summer months when families that rely on free meals at school suddenly lose a vital meal source. As the Collaborative Summer Library Program writes in their Libraries and Summer Food Toolkit:

> Every summer, 22 million U.S. children who receive free or reduced-price school meals, including 12.5 million who live in food-insecure households, lose access to the daily breakfast and lunch served in school. During the summer, many students also lack the other benefits of school, including engagement, learning, the presence of adults, a temperature-controlled environment—things libraries can provide. The USDA's Summer Food Service Program (SFSP) makes free healthy meals and snacks available to young people in communities with high rates of poverty. Many public libraries already participate as meal or snack sites or provide programming to nearby feeding sites. Libraries can incorporate their summer library program into this program to support healthy living and to send children and teens back to school ready to learn. Your library can be part of the solution to childhood hunger. Become a meal site or partner with existing sites, publicize the program, and connect young patrons to healthy food. (CSLP 2019)

You don't necessarily have to work with the USDA program. If your community is not eligible for this program, you have other options for helping feed young people. Some libraries work with local food banks, for instance, which allow them to serve meals not only for youth (the USDA program is limited to those under the age of eighteen) but for caregivers as well. At the Madison County Public Library in Berea, Kentucky, a partnership with a local food bank enables the library to serve meals every day of the week during the summer. On weekdays, meals are available for those aged eighteen and younger. On weekends, anyone who wants a free meal gets one, no questions asked. Explore your options and join the more than one thousand public libraries that already offer summer meals at the library.

The advice given by the Medway, Massachusetts, Public Library is very much on point, echoing what I have found across the country:

- We were amazed at how many businesses and organizations were happy to donate. Don't hesitate to ask, even if the business is unrelated to food.
- Start out small—one meal a week worked well for us.
- We found that it was not necessary to ask people to sign up when we offered lunch one day during February and April vacation without a sign-up, we still had a good turnout.
- We planned for twenty to thirty people each week. Had a larger number showed up, we planned to make a quick run to a local pizza shop or to a deli for more sandwiches.
- Make sure you have enough volunteers with driver's licenses to pick up the food. We had no problem finding wonderful volunteers of all ages to serve the lunches. (Eberle 2018)

In rural areas it may be necessary to bring food to patrons through outreach initiatives. Consider providing food through bookmobile stops and other outreach programming. In the small town of Pendleton, Indiana, the library teamed up with the United Way to start a "Read 'n' Feed" program, which "is a combination bookmobile/food pantry that visits our neighborhoods every Thursday." According to the library, "patrons wishing to use the services on the trailer simply need to provide their name and address. You are then welcome to take 10 food items of your choosing. No gimmicks. No catch. No questions asked" (Pendleton Community Library 2019).

From Summer Meals to Summer Programming

Hosting summer meals at the library is the perfect example of libraries embracing the principles of "shared use" we discussed in part II. Many libraries have gone beyond feeding kids to also provide programs that increase healthy living. **Alliance for a Healthier Generation**, a national nonprofit focused on empowering kids to develop lifelong healthy habits by ensuring the environments that surround them provide and promote good health highlights a lunch program at Bristol Public Library, in Connecticut. This program focuses on developing what they call "Sound Minds, Sound Bodies" in summer programming:

We introduced exercise, mindfulness, and creative food preparation activities to lunchtime. Children were thrilled to not only participate in the free lunch program but to also explore something new and "good for you." We launched a "Yoga after Lunch" program, where children discover the relaxing art of stretching and the beauty of calming thoughts. The yoga instructor encourages children to participate in the rhythm of a story by listening to words and moving to action. They love it! For our young adults, we aim to provide opportunities to connect with one another and take a break from screens. Older kids hang out in a designated teen area and enjoy "Dudes' Day Out" or "Girls' Day Out" activities that promote safe and healthy socialization. They also love to get their hands dirty, making slime, painting on canvas, and experimenting with healthy ingredient cookbooks. (Toner 2018)

You don't need a big budget or a big space to incorporate healthy living into your summer meal programs. In the tiny town of La Cygne, Kansas (pop. 1,149), the library feeds the children every day, and then once a week, a local retired PE teacher drops by to get kids moving in what the library calls Fitness Thursdays. The library also provides cooking and nutrition programs on other days, also led by local volunteers. According to librarian Janet Reynolds, the Fitness Thursday program is the biggest draw of the week, routinely attracting more kids than other programs offered on other days after the meals are served. It's all about community! Learn more at http://nlcblogs.nebraska .gov/bigtalk/previous-conferences/2018-presentations/more-than-summer -lunches-social-cultural-and-healthy-connections.

For more ideas, the California Library Association has, as part of its Lunch@ the Library initiative, highlighted the importance of organizing healthy living programs around summer meals, most recently in its tool kit on "Lunch at the Library: Linking Early Learning and Nutrition for Young Children." Getting kids (and caregivers!) learning about the importance of smart eating and active living is quickly becoming an integral dimension of many library summer meal programs. Learn more about how to add healthy living programs to your summer meals at https://recordings.join.me/sP5xGsbEDk-tJq8_Hq3gDQ.

At least one library system has completely transformed its programming around summer meals. In Washington state, Carolyn Peterson, rural library consultant for the Washington State Library, has worked with two rural libraries in Lincoln County and one in Adams County to help them develop programs that simultaneously meet three community needs: (1) the summer slump, (2) summer hunger, and (3) summer enrichment activities. Peterson said that these communities, like many rural and small communities, lack daycare and summer recreation facilities, so the libraries have stepped into this void, offering structured day camps for six weeks from 8:00 a.m. to 5:00 p.m.

The library day camps also highlight the importance of staying active during the summer, with walks and afternoon physical activities as part of the program. In total, according to Peterson, the programs have engaged nearly 50 percent of the kids in these rural communities.

I'm not suggesting that you go out and immediately start a summer camp at your library, but *do* start thinking about how you and your library can get on board with summer meals. Maybe you're not a summer meal site yourself, but can you go to where the meals are being served? In Raleigh, North

Carolina, the Wake County Public Libraries recently received an award from the National Association of Counties for its partnership with the county's Parks and Recreation Department:

> Historic Oak View County Park and Wake County Public Libraries part-nered to address issues of food insecurity and the summer slide by serving at-risk youth in South Raleigh through the USDA's Summer Food Service Program. SFSP ensures low-income children receive nutritious meals dur-ing school breaks. Offered since 2016 at HOV in collaboration with the Wake County Public School System, 2018 saw 64 volunteers provide lunches to 945 youth. Studies find that when activities are offered at SFSPs, participa-tion increases. WCPL created the Thompson Fellowship, an eight-week paid work/study opportunity for teens who completed service with the Librar-ies Teen Leadership Corps to offer educational and recreational activities to SFSP participants at HOV. Activities were designed to help participants avoid the "summer slide"—when students forget skills learned the previous school year—more common in at-risk children. The teens also met weekly with community partners and WCPL staff to enhance their personal and professional development. The program is an example of a partnership that fed both bodies and minds of Wake County's most vulnerable residents. (National Association of Counties 2019)

Active Storytimes

Full disclaimer: I am not now nor have I ever been a children's librarian. In fact, most of my work over the years has been with adults, specifically, older adults. Nonetheless, I would be remiss if I didn't highlight the amazing ways that children's librarians infuse physical activity and healthy living into their storytime programming. In many ways, these librarians raise the bar for us all. We can learn so much from their successes, and get the inspiration and infor-mation we need to bring healthy living into *all* of our programs. For instance, Kelly, from the Youth Services Section of the Wisconsin Library Association, writes,

> Have you ever finished a program and thought, "I needed that as much as the kids"? That was my feeling after our dance party yesterday. Dancing for 30 minutes was a great stress relief! Now I'm thinking I need to add dance parties to the regular schedule and not as a special storytime break activity. They are easy to plan. There's lots of fantastic librarian-curated playlists to get you started. And they help promote your music collection! (WLA YSS 2017)

We could all use a dance break! Let's let go of our adult inhibitions and embrace this ethos of fun physical activity across our programming for all ages.

I'd like to highlight some examples of children's librarians leading the way in their efforts to infuse healthy living into their existing programming.

When we think about parks and recreation, we tend to think about natural amenities. However, most departments also have indoor recreational facilities as well. The Wood River Public Library and its local parks department offers a kids' storytime and tumbling program, called Roll-n-Read, at a rec center. Each week the librarian shares stories with children and engages the kids in gymnastic activities.

Where to start with such an active story program? According to Lindsey Herron, the director of the Wood River Public Library, it all comes down to building relationships:

> What makes our partnership great is we have mutual respect for each other and try to eliminate having the same programs going on, Herron said. "By collaborating on all of our events we save money (split the costs) and hit up a larger crowd (we advertise at our respective locations). The Parks and Recreation Department has several large events that have been going on for decades. Rather than trying to compete with them, we simply have joined in and helped to promote their event while getting our own names out there.... My advice for those looking to reach out would be to check their websites, check their Facebook pages, etc. and see what BIG events they are doing. Then come up with a way to be a part of it. Find out who does the different monthly events and see if they want to partner. Find out what gaps you have in the events you both provide and see how you can fill them together."

There are all kinds of variations on this basic program idea. Yoga storytime is among the most common, and dozens of children's librarians across the country have become certified children's yoga instructors to do this program themselves. Librarian Katie Scherrer's "Stories, Songs, and Stretches" curriculum focuses on preparing children's librarians to do this program. Learn more at https://www.storiessongsandstretches.com.

Other variations include

- Music and movement programs
- Swim and read programs, storytime at a pool
- Story ride, community bike ride with stops for stories

The best programs don't just get kids moving; they get caregivers moving as well. This topic is so well developed among children's librarians, that back in 2014 *Storytime Underground* featured a blog post titled "Getting Parents Moving," focusing on subtle and not so subtle ways to make sure that active storytime programs are impacting not just kids but also their caregivers. Learn more at https://storytimeunderground.wordpress.com/2014/05/06/ask-a-storytime -ninja-getting-parents-moving.

So, if your library already has active storytime programs, great! You may want to take things to the next level and make a concrete strategy to try to get caregivers moving as well. Get the whole family moving at the library! And then get everyone moving, whether or not they have kids.

Healthy Living Book Clubs and Heritage Walks

When it comes to adult programs, possibly the most common way to infuse healthy living into programs is to add in some walking. There are two ways librarians typically do this:

- Heritage walks
- Walking book clubs

Heritage walks involve librarians weaving together local history, heritage, and walking. In 2017 the American Library Association highlighted the spread of these programs. A branch of the Baltimore, Maryland, library hosts regular historic walking tours. The library in La Crosse, Wisconsin, does ghost-oriented walking tours every fall. In New Jersey, the Red Bank Public Library celebrated its eightieth anniversary by conducting a walking tour of the town, and in Effingham, Illinois, the library helps organize an annual sculpture walk. Learn more at https://americanlibrariesmagazine.org/2017/09/01/walking -history-library-sightseeing-tours.

These programs also take place outside the United States. The public library in Innerpeffray, Scotland, launched a heritage walk to showcase its local history. Walking history programs have been a major initiative at the library in Winnipeg, Canada, where the library regularly offers historical walks, literary walks, gardening walks, and walking book clubs to expose people to the history and resources of the city that can be accessed through walking. These programs can also be a great fit for academic and school libraries, where history- or public-art-oriented tours of downtown or of campus can be great programs for librarians to do either by themselves or in partnerships.

Librarians also connect stories and healthy living through walking book clubs. Librarians have been offering these programs for at least a decade. In the late 2000s the public library in Elgin, Illinois, launched its walking book club. According to the librarian that organizes the program, "We read and exercise, build community and friendships, and hold lively discussions along the way" (Gail Borden Public Library 2017). One participant said that "the friends

I have made will last me longer than the books I have read" (Haggard and Henson 2011).

In Kokomo, Indiana, participants walk around downtown, discussing what they are reading. In Middletown, Connecticut, "Book Talk with a Walk" programs are held Mondays from noon to 1:30 p.m. Participants walk from the library to the river and back, two miles round trip. Librarian Ann Smith said, "Even if you haven't read the book, everybody has something to contribute because you have an opinion about . . . whatever the book's theme was: everybody's got something to offer, whether it's related to the book or not" (Day 2018). This quote illustrates how these book clubs tend not to be overly focused on the books themselves.

Libraries can also have book clubs focused not specifically on walking but on healthy living in general. My favorite example comes from the Brainerd Memorial Library in Haddam, Connecticut. For years, one of their signature programs has been the "Healthy Exchange Book Club," which meets the first Wednesday of the month at 6:30 p.m. Here is how they advertise the group: "Enjoy reading about health, nutrition, fitness, & emotional wellness? Would you like to share details with other like-minded individuals?" Learn more at http://www.brainerdlibrary.lioninc.org/adults.

During the summer months, the library mixes it up by going on fun excursions. The Healthy Exchange Book Club has gone to a pickleball court to learn to play this low-intensity sport, they've gone to a lake to learn stand-up paddleboarding, and they've played mini golf together.

Here are some other ideas for healthy living book clubs:

- Outdoor explorers book clubs, such as the one offered in Orange County, North Carolina. Read about outdoor adventures and then meet at a park to go exploring and discussing what you read.
- Cookbook club., Challenge members to check out a cookbook, try a new recipe and then discuss how it went together. You could even ask people to bring in their dishes, potluck-style, or create a library cookbook based on the favorite recipes of members. Learn more at https://sparks.winnefox.org /node/380.
- Couch-to-5K reading group. At the Mint Hill branch of the Charlotte Mecklenburg Library, an adult services librarian ran a Couch-to-5K running and reading group, in which short articles on running were read and briefly discussed before everyone went out together on a fun run, to prepare for their first 5K.
- Nutrition motivational group. Members in a motivational group can encourage each other to improve and maintain healthy food-shopping and cooking strategies. Keep members engaged with inspiring stories and news articles,

using the readings as jumping-off points to keep this peer-to-peer support group connected and growing. This group could also highlight and help members learn more about community agriculture and gardening, farmers markets, food insecurity, and more. Excursions could include a group trip to volunteer at the local food bank or to pitch in at a community garden.

Exercises

1. Thinking about the programs your library currently offers, are there ways you could integrate healthy living into them? For example, could you mix up the foods that you provide or take an instant recess dance or stretch break?
2. What resources or support would you need to integrate healthy living into your library's existing programming?

10

All Ages Play, or Why Should Kids Have All the Fun?

Over the past two decades, children's librarians have led the play revolution within librarianship. More and more embrace the power of play for learning and child development. Nowhere is this more evident than in the American Library Association's "Every Child Ready to Read" initiative, which lists "play" as one of the five key dimensions of early literacy services.

Well, guess what? ***Play is essential for all forms of lifelong learning***, so if you really want to help your community embrace healthy living, you should embrace the power of play. This chapter focuses on how to do that, highlighting play-based programs for all ages, giant games, and healthy living games. It ends by going over the "Fun Palaces" program model, which hundreds of British libraries offer every October.

The Power of Play in and around the Library

On September 13, 2018, the Madison Public Library published a blog post called "Wild Rumpus: Flying," featuring children who, as part of a library program, made three-dimensional play spaces from which they then launched their bodies into the air. Around the same time in Connecticut, Kari Ann St. Jean, children and teen services manager for the Avon Free Public Library, started a series of storytime programs focusing on integrating yoga, movement, and stories. She writes, "By asking participants to *embody* the movement in stories and rhymes . . . we invent our own actions, and storytime is transformed! . . . The result is an interconnected experiential set of imaginative activities that only exist in the here and now" (Fletcher 2019, 2–3).

Play refers to engaging in activity for enjoyment and recreation rather than for serious or practical purposes. Scientists increasingly recognize that play constitutes a vital dimension of learning. MacArthur Foundation Genius Grant awardee Angela Duckworth says that we can't develop our passions without it: "Before hard work comes play. Before those who've yet to fix on a passion are ready to spend hours a day diligently honing skills, they must goof around, triggering and retriggering interest. . . . At this earliest stage, novices *aren't* obsessed with getting better. . . . More than anything else, they're having fun" (Duckworth 2018, 106–7). She goes on to quote psychologist Benjamin Bloom, who discovered that the best teachers make "the initial learning very pleasant and rewarding. Much of the introduction . . . was as playful activity, and the learning at the beginning . . . was much like a game" (Duckworth 2018, 107).

The implications of this science for library programming are that we need to focus our healthy living programming around play. If we want to change people's habits and make a lasting impact on community health, we need to embrace the power of play.

Active Play Bridges Makerspaces and Healthy Living

There really is no wrong way to embrace play in your healthy living programming. Take a playful approach to programming! We can see these principles in action in innovative library programs that combine the makerspace ethos with healthy living. The Ballyfermot Library in Dublin, Ireland, organized, as part of the Dublin City Council's "Children's Art in Libraries" (CAL) initiative, a program in which children "watch professional dancers in their local library, then respond and create their own work which they perform in front of a local audience" (Derenthal 2018). Similarly, in Ithaca, New York, Tompkins County Public Library teams up with Cornell University and Ithaca College for "Ballet and Books," in which college students are paired with local youth for dancing, reading, and one-on-one mentoring.

A more unstructured play program can be seen in a program created by Beth Smiley, school librarian in the Charlotte Mecklenburg Schools in North Carolina. She provides her students with prompts that she asks them to "make" using their bodies. For instance, in 2016 the North Carolina Children's Book Award winner was *Giant Squid* by Candace Fleming. The students were charged with figuring how to use their bodies to make a giant squid on the floor of the library. By working together, students laid down on their backs across the library floor, creating the shape of the titular character from the book.

You could do these types of programs at your library through in-house and outreach programming. As an outreach program, Kat Cook in Keokuk, Iowa, developed a "Lego Days at the YMCA" program through a collaboration with the Hoerner YMCA in November 2017. The library and the Y discussed the need for more after-school activities and their shared desire to reach more young people. Out of this came Lego Days at the YMCA. Essentially, librarians take their Legos to the Y once a month and offer building challenges as well as open time for kids aged five and up to, as the Y puts it, "stretch their imaginations as much as their bodies" (Lenstra 2019a).

The YMCA is a great partner for any active play-based programs, since healthy play is one of their core values. The Williams County Public Library in Bryan, Ohio, worked with their Y for National Library Week 2018 for a special "Swim & Story Family Night" at the Y. The free event featured a pool party as well as a storytime in the pool for younger kids, plus crafts, swimming races, and a free showing of the movie *Coco*.

A Playful Approach to Librarianship

Play programs for all ages are also a wonderful way to gently challenge stereotypes of librarians and of librarianship. In Milwaukee, the public library's embrace of play appears in their "Library Loud Days," in which they encourage patrons to "Go Ahead, Be Loud in the Library":

> Gone is the notion of the sleepy, quiet library, where all you hear is "shush." We're changing the Milwaukee Public Libraries into lively, vibrant gathering places. And our Library Loud Days (an ongoing series of free events) is leading that change. So come see what the new definition of a library is all about. And leave your inside voice at home.

Learn more at http://mpl.org/special_events_and_programs/libraryloud.

A librarian in Mobile, Alabama, told me these programs are offered "to do different things in the library . . . to break down the stereotype that libraries are quiet places only." Another Alabama librarian said these programs "promote the idea that the library is a community gathering space, that it is a fun place to be (regardless of age), and that there is more to learning than just reading a book quietly. We are trying to break stereotypes" (Lenstra 2018k, 198). A librarian in rural South Carolina said their play programs are offered so that "participants may see the library differently—more active, more fun." A librarian in the St. Louis area said, "Offering [this] programming I think allows your community to start seeing the library's role differently. Beyond books and material. That's a positive" (Lenstra 2018k).

This approach to healthy living at the library can be vividly seen at the Burlingame Public Library in California. Their "Get Jazzed about Healthy Living Open House Extravaganza" on August 9, 2018, invited participants to "get dressed in your favorite workout clothes, the crazier the better" (Burlingame Public Library 2018). This variant on a typical health fair focused on fun play, with exercise intros, live music, healthy snacks, nutrition information, and a fun, festival atmosphere designed to encourage people to come in and try out new healthy living activities.

Playing Around in Early Literacy Programs and Beyond

Movement is now broadly recognized as a core part of early literacy programs in libraries (Kaplan 2014). The idea behind these services is that very young children need to learn how to move (i.e., use fine and gross motor skills) as well as read and that libraries can help with both learning needs. In "Public Libraries Harness the Power of Play," the researchers who evaluated the American Library Association's **Every Child Ready to Read** initiative examined "if and to what extent free play, music, **large muscle movement, and/or small motor activities** were incorporated along with storybook reading" (Celano, Knapczyk, and Neuman 2018, emphasis added) and concluded by stating, "Libraries are changing traditional story-time programs to reflect the importance of play, especially with toddlers and preschool-age children" (Celano, Knapczyk, and Neuman 2018).

This playful attitude toward library programming has more recently spread from early literacy services to youth services and now into adult services. In a recently published handbook on youth services written by a past president of the ALA's Young Adult Library Services Association (YALSA), Flowers (2017) notes that libraries are now "a safe place to try something new. As teens are finding themselves, library programs can give them the opportunity to try a new skill in a place of relative safety. Some examples are . . . physical activities. Teaching various types of dance, martial arts, yoga, or whatever you have the space and expertise for" (37).

This quote very clearly echoes some of what we read above, from Dr. Duckworth and her advocacy for the importance of play when introducing people to new things and activities. Here we see the expectation that librarians should support young people's bodies as well as their minds by extending access to healthy living practices (and different forms of food preparation and food growing would be great additions to Flowers's list).

Similarly, in response to my survey, a librarian from rural Maine wrote that it is important to "expose kids to activities which they may otherwise not have an opportunity to experience. Not all kids are team sport oriented and having the opportunity to experience other ways to remain active is important" (Lenstra 2018k, 191).

In these examples we see librarians supporting the whole person by creating opportunities for individuals to playfully explore new things and practices.

A recently published story on NPR shows that this orientation toward play in library programming has spread into adult services as well. The article

"Xbox Bowling for Seniors? Visit Your Local Library" discusses the "Library Lanes Bowling League," a program that has been offered at multiple branches of the Brooklyn Public Library for years. The program is organized and coordinated by the library's Services for Older Adults department.

Members of the primary audience for the program are invited "to join a team, learn how to bowl using a Microsoft Xbox One, and compete with neighborhood libraries and senior sites in the community" (Jaffe 2017). Two of the participants interviewed for the NPR segment said they enjoy bowling at the library rather than at a senior center because, in the library, all ages are present. The program continues to grow. NPR reported in 2017 that there are twice as many Xbox bowling teams for seniors in the Brooklyn Public Library System as there were the year before. The Library Lanes program also caught the attention of sociologist Eric Klinenberg, who prominently features this program in his book, *Palaces for the People*, an example of the vital roles of public libraries in community life. Klinenberg has also tweeted out a video of the Library Lanes program that he collected as part of his fieldwork, to illustrate how playing in libraries forges healthy social connections (as well as gets older adults moving!). Learn more at https://twitter.com/EricKlinenberg /status/1136954238339358721.

Your library might not start a bowling league for older adults, but there are lots of other things you could try to create opportunities for senior citizens and other adults to play together in the library, and to playfully gain exposure to potentially life-saving forms of healthy eating and active living.

Other play programs for adults take things that have worked well for youth and tweak them for adults. I'm thinking of NERF wars at the library. At the public library in Dubuque, Iowa, a group of adults of all ages meets once a month on Saturday night to play after-hours NERF Capture the Flag at the library. Things like this may seem frivolous, but I assure you they are not. We all need to think playfully when we think about how to push the needle regarding healthy habits.

A great way to support play among adults is to focus on programs that foster joyful movement, whether through Xbox Kinect, NERF wars, or something more contemplative, like tai chi. Testifying to the power of these programs, a librarian in rural Iowa wrote this, in response to my survey:

> I have to say, I think that the tai chi series [at the library] really gave people a new way to think about exercise and their bodies. I think that too, for many people this was a first attempt at exercise after a stretch of doing without, and it probably gave them courage to continue with tai chi, or begin a new type of exercise. In my twenty years of programming, I don't believe I've ever before seen such happy, excited people after any program. (Lenstra 2018k, 192)

By fostering joy through play-based programs for all ages, patrons reimagine healthy eating and active living. Rather than see these things through the lens of prescriptive things like diets or idealized bodies, things that seem so daunting and out of reach and damaging, we instead reconceptualize healthy living as something fun, collaborative, and full of joy. By embracing play in our programs, we change the conversation about how to become a healthier society.

Big Games

When we think about play, one of the first things that come to mind is gaming. But did you know that the boundary between gaming and sports is pretty fluid? Some (including me) would argue there is no boundary. Entire books have been written about gaming in libraries, but what is less acknowledged is that sit-down board games are just the tip of the iceberg when it comes to library gaming. Library game guru Scott Nicolson devotes an entire section to what he calls "Big Games," in *Everyone Plays at the Library: Creating Great Gaming Experiences for All Ages*: "The basic concept of big games is that the game board is the real world and the players are the game pieces. . . . A game of Kickball, Four-square, Nerf Wars, or Dodgeball out in the library parking lot is certainly an action gaming experience that can be part of a program" (Nicholson 2010, 102). These types of play programs are great ways to get people moving, experience joy, form new social connections, and develop healthy living habits.

More and more libraries host programs that bring people of all ages together for "in real life" or IRL gaming. Building on the popularity of online gaming, these events help get people off the couch and away from their screens, provide healthy physical activity, and increase face-to-face social connections. Tiffany Fay, youth services specialist at the Emporia Public Library, Kansas, hosted a Fortnite IRL event at her library, and she shared with OCLC/WebJunction how she planned and implemented the program:

> Participants scavenged for building materials and weapons (i.e., bean bags) to aid them in the endeavor of being the last person standing. When kids arrived, they were given a lanyard which they had to wear for the duration of the program. On this lanyard was their player badge and a map of the library. The player badge has a number; this allows staff to keep track of how many kids are playing. It's also helpful if player names are not known. The object of the game is to be the last one standing. Like the video game, kids are given the opportunity to scavenge for hidden materials that might help them in their endeavor.

Learn more about the nitty-gritty details of this program at https://www.webjunction.org/news/webjunction/fortnite-in-real-life.html.

Technology can also play a big role in these programs. In 2010 Fresno County Public Library (2011) purchased Wii gaming systems for six of its branches to "promote safe, indoor physical activity." They won an award from the Urban Libraries Council for their efforts to promote healthy living in this way.

Sports programs are another great way to embrace big games at the library. The Twin Falls Public Library, in Idaho, partnered with the College of Southern Idaho's volleyball team for "Active Kids," an initiative designed to get elementary school students moving. And of course, dozens of libraries have now offered Quidditch programs as part of summer at the library. So what are you waiting for? Embrace your sporty side and try a big-game program at your library.

Healthy Living Games

Play can also orient food programs. In Crandon, Wisconsin, the library organized an "Iron Chef: Healthy Fruits and Vegetables" edition to see which families could make the best-tasting dishes using healthy ingredients. To organize the program, the library teamed up with partners including the local health department (and in particular their council on activity and nutrition), the school district, restaurants, and a local nonprofit.

The library didn't have the facilities to host this program, so they took it off-site to the local school. Using space at the cafeteria, participants were given thirty minutes to create a unique panini dish, using an eggplant and other pantry items provided by the library and their partners. Participants competed in three categories: adults (18 and older), teens (12–17), and youth (11 and younger) and adults working together. Local restaurant owners participated as celebrity judges. The library was able to display more than twenty-five items related to cooking and nutrition from its collection as part of the event.

Fifteen competitors developed culinary creations, and each took home a panini maker donated by the local health department. The grand-prize winner took home a Ninja® blender, donated by a local nonprofit.

This program's success depended upon the dense web of partnerships that the library had developed and fostered (much like a gardener) over the years. Owing to these partnerships, the library's three full-time staff members were able to efficiently plan and deliver a healthy living game centered on increasing nutritional knowledge. Everyone involved took a very hands-on approach, including shopping for and prepping fresh ingredients. Before the event, planners walked through the participant experience from start to finish and considered details such as how to set up the cafeteria space, what rules would be provided in advance, and the criteria used for judging. Wrote the librarian, "Thinking about all aspects of the participant experience enabled community members to connect, engage and learn in an atmosphere of positive collaboration" (Crandon Public Library 2015).

You can also think about more passive healthy game programs. The small town of Concrete, Washington (pop. 732), offers a "Winter Reading Fitness Bingo" program. Community members are invited to try to complete a row of challenges to earn one entry toward the grand prize, and to black out the entire card for three entries. A grand-prize winner receives a fifty-dollar gift card at a March drawing.

Other types of healthy living games include walking and pedometer challenges to see who can get the most steps in, which can be either a group or individual challenge. Or you could make it a collaborative game, rather than a competition, to see how long it takes all the program participants to say, walk across Texas (which they did at Victoria Public Library, in conjunction with the library's monthly Walking Book Club) or even walk to the moon, which three library systems did together in New York state. Learn more at https://librarymoonwalk.sals.edu.

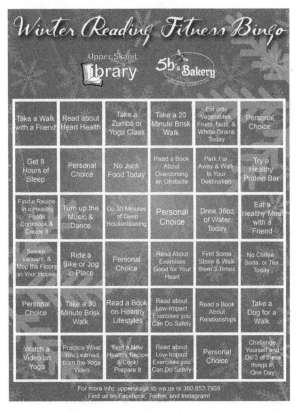

Winter Reading Fitness Bingo card. Reprinted with permission from Tess Caroll, Upper Skagit Library.

Get really creative and embrace the makerspace ethos such that your patrons *create* a healthy living game. School librarians have started to do this, and the results have been phenomenal! In a school library in Guelph, Ontario, the librarian challenged elementary school–aged children to create a big board game all about exercise. When students land on a spot they have to act out whatever exercise the spot has. All the rules, and the entirety of the game's structure, was created by the children. Similarly, an elementary school librarian in Michigan developed a "Code to Move" program, wherein youth make their own "codes" using action cards and computer code sequences to string together a series of actions that they and their classmates then enact. Kelly Hincks explains how it works:

> Each child decided on a motion that they could represent in a picture. The pictures were placed in a SMART Notebook. Under each picture, words were added to describe the motion. Then a box was drawn around the picture and word combo. These items were then grouped as one. Finally, using the infinite cloner tool allows for each of the coding blocks to be used multiple times in the code. Now, one of the choices, when students need a brain break in the classroom, is for one of their classmates to build a code with the motions they created. The students then act out these motions together. (Hincks 2018)

Learn more at https://knowledgequest.aasl.org/code-to-move-mixing-coding-with-brain-breaks.

The great thing about embracing play in your healthy living programs is that the possibilities are only limited by your imagination and creativity. Embracing play is a wonderful way to weave the library's mission of fostering lifelong learning and creativity into healthy living programming.

Fun Palaces

I want to end this chapter on embracing the power play by highlighting a program model that has become hugely popular among public libraries in the United Kingdom, but which has, up to now, not had much adoption outside of the UK. I'm talking about Fun Palaces. On October 7, 2017, the Huntington City-Township Public Library became the first public library in the United States to do a "Fun Palaces" program. During the weekend, the library was filled with fun activities led by community members. At different stations inside and outside the library building, you could learn ballet, how to ride a bike, hula dance, stretch your body, start your family tree, paint like Jackson Pollock, discover Dungeons & Dragons, cross-stitch, decorate cakes, paint rocks, and much, much more. According to Devon Henderson, the library

Due to the Fun Palace,

the library will be very noisy

Saturday, October 7
between
10 a.m. and 4 p.m.

Thank you for your understanding.

Flyer for Fun Palaces at the Huntington City-Township Public Library. Reprinted with permission from Devon Henderson.

"ended up with 68 volunteers, 24 unique activity stations and over 500 in attendance" (Quoted in Lenstra 2018h).

Jessi Brown, the library's assistant director of library services, wrote in the wrap-up report:

> It allows us to be seen as a space for art, for science, for learning new things and excitement. Fun Palaces are important for my community because it allows them to share their passion, and perhaps find someone to share that passion with that they might not have ever found. It allows them to take a risk and try something new and no cost to them. And, it allows people to experience something that they might not ever have experienced because of a lack of someone in their life to teach it. (Quoted in Lenstra 2018h)

The library found that they did not have to invest an inordinate amount of time in planning the event. Devon Henderson stated, "We spread word around the community around August that we'd be hosting it, and that we were seeking volunteers from the community to lead sessions during the two day festival," and many people stepped forward to share their skills. Given that the programs were all led by community members, those presenters did a bunch of word-of-mouth advertising, driving attendance to the event.

History of Fun Palaces in Libraries

Let's back up. Where did this idea come from, and how has it developed in British libraries? Although the idea of "fun palaces" dates back to the 1960s, it was not until 2014 that the idea came to fruition on a national level in the UK. Then venues as diverse as the Royal Shakespeare Company and a Canadian radio station opened their doors the first weekend of October for a pop-up laboratory of fun in which community members share the activities they love to do with other community members.

Since then, Fun Palaces have become a "worldwide campaign for culture made by your community, for your community" (for the source of this and other quotes in this section, consult Lenstra 2018h). Every year the number of venues that participate in the weekend of action—the first weekend of October—has grown, and from the beginning public libraries have been key participants. In 2014 Britain's Gladstone's Library offered a Fun Palace, and the librarians found that "every single person [who participated] was new to the library." Fun Palaces pull people in to engage with libraries (and with other community members) in new and exciting ways.

One of the best parts of Fun Palaces is the unexpected discoveries that arise when so many people are sharing so many passions all at once in one place. For instance, in 2017 librarian Mark Heaton of Rotherham Libraries, in England, tweeted a picture of someone learning martial arts at the library with the caption "Didn't expect to see this in a library! #FunPalaces."

Bolstered by success stories like these, libraries have enthusiastically joined the Fun Palaces movement. Indeed, in 2017, 54.97 percent of the 362 Fun Palaces offered worldwide took place in libraries. In *CILIP Update*, the British equivalent of *Public Libraries*, Matt Finch wrote, "Libraries are inspirational spaces where people can experiment creatively and engage with knowledge, culture and self-directed learning," thus making them the perfect setting for Fun Palaces.

In 2016 Stella Duffy, the co-director of Fun Palaces (now a not-for-profit unincorporated association), gave a keynote on the movement for the Society of Chief Librarians in England. She said that talking with librarians about Fun Palaces "made a massive difference to libraries taking us on." At first, some libraries in the UK were wary of the staffing obligations associated with this program, but after they saw the impacts that Fun Palaces were having in libraries, how much support they received from Duffy, and the resources she and her staff have put together, even more libraries got involved in the movement. Duffy remains an asset for librarians anywhere around the world who want to give this program a go. The first weekend of October is also the ideal time for a program like this, as it typically does not overlap with any major program. Academic libraries could do Fun Palaces to help students de-stress around mid-terms. School libraries could partner with other school units to open up the schools for a new use on the weekend. Finally, by joining in the global Fun Palaces movement, you enter into a community of practice that can give you lots of support and inspiration. So give it a go!

Get involved and have fun at http://funpalaces.co.uk.

Exercises

1. How does a play-based approach to learning healthy living differ from how you typically think of learning about health?
2. How does your library support play as part of its commitment to lifelong learning?
3. If you offer play-based programs for very young children, are there things you could adopt from the programs offered for this age group to programs for other age groups? What are they?

11

Immersive Cooking and Fitness Classes

This chapter goes over cooking and fitness classes in libraries. Before we break them apart into different program models, let's first take a look at how you can bring them together in one overarching program series focused on healthy living. That is exactly what they've been doing at the Phoenix Public Library in Arizona since 2014, in a program called "FitPHX Energy Zones." This program is a collaboration between the Phoenix Public Library and Arizona State University, with additional support from Phoenix Parks and Recreation and the Mayo Clinic, among other partners. In essence, university students from a variety of disciplines visit multiple branches multiple days a week to engage middle-school students after school in immersive programs focused on such topics as fitness, nutrition, portion size, body image, and stigma. Let's take a look at how it works, so you can consider trying something like this at your library.

It all started in 2014 with an obesity prevention initiative funded by James Levine, one of the initial designers of the treadmill desk. His original vision was to put walking desks into places like libraries, along with programs that could impact healthy living practices among middle schoolers. The FitPHX Energy Zone program focuses on ages eight through fourteen in four branches of the library system and targets those in this age group that already hang out at the library after school and during the summer months. About 90 percent of the young people who participate in the program participate in the federal lunch and breakfast programs. A lot of these youth already spend huge amounts of time on library computers, so enabling them to walk as they used the computer made a big difference in their habits. The walking desks are also available whenever the library is open and have become highly successful, usually with a waiting list to use. When the program is not in session, adults are welcome to use the walking desks.

The walking desks were just the beginning of the FitPHX Energy Zone program. At each of the four branches, the program has been customized and tailored to the unique needs of each community. Across all branches, programs focus on nutrition and physical activity in a very engaging format. The programs are led by university students who commit to participating from 4:00 to 6:00 p.m. on Tuesday and Thursday afternoons for a semester. The program has been very impactful both for the college students and for the youth. Some students even switched majors to focus on community work, and all now see libraries in a new light. One college student stated, "This internship experience has been one of the more rewarding experiences I've participated in throughout my academic career. . . . It has challenged me to call upon my creativity and understand how to present exciting activities in a library setting. I think my future career in public health will benefit from creativity. Thinking outside of the box can manifest fresh, and oftentimes successful, ideas" (Lenstra 2018j).

The students work from curricular modules created by Arizona State, which they use to teach cooking classes, lead kids in exercises, and go over other aspects of healthy living in a fun, lively format. If you're looking for programs like this one to do in your library, I recommend the resources gathered together by the U.S. Department of Agriculture in their SNAP-Ed Connection database: https://snaped.fns.usda.gov/library. You'll find a ton of resources here for creating healthy living programs in community settings likes libraries.

In any case, over the years, the FitPHX Energy Zones program has seen more than 600 kids work with more than 140 college students from 19 different majors. For many of the youth, interacting with college students is one of the things that attracts them to the program and keeps them participating.

The branch located in the poorest neighborhood of the four that participate in this program—median income, $18,000—partnered with Arizona State University to create a summer reading program linked to the walking desk; young people get points when they go walking on the desk. That library also offered a bike-repair program, because it is located in a part of the city where you can bike or walk to the library. The key to this branch's success in expanding the program beyond the academic year was having a very engaged branch manager (see chapter 5). The branch manager's passion led to even more spin-off programs, including setting up a garden at the library, cooking salsa with herbs from the garden, and teaching kids about native seeds and culinary heritage. That branch was also able to set up a bike program on Saturdays in partnership with a bike co-op.

At two other locations, the partnership led to the Fresh Express Bus (a nonprofit focused on getting fresh produce into food deserts) making regular rounds at the library. The college students would then unload from the bus the fresh produce, which was made available at the library. However, in one branch, the program struggled to get buy-in from staff. As a result, the FitPHX Energy Zone there remains a program mostly disconnected from everything else happening at the branch. This finding again illustrates the importance of *getting your library team on board*. It isn't enough to have a great idea. You need to build enthusiasm as well.

The major limitation of a program like this one is that in order to do it, you need a project coordinator. The FitPHX Energy Zones have been lucky to have a long-term relationship with Arizona State University, which provides the coordination to keep the program running from year to year. A program like this one would be a great one to suggest to your local university, college, or even community college. College students typically love the opportunity to apply their skills in the real world, and youth love hanging out with college students after school. In Phoenix, the college students are a big draw for kids. The kids love them and are sad when they leave.

The actual cost of the program is pretty minimal. According to the project coordinator, the actual costs (most of which go toward food for the youth) are only about $300 per year per site, but without a coordinator, it can be difficult to manage and keep everything going. In some locations, the libraries are also able to offer healthy snacks as part of the program, through a partnership with local food banks. Local foundations have also been more than happy to chip in and help get needed supplies. The **key**, though, is a project coordinator, or project champion, willing to put in the time and energy to sustain the momentum from year to year. The benefits are huge, but finding a way to coordinate it all does take time.

I have started with this example to show what one large urban library system is doing to impact healthy living in a big way through programming that combines new equipment (walking desk) with immersive cooking and fitness classes, all tied together with a multiyear partnership with another institution.

Teaming Up with Academic Institutions

According to the National Center for Education Statistics, there are 4,360 colleges and universities in the United States. More likely than not, there is a college or university close to you—and partnering with it would be a great way to bring high-quality healthy living programming to your library. Conversely, if you are an academic librarian, there is surely a public library close to you. Let's collaborate!

One of the biggest hurdles associated with partnering with colleges and universities is figuring out where to start. You can't (usually) just call up the provost and ask if the school would want to work with you.

Thankfully, some institutions are trying to make the process simpler. At the University of North Carolina at Greensboro, the University has a "collaboratory," a publicly searchable, online database that shares information about what faculty are doing, so off-campus entities can identify appropriate partners. The collaboratory is also available at five campuses of Indiana

University as well as Mercyhurst University in Erie, Pennsylvania, and hopefully will be more broadly available in the coming years. Learn more at https://cecollaboratory.com.

Your local college or university may not have a collaboratory, but it may have an office of public or community engagement. You could also reach out to your local academic librarian for help. Academic librarians typically have a deep understanding of the institution's structure and should be able to direct you to units and individuals on campus who might make excellent partners.

Furthermore, if you're lucky enough to have a health sciences academic librarian nearby, that librarian may be interested in working directly with you, which is exactly how the St. Louis Public Library and librarians from Washington University's School of Medicine started working together on health programming offered throughout the public library system.

In any case, common partners within academic institutions include:

- Health departments (which may have different names, from kinesiology to public health to gerontology to nursing to medicine)
- Sports teams and athletics departments
- University hospitals
- Education departments (especially early-childhood education)
- Agriculture extension units

Don't rule out other, more unexpected partners. Obesity Solutions at Arizona State University (the initial partner for the FitPHX Energy Zones) represents the type of interdisciplinary unit that is becoming more and more common in colleges and universities across the country, as older, more traditional disciplinary boundaries give way to new structures.

And finally, don't forget about library and information science (LIS) departments. As more and more LIS education is offered online, you may discover LIS students living nearby who may be excited to work with you to develop and deliver health and wellness programming as a practicum or internship. Reach out to the LIS program in your area to get started.

Collaborations work best when they play to the respective partners' strengths and interests. In Phoenix, FitPHX works so well because college students see the experience of working directly with the public around health matters as invaluable preprofessional experience. Furthermore, the structure of these initiatives allows the libraries to count on steady streams of trained students ready and enthusiastic to make a difference.

Cooking at the Library

When I talk about cooking classes in libraries, the feedback I typically receive is along the lines of "I'd love to do this in my library, but we don't have a kitchen or cooking equipment." The space issue can be a tricky one. But librarians are creative people, and we've found all kinds of ways to offer our communities immersive cooking and nutrition programs by taking advantage of the spaces and equipment we do have or by cobbling something together through community partnerships.

Here are just a few of the creative solutions I've found:

- Prep the food ahead of time so all that remains is assembly. Salsa making is a great option for this sort of program as—if you don't mind chunky salsa—you can easily do this program in any library meeting room with some bowls, spoons, and your favorite fresh ingredients (e.g., tomatoes, onions, garlic, cilantro, lemons, limes, etc.). Librarians Kristin Grabarek and Mary R. Lanni (2019) report that in some smaller, family programs they even invite caregivers to chop the veggies themselves at the program (don't forgot those waivers of liability!). Other options for no-cook, no-special-equipment-needed recipes include things like fruit-based and sandwich recipes (e.g., healthy banana splits, fruit kabobs, and cucumber sandwiches), and no-bake cookies and pastries.
- Try tasting programs. Working with a partner, you may be able to arrange programs focused on exposing your community to new culinary experiences. A great example is a cheese-tasting session (make sure you have some non-dairy cheeses). You could also do tasters around fresh veggies and fruits or really anything that is simple to prepare or that is in season.
- Blenders are your friends. I've seen so many libraries embrace the ethos of blending in cooking programs. You can do a lot with just a couple of blenders and extension cords: basic juicing classes, smoothie sampling—you could even challenge participants, asking, "Will it blend?" to engage in some culinary creativity. This is a fun one for teens, similar to the "Will it waffle?" challenge, which is the same idea but with a waffle maker.
- Make your own trail mix. This one is pretty self-explanatory: get a bunch of different trail mix ingredients and encourage people to think about how putting together different flavors and textures (seeds, salty snacks, sweets, fruits, nuts, etc.) leads to different taste sensations. Don't forget to talk about the nutrition behind trail mixes.
- Consider hot-plate programs. For more complicated recipes, you may be able to bring hot plates into your meeting rooms. Some libraries do a lot with hot plates, but I would not jump into using them right away. Build up your experience with cooking programs, first, as anything involving heat increases risk. Get comfortable doing cooking programs at your library before bringing in hot plates or other heat-generating devices.

Other libraries address this issue by taking their cooking programs off-site. That is what Clancy Pool, the branch manager of the St. John (pop. 537) branch of the Whitman County Library in Washington state, does. Her cooking class for teens and tweens occurs off-site in a church kitchen, where they have the facilities needed to successfully run the class. A church member always checks in before and after the program. Normally the church would charge a cleaning fee for a public event, but they waive it because the attendees leave everything the way they found it. This is a monthly summer program, but the library has occasionally held it during school vacations as well. Clancy told me, "We've had decent luck getting small grants to support these programs from banks and community development agencies. The program in the picture was supported by a memorial donation. The donors mentioned that 'Grandma was a great cook and always said it was too bad that nobody knows how to fix a meal from scratch anymore.'" Appealing to the popular desire to spread culinary literacy as a basic life skill is a great way to build support around your library's cooking programs. To access a photograph of this class, visit the book's online supplement at http://letsmovelibraries.org/healthy-living-at-the-library.

The sad fact is that many Americans of all ages have never had the opportunity to learn about even basic food preparation. An even larger number of Americans do not understand where food comes from. So some simple things you can do with minimal equipment may be completely eye-opening and transformative for community members. There will be costs involved—food isn't free—but if you work with partners (I especially recommend food banks, extension agents, farmer's markets, and even grocery stores), you may find the supply costs will be minimal.

As your cooking programs develop, you may want to invest in more equipment. You could even think about checking out cooking equipment when not in use in programs (think: cake pans and the like).

And bear in mind a few important logistical items: when handling and/or serving food in a library, you want to make sure you have the appropriate approval. A food-handling certificate is typically not too difficult to acquire, and is something a librarian could achieve. It can become more tricky when you move to *serving* food (e.g., Serv Safe® Certification training may be required). In many jurisdictions serving food prepared on-site, as opposed to food served elsewhere (the typical case for summer meals), requires even more layers of approval. Just be safe and informed before branching out into serving food prepared at your library. Call up your local health department to help you figure out what is necessary to bring a particular food program to your community. One good work-around if you run into obstacles is to team up with a local nutritionist, chef, registered dietician, extension agent, or other food professionals who may already have the appropriate clearance to lead such programs.

After you've worked out these logistics within your library team, the next step is thinking about what you'll be cooking or preparing. When you think about ingredients, you need to consider factors like cost, feasibility, and the outcomes you hope to achieve. Another concern relates to allergies. At the very least you need to make sure that all ingredients are transparently communicated. In the best case, you want to make sure there are alternatives.

Now that we've got some of the logistical issues out of the way, let's focus on the program itself. The best cooking programs cater to community interests and needs. Cooking programs can cover a wide range of topics and take on a variety of formats and can include everything from cookbook-author events—in which authors come and demo a few recipes from their books—tasting programs, preserving and pickling classes, basic knife skills, cuisines from around the world, and even gardening programs, like an heirloom seed swap (an especially good one to do right before gardening season starts).

Some good ways to get started with a cooking program are: (1) ask a local chef or extension agent to come and lead a class, (2) email a cookbook author or publisher to see about scheduling an author event (there may be self-published cookbook authors in your area, so don't overlook them), or (3) lead programs yourself. A fourth option would be to invite local cultural institutions to come to the library to demonstrate how to prepare different cuisines (as well as share a bit about the heritage behind them). If you do this, make sure to tell the presenters to keep it simple. Food can really bring a community together and even more so when 'everyone is working together at the library to help prepare it!

If you decide to take the DIY approach to cooking at your library, you will need to start small. Lead a program on something you know how to do really well and that you can make work given whatever logistical constraints you have in terms of space and equipment.

You'll also need to think about how to get your cooking supplies. Libraries have found three ways to procure ingredients for cooking programs:

1. If working with a partner, ask the partner to purchase food supplies, and then reimburse the partner or ask the partner to cover the costs.
2. Purchase the ingredients out of the library budget directly. When you have control over the purchasing of your ingredients, you can use a food-delivery service or even think about purchasing a share in a local community-supported agriculture (CSA) program. If you join a CSA, you'll have a variety of fresh produce throughout the growing season that you can use in programs focused on exposing your community to new tastes as well as on educating about food systems and ecology. When you join a CSA, they'll bring you (or you'll have to pick up, depending on the program) a fresh box of produce throughout the growing season. Of course, you can also just pick things up from the store or farmer's market.
3. There is nothing better than using ingredients you grow yourself at the library—another reason to branch out into gardening at your library.

Another great way to bring cooking classes to your library is to join the librarians across the country who have started participating in the Charlie Cart Project. In South Carolina, Lyndsey Maloney of the Horry County Library used a Charlie Cart to demonstrate food preparation at her library. A photograph of Lyndsey cooking at the library with the Charlie Cart is at http://letsmovelibraries.org/healthy-living-at-the-library. She told me,

> I made veggie and black bean quesadillas. I had six- and seven-year-old children eating spinach, so I call it a win! It was a pop-up event so it wasn't advertised; instead we just had people who sat and watched or stopped by to ask questions. There were about fifteen people total!

> I had so much fun doing this and hope I can do it again soon. Food literacy is a growing trend across the country, so picking a budget-friendly but tasty meal and allowing people to taste-test and take the recipe home was a fantastic experience!

The Charlie Cart Project focuses on increasing food literacy among Americans through a "program-in-a-box" (or, in this case, a cart). Although designed for a K–12 setting, libraries from Oklahoma to South Carolina to Pennsylvania have started acquiring Charlie Carts for pop-up programming. The carts contain most of the basic supplies you need for simple cooking classes, can be transported easily, and have recipes you need to get started. A Charlie Cart is a great thing to ask for in a grant (that is how the staff at Stillwater Public Library in Oklahoma got theirs), or to organize a fundraiser around. You could even think about possibly acquiring a Charlie Cart through a regional library consortium, which is what they did in South Carolina. The South Carolina State Library's "Read, Eat, Grow" campaign purchased a Charlie Cart that librarians from across the state can now "check out" to bring cooking classes to their libraries. Learn more about the Charlie Cart Project at http://charliecart.org.

Little University Program: Healthy "Cooking" Class

One of our most popular Little University programs is our healthy "cooking" class. We put the word "*cooking*" in quotation marks for the obvious reason: while babies, toddlers, and preschoolers will be slicing, dicing, pouring, and mixing, we do not actually allow them to use an oven or stove.

Instead, we host a variety of programs that feature healthy, no-cook recipes. Most recently, we introduced our young program attendees to tropical fruits by making a fruit pizza.

We employed thin, round slices of pineapple to serve as the crust. We used vanilla yogurt, including nondairy options, for the sauce. The "pizza" toppings provoked the most interest from our participants, as that was when our little chefs got to use their "knives." Slicing precariously and messily with butter knives, we managed to cut and/or mutilate a full basket of unsuspecting fruits, bananas, kiwis, and mangoes, in particular. We topped the whole project off with shredded coconut, which served as our pizza "cheese."

The learning opportunities here are not to be missed. Toddlers and preschoolers were asked to deduce which parts of each fruit they should eat, and which parts they should not eat. My copresenter and I encouraged them to only plan on eating the "delicious parts" of each fruit. So we discarded the spiny pineapple outside, the too-tough banana peels, the fuzzy kiwi parts, the too-chewy mango outsides, and the too-hard mango insides.

Most importantly, though, babies, toddlers, and preschoolers were invited to take ownership of making their own snack, which in turn highly motivated babies, toddlers, and preschoolers to eat their own snack. Combine this motivation with the obvious fact that the snack is healthy, and we have a tremendously positive result around a task parents often confront as a battle: encouraging little ones to eat healthy foods.

We boosted this motivation further by including enough supplies for grown-ups to make a fruit pizza for themselves. These, generally, turned out looking like pizzas, whereas the projects assembled by the little ones more closely resembled slop. We leveraged this to our advantage, however, by asking our young participants if they would like to feed their pizzas to their grown-ups, and vice versa. The result was that all participants in the program had a solid dose of vitamins, minerals, and fun.

Three helpful hints:

1. Ask about allergies and aversions. A well-advertised program, though, usually helps concerned parents self-select whether the content and ingredients will be appropriate. Still, ask to be sure.
2. Remember the babies! We lugged a blender into the room and blasted a quick smoothie concoction, using the abovementioned ingredients, for the babies to try.
3. Avoid the big allergens. We simply never do peanuts or honey; better safe than sorry!

Teaming Up with the Extension for Cooking Classes

In the United States, there are few partners better than the Cooperative Extension System for cooking classes. The Cooperative Extension System, an agency of the U.S. Department of Agriculture, exists to "encourage healthful lifestyles" by providing "non-formal education and learning activities to people throughout the country" (read more at Lenstra 2018b). The system emerged alongside the land-grant university system and, over time, evolved from a focus on agricultural education in rural areas (including 4-H, Master Gardeners, and

Master Naturalists) to a broader focus on healthy food and agriculture in both urban and rural parts of the country.

A library seeking to partner with the Extension System on cooking programs can do so by reaching out directly to Extension agents in your state. Find yours at https://nifa.usda.gov/land-grant-colleges-and-universities-partner -website-directory. This website will enable you to drill down to your particular state's Extension office, but then you will have to find the local Extension agent that serves your county or region.

Here are some examples of librarians working with extension agents to whet your appetite. In Georgia, the Cobb County Library partners with the University of Georgia Extension's Cobb County Office for a variety of health and wellness programs targeted at both youth and adults. In Summer 2018 the library worked with the local 4-H chapter to develop summer reading programs focused on improving youth nutrition and physical activity. This recurring program series was called 4-H Yoga & Healthy Living Program and featured Extension agents coming to the library to lead yoga programs and to educate about nutrition. For adults, the Extension offers programs at the library on how to become a Master Gardener, as well as a THYME to Read Book Club, in which participants read and discuss books related to food, agriculture, and gardening.

Extension agents no longer only focus on rural America; urban areas across the country also have Extension agents. For instance, the New York Public Library has worked with Cornell University's Extension Agents to offer Cornell@NYPL. The program has brought more than seventy-seven programs into the library's branches on health, nutrition, and financial literacy, taught both by Cornell faculty and by New York City Cooperative Extension experts.

In urban Nevada, the public libraries in Reno and Las Vegas work with the University of Nevada Cooperative Extension to offer a program called Little Books and Little Cooks. The program focuses on preschool children and their caregivers to boost healthy eating, literacy, parent-child interaction, and school readiness. Since 2012, the program has provided families with opportunities to cook and read stories together. You can read more about this program and how it works on the University of Nevada Cooperative Extension's website: https://snaped.fns.usda.gov/library/materials/little-books-and-little-cooks.

These partnerships do not materialize out of thin air. Librarians and Extension agents meet multiple times to figure out how best to work together. To better understand how this process works, I asked the Programming Librarian Interest Group (see chapter 7) what its members had done with their local agents.

Librarians reported developing nutrition programs, including Cook Smart, Eat Smart; food prep and canning; Instant Pot and pressure cooking; dehydrating food; pickling vegetables; composting; cooking for teens; budgeting to make sure you have enough money to eat healthy and well; and general nutrition and cooking programs using healthy ingredients. (Multiple librarians noted that Extension agents are typically certified to prepare and serve food.)

Librarians also reported working with Extension agents to develop programs focused on how to grow your own food, including programs on starting a home garden, starting a community garden at the library, starting a seed library, and kids' gardening. One librarian said that they worked with their Extension agent to develop five programs during summer reading in which kids plant pole beans and track their growth during the length of the program. Another librarian recommended working with the Extension agents to set up a local farmers market at the library, an idea that the Public Library Association/Institute of Museum and Library Services recently highlighted in Richland County, South Carolina. These examples all illustrate that if you want to start cooking at your library, and you live in the United States, a great starting point is to reach out to your Extension agent.

Fitness Classes at the Library

In my survey of movement-based programs in North American public libraries, the most common types of fitness programs offered were (in order of frequency): yoga, dancing, Zumba, and tai chi. In addition, a large percentage of respondents said they had offered "other," which they specified as including everything from Pilates to Jazzercise to CrossFit. There is no shortage of ways to get people moving together in a group setting, which is the focus of this section.

Leading an immersive fitness class in a library, or in any other setting, typically requires one to undergo training. As such, we will focus here on how you can organize these programs as partnerships with volunteers, individual instructors, and institutions. Even if you happen to be in the position to pay your instructor as a performer, you should *still* approach it as a partnership, because typically the fitness instructors who teach in libraries do not do so to become rich, but as a way to give back, typically offering deep discounts on their going rates because they want to extend access to more individuals.

No Instructor, No Problem!

Most fitness classes in libraries are taught by certified professionals. However, during the last few years, I have seen a growing number of libraries offer fitness classes without instructors. These programs are of two types:

1. Peer-to-peer group classes.
2. DVD or streaming video classes.

These programs can be very effective but, be warned, there really is no substitute for an expert in the room going through the moves with you. Programs without certified instructors can help introduce people to new ways to move, but if they want to go further in their training, they will definitely want to seek out a certified instructor (and you should tell them that!). Also, make sure you tell participants there will be no instructor to check in on them, and include that fact in the waiver of liability they sign (see appendix).

You will also be responsible for the setup of the room, which means, at a minimum, you'll want to have watched the video in advance (or reviewed any supplementary notes), or consulted with the peer leader, to make sure you have all the equipment participants will need (e.g., certain types of chairs, mats, weights, bands, etc.). Or you could tell them to bring in their own supplies. These classes work best for what I call gentle exercises, in particular, chair-based exercises in which there is minimal risk of anyone falling over or sustaining an injury due to exertion.

A video-based exercise class can also focus on fun and play. At the Fargo Public Library in North Dakota, librarians offered "Flashback Fitness" in Summer 2016: "Start out your Saturday with an 'active' sense of humor and revisit some past fitness trends from the 80s & 90s (think 'Sweatin' to the Oldies' and the Tae-Bo workout). Healthful treats or smoothie samples from local businesses will be served to participants post-workout. Retro fitness gear (legwarmers & neon T-shirts, anyone!?) and fun encouraged!" (Fargo Public Library 2016).

Here is how to offer a fitness program at your library if you don't have an instructor:

1. If you are using a DVD or streaming media, you have three options:
   a. Purchase public performance rights
   b. Purchase public performance rights for *particular* exercise programs.
   c. Utilize the creative commons and public domain
2. If you're *not* using streaming media, a few options include:
   a. Exercise support groups (with simple exercises)
   b. Peer-to-peer exercise groups.

Public performance rights can be purchased through a service like Swank: https://www.swank.com/public-libraries/licensing-options. Securing annual Public Performance Site licensing enables you to screen a wide variety of streaming and DVD fitness content in your meeting rooms.

You could also purchase public performance rights for particular exercise programs. In Spring 2019, I worked with Fran Fischer, the head of Geri-Fit, LLC, an evidence-based exercise program for older adults, to launch a trial of DVD-led exercise classes in rural and small-town libraries across the country. Fran gave participating libraries free access in perpetuity to the exercise DVDs she had created, and in exchange we collected data from the participants. The trial went off almost completely without a hitch, despite a particularly nasty January! What we found is that with a small amount of training, library staff feel comfortable setting up a digital fitness program like this, and older adults love it. Many of the participating libraries plan to keep offering the program, which for many was the first exercise program they had *ever* offered in their libraries. Learn more about Geri-Fit here: https://www.gerifit.com. There are other branded, evidence-based exercise programs that you can purchase to offer at your library. Consider making the purchase with help from Friends, donors, or by teaming up with other libraries in your area.

For a free video option, a lot of governmental agencies post free, evidence-based workouts online. For older adults, I recommend the workout videos produced by Go4Life, an initiative of the National Institute on Aging. These videos, and other Go4Life content, are already being used in a "Bend & Stretch" program at the Birmingham Public Library, in Alabama, where they use these videos and free booklets provided by Go4Life, for volunteer- and staff-led "gentle exercise routine, primarily sitting in chairs, to promote strength, flexibility, balance, and endurance" (Birmingham Public Library 2019). The classes have been offered for years by volunteers and by librarians and have gone very well. A similar program is offered at the Southwest Branch of the Orange County Library, in Florida. Learn more at https://go4life.nia.nih.gov.

Finally, you can find additional creative commons workout videos by searching Vimeo; their advanced search feature allows you to look for CC videos.

Support and Peer-To-Peer Exercise Groups

In the small town of Boonville, North Carolina (pop. 1,222), every Wednesday for over a decade, a group of local residents have gathered at the library for a healthy living support group. Participants share what they've been doing, hold each other accountable, swap recipes and cooking tips, and typically engage in some easy exercises together. These exercises are often led by one of the participants or are based on a short clip from an exercise DVD the library owns. Other times, the group will take advantage of the good weather and go for a walk. An exercise *support* group, with a little bit of immersive exercise thrown in, is a great way to get started with exercising at the library.

Sixty miles west of Boonville, in another small town, West Jefferson, North Carolina, the library has for years hosted the town's yoga club. This club doesn't have a formal leader per se but instead consists of a group of people who gather at the library every Monday night to do some simple yoga moves together. The classes are peer-led, with people leading them who have been practicing yoga for a longer period of time. The library is careful to call this a *club* and not a *class*. Individuals seeking detailed introduction should look elsewhere. Nonetheless, this is a great example of peer-to-peer learning in the library! Library staff will also typically join in the club as well.

Fitness Programs with Live Instructors

For all kinds of logistical, theoretical, and other reasons, the *best* immersive fitness classes have live instructors in the room able to give real-time feedback, advice, and monitoring of participants to ensure no one pushes too hard and risks injury. In Spring 2019, in collaboration with the National Institute on Aging's Go4Life campaign, I asked libraries to tell me about how they have worked with partners to bring exercise activities to their libraries. The findings from this report—freely available online—include lots of great advice on how to form and sustain partnerships with the volunteers, paid instructors, and partners that you will work with to extend access to fitness at your library. Learn more at https://go4life.nia.nih.gov/libraries.

Libraries that work with partners to offer exercise programs typically offer them about once a week. Some do monthly programs, some do twice a month, but weekly programs seem to be the norm. Common partners for free exercise at the library include recreation and community Centers (typically parts of parks and recreation units), private fitness studios and individual instructors, Ys, and a huge number of other options. On campuses, the athletics departments and university wellness units, among other entities, will often offer free exercise classes in school and university libraries. You can also be creative. Libraries have brought in retired PE teachers to lead fitness programs, while others work with high school teachers, faculty members (and students) in the kinesiology department from the local university or college, public health departments, and even hospitals. In Catawba County, North Carolina, the local hospital supplies the library with a Zumba instructor. The hospital pays the Zumba instructor as part of their preventive medicine outreach, and they are constantly seeking sites in which to offer this program. So don't think you have to work with just one individual or one entity to bring exercise classes to your library. There may be someone literally just waiting to receive a call. If it doesn't work out with one partner, try another! To see a postworkout photograph of a library Zumba group, visit this book's online supplement at http://letsmovelibraries.org/healthy-living -at-the-library.

Teaming Up with the YMCA

Bringing a YMCA fitness instructor to the library is cost-effective for the library and good promotion for the Y. Bring one of the YMCA's 20,000 full-time staff or 600,000 volunteers to your library to lead free fitness programs. The "YMCA of the USA" is "a leading nonprofit organization for youth development, healthy living and social responsibility" (Lenstra 2019a) that includes approximately 2,700 local entities that together engage 21 million Americans. They are also the perfect partner for any public library interested in developing healthy fitness programs.

In Connecticut, the Danbury Public Library hosts a Zumba instructor from the local YMCA every Wednesday night for a free, fun, family-friendly workout at the library. In Superior, Wisconsin, Jen Rosnau, the Superior YMCA wellness coordinator, leads a free yoga class at the library once a month on a Saturday morning.

In Decatur, Illinois, the library teamed up with the Decatur Family YMCA to offer a series of free exercise classes and demonstrations at the library in January as a way to jump-start healthy New Year's resolutions. And for Black History Month 2018 in Brooklyn, New York, the library invited Princess Bey, the healthy living program coordinator for the YMCA of Greater New York, to come down to its Clarendon Library Branch to demonstrate the importance of physical fitness for young people.

Finally, think about teaming up with the YMCA to celebrate special health-related holidays. As part of the National Institute on Aging's annual Go4Life month programming in September 2018, the Ferdinand Public Library, in rural southern Indiana, teamed up with the Tri-County YMCA and the Purdue Extension for a series of free exercise programs for older adults. The classes took place at the YMCA. The library helped advertise them and made available information packets about the importance of exercising as you age, which included a free exercise guide. For youth, one idea is to team up with the Y for their Healthy Kids Day event. Held each April, Healthy Kids Day is a national initiative to improve the health and well-being of kids. Dozens of public libraries across the United States have participated in Healthy Kids Day programs sponsored by their local YMCAs. If your library does not already collaborate with the Y for this event, reaching out to them to express your interest in doing so would be a great way to begin the conversation and collaboration.

How Do I Form These Partnerships?

My data show that library staff themselves, rather than outside entities, usually are the driving force in starting partnership-based exercise programs. Most people in the fitness world haven't (yet) thought of the library as a venue to promote learning about active living, so the onus to start these partnerships falls on us. If you're interested in offering exercise programs at your library, take these steps:

- Emphasize to potential partners that exercise programs are quickly becoming more and more common—and popular—in the public library setting.
- Suggest a mutually beneficial partnership.
- Explain exactly what the library has to offer (space, an audience, marketing, etc.).

It can also help facilitate forming and sustaining partnerships if you can articulate *exactly* what your needs are and *exactly* what you bring to the table. Here are some of the common concerns of librarians as they seek out partners:

- **Communication.** A well-developed proposal and clear communication with library staff about policy, expectations, and assessment.
- **Budget**. Agreement on a reasonable price and/or the potential for free or donation-only classes.
- **Instructors.** Professional qualifications, credentials, insurance, understanding of different individuals' physical skill levels. Instructors must have the skills, experience, reliability, and consistency to create a program that is welcoming to all, and the commitment to stick to a plan and schedule, with flexibility to adjust as needed.
- **Scheduling.** Advance planning, timing that suits the schedules of different audiences, and a commitment to a designated schedule.
- **Marketing.** Multiple approaches, including co-promotion with library staff and working with outside organizations to help spread the word. Partners should be willing to work with the library around good marketing strategies that attract the targeted community.
- **Needs assessment.** Assessment of community needs, interest, adequacy of space; ability to adapt programs to the unique needs of different audiences. Instructors should be willing to offer a test class (or classes) to determine interest and get feedback.
- **Legal issues.** Experience with liability waivers, discussions with library insurers and attorney, medical clearance from doctors, where necessary.
- **Teamwork and mutual understanding.** Realizing the importance of meeting the needs of all concerned: instructors, library staff, and class participants.

Even with all these details worked out, partnerships do not always go smoothly. In fact, in interviews and surveys, I have frequently heard growing pains along the way. Common challenges reported included cost, space, community interest, concern over legal liability, and staff oversight. Here are some of the tactics librarians use to overcome these obstacles:

- **Funding.** Use donations, fund-raising, Friends of the Library efforts, and more. If you can tell the story well, you'll be able to convince people to help pay for the program.
- **Legal and liability issues.** Use disclaimers, waivers, and liability forms, and consult with library insurers and attorneys.
- **Partnerships.** Negotiate with individual instructors, volunteers, and outside groups; also adjust class schedules and locations to find mutually agreeable times.
- **Marketing.** Frame this activity as a dimension of the partnership. Partners are expected to help promote the classes they lead in the library. Use multiple communication sources and strategies, including advertising, social media, and outreach to community groups.
- **Space.** Use early room booking; find alternate/additional spaces both within and outside the library setting (e.g., an open children's room or a nearby church kitchen).
- **Program Expansion.** Add programs based on demand; secure space at other library and nonlibrary locations, if needed.
- **Staffing.** Use a designated staff liaison as the point person for the partnership and to collect paperwork (e.g., liability forms and assessment forms). Also, use library organization and scheduling to make sure staff time is delegated to oversee the program.
- **Timing of Programs**. Rotate schedules to attract new audiences, vary time for participant convenience, or keep them the same for consistency.
- **Community Interest.** Test interest, eliminate programs of low interest, try a different program or instructor if needed.

I've also heard numerous examples of many long-term successful partnerships. Most libraries that responded to my survey have been offering exercise classes for between three and five years, although many have held them much longer. Said one respondent, "We have offered yoga for over thirty years," and there was a significant number who said they've done these programs for more than ten years (Lenstra 2019b).

Working Out in the Academic Library

Although comprehensive data does not exist, there is evidence that more and more academic libraries also offer exercise classes, particularly during finals and specifically in partnership with other campus agencies, like wellness or athletics. Meyers-Martin and Borchard (2015) surveyed a self-selecting sample of 279 academic librarians about their finals-week programming. Their survey did not explicitly ask about physical activity programming; options provided included therapy animals, movies, nap spaces, arts and crafts, social media, gaming, or other. Nevertheless, fully 47 percent of respondents selected the "other" category and wrote in that they offer programs ranging from chair massages to "dance and exercise breaks including yoga, Zumba and hula hoops" (2015, 518).

To investigate the prevalence of this type of programming, I conducted an informal study during December 2018 to see how physical activity was being supported during academic finals. Using Twitter, I conducted nightly keyword searches during the first three weeks of December for terms like "libraries" and "finals," or "libraries" and "yoga" to see what types of special programs academic libraries were offering (Lenstra 2018c). Among the results of this study were the Brain Break program at the University of Toronto's Robarts Library that invited students to enjoy fun fitness activities led by staff from campus rec at the library. In Scotland, the University of Glasgow Libraries invited students to meet at the library at noon every day during finals for a one-mile run. Academic libraries also had special exercise bike programs at Nicholls State University's Ellender Memorial Library in Thibodaux, Louisiana, and at Merrimack College's McQuade Library in Massachusetts. Yale University's Bass Library invited students to "Recharge . . . with a free Zumba class at the library" (Bass Library 2018).

Finally, it seems that yoga was being offered everywhere, with special yoga programs at the University of Lincoln (United Kingdom), the Old Dominion University library (Virginia), the University of Michigan at Flint's library, the Arapahoe Community College library (Colorado), Adelphi University Libraries (New York), the Georgia Tech library, Jacksonville State University's Houston Cole library (Alabama), Marquette University's library (Milwaukee), Saint Anselm College's library (New Hampshire), the University of Nevada–Las Vegas library, California State University–Chico's Meriam Library, the Mount Royal University library (Calgary, Canada), the University of North Carolina at Chapel Hill's SILS Library, the Lone Star College Library (Texas), the University of Wisconsin–Madison's art library, the University of Maryland–Baltimore library, and Brandeis University's library (Massachusetts).

Even though we still do not know how common these types of special programs have become, we do have clear, if anecdotal, evidence that these types of programs are being offered and enjoyed in a wide variety of academic libraries in many parts of the United States and Canada and beyond. More research is needed to generate more comprehensive data on this trend.

Some academic libraries have even started offering ongoing exercise classes. At Cal State University's Los Angeles campus, the library now offers free weekly yoga classes throughout the year. Similar programs are now popping up on campuses across the country, especially when there are no other exercise options near the campus library. School libraries are getting in on this trend as well. A middle school librarian in Johnston County, North Carolina, created what she calls a "Namaste Nook" in her library. In this space for students to de-stress, the librarian sometimes offers simple yoga classes.

Engage New Users through Fitness Programming

Free fitness at the library can also bring in new users. Jessica Zaker, a librarian in Sacramento, focuses her fitness programming on a specific population iden-tified as underserved by her library: adults in their twenties and thirties (Zaker 2014). Zaker and the library started an alternative library, or alt+library, ini-tiative by forming a special Friends of the Library group composed of these younger adults. Zaker and this Friends group then organized such unortho-dox fitness activities in the library as punk rock aerobics, alterna-Pilates, brutal yoga, holidaze yoga, zombie survival aerobics, and Riot Grrrl Plyo. The library has since seen more adults of this age group using the library.

Most libraries find that once they start offering fitness programming, their communities want more of them. As part of Health Happens in Libraries, OCLC/WebJunction supported free Zumba classes at the Hampton Public Library, in Virginia. A postproject survey found that "participants expressed a desire for more exercise opportunities at the library, including Zumba and yoga instruction." The report also quotes a librarian involved in the initiative, who found as follows:

> Health programming at the library is an opportunity for community mem-bers to have an experience together. Strictly informational programs, while useful, might attract a more self-selected audience. As we learned in pro-viding our Zumba class, activities and events for all ages and skill levels truly excite and positively surprise patrons and partners, and pave the way for them to learn more about all the library has to offer. (Hampton Public Library 2015)

Similarly, in St. Louis, Missouri, health science librarians from Washington University partnered with the local public library system to administer a com-munity needs survey on health information. The survey found that "exercise" was the topic the public most wanted to see more of at the library (Engeszer et al. 2016, 64). In response, the partners developed a series of programs that included yoga, beginning exercise, and Zumba, which were subsequently offered throughout the library system.

Yoga for All at the Library

Yoga is one of the most impactful programs I've offered at my library. A blend of movement and mindfulness, it is a perfect something for families to do together. Unlike most yoga classes, the ones that I have offered in my community are family-friendly, encouraging participants to leave the comfort of their mats in order to venture out into the space occupied by others. While the children are usually ready to do that, it is clear that the parents, often, are not. However, thanks to some gentle encouragement from the instructor and the example set by their children, these parents gently step out of their comfort zones to find themselves moving with those around them.

Entering the imaginative space occupied by their children, parents practice balance as they move on tiptoe like giraffes, increase cardiovascular output while prancing like horses, and build muscle strength by lumbering like elephants. Even traditional yoga poses like boat pose and goddess pose can be the foundation for parents to lift their children in an atypical way. The more fun these poses are, the more likely they are to be requested again outside of the library.

In one program, the instructor asked everyone to sit "criss-cross applesauce" on their mats as she distributed a length of yarn to each person. She had them hold the yarn out in front of their faces and asked them to blow: once to make the yarn move far, once to not move it at all, and once to move it somewhere in the middle. To my delight, everyone participated, even if they weren't yet old enough to be adept at executing the concept. This activity helped increase focus and calm and was a tool that could be carried out into the world. I watched as parents who, no doubt, had a laundry list of worries and needs on their minds, immersed themselves in this moment with their children. Especially when things at home are stressful, tools like these help keep families grounded and connected.

Our hope is that by participating in movement programs together in the library, families will be more inclined to move and play together outside of the library as well. Regular, repeated attendance by families is proof of their enjoyment, and increased comfort is observable from one program to the next. Though we don't always know how families interact when we can't see them, the indicators that we *do* have show that the foundation, at least, has been laid.

Next-Level Libraries

As discussed in part 1, for over a decade the Urban Libraries Council has given awards and honorable mentions to the activities that member libraries have undertaken to improve health, safety, wellness, and sustainability. To inspire you to dream big, I'd like to end by highlighting a handful of examples of libraries in this database:

- In Ohio, the Public Library of Cincinnati and Hamilton County started a Healthy Kids Zone in 2009. Weekly programs included a thirty-minute fitness activity. Nearly forty thousand children participated in the program. According to librarians, "parents also commented that their children were encouraging them to eat better at home and exercise more."
- In New York City, Queens Library launched Queens Connect Care in 2011. The initiative led to exercise classes being offered throughout the library system.
- In Missouri, the Kansas City Public Library started "offering free cardio kickboxing and aerobics classes along with a 12-week weight loss challenge for all fitness levels and ages" in 2012. The award notes that "attendance at cardio and aerobics classes is averaging more than 40 each week. Participants range from those with excellent fitness to those confined to wheelchairs, the elderly, and families" (Kansas City Public Library 2013).
- In Texas, the Houston Public Library started offering, in 2013, programs for families "focused on intergenerational learning—parents and children learning together through interactive, literacy and technology infused educational activities ranging from Zumba to cooking demonstrations" (Houston Public Library 2014).

The activities of our nation's largest libraries should inspire us all. Not all of us have the resources and time to build such award-winning programs, but *we should do something!* That really is the message of this section and of this book. Get out there, get in the mix, and make sure that the library is at the table when discussions of how to improve healthy living through access to nutritious food and physical activity take place.

Exercises

1. What types of cooking demos or exercise classes do you think you could offer at your library?
2. What support would you need to feel comfortable offering immersive cooking and fitness programs at your library?
3. Are there partners, members of your library team, or other librarians you could reach out to, to get this support? Who are some likely candidates?

12

Creating Health-Supporting Spaces and Collections for Your Programs

As healthy living becomes more central to library programming, some libraries have started developing spaces and collections to support it. This chapter provides only a cursory overview of how to develop these collections and spaces. If you'd like to dig deeper into this topic, I recommend *Audio Recorders to Zucchini Seeds: Building a Library of Things*, edited by Mark Robison and Lindley Shedd. Unfortunately, there isn't (yet!) a whole book on how library spaces can support healthy living, but good starting points for further reading include the following:

- Carrie Scott Banks and Cindy Mediavilla's *Libraries and Gardens: Growing Together* (ALA Editions, 2019)
- "Get Moving: Library Design," library architect Traci Lesneski's article from *Library Journal*, September 26, 2017
- San Diego public librarian Jeffrey Trapp Davis's *The Collection All Around: Sharing Our Cities, Towns, and Natural Places* (ALA Editions, 2017)

What do health-supporting spaces and collections look like? Broadly speaking, table 12.1 shows what I've found. Librarians are developing kitchens for cooking classes, and bike fix-it stations to create bikeable libraries. They're developing seed collections to support sustainable community agriculture, and gym passes to enable local residents to check out the YMCA without having to purchase a membership first.

What we'll do in this chapter is give you the information you need so that you can get ***started*** developing spaces and collections to augment and to

TABLE 12.1   Examples of new spaces and new collections developed by libraries to support healthy living programming

Spaces		Collections	
Indoor	**Outdoor**	**Food**	**Physical Activity**
Kitchens/ Kitchenettes	Gardens	Cooking supplies (e.g., cake pans)	Fitness equipment
Play spaces and equipment	Play spaces and equipment	Gardening tools	Bike and walking equipment (e.g., bike locks, walking poles)
Exercise equipment (e.g., FitDesk)	Walkable spaces (e.g., greenways, StoryWalk®)	Gardening plots	Sports and recreation equipment (e.g., Frisbees)
Flexible spaces (e.g., SkillShare)	Bikeable spaces (e.g., bike racks, Fix-It stations)	Seeds	Nature and hiking equipment
Yoga and reflection spaces	Mobile kitchens/ farmers markets	Food itself (e.g., Little Free Pantry)	Gym and park passes

support your programs, and as such to holistically turn your library into a healthy living hub. Unfortunately, we don't have time for a deep dive into all the different ways library spaces and collections can support healthy living, so we'll use selective examples to illustrate *some* of the possibilities.

Libraries: Spaces for Movement

If you were going to build a new public library from the ground up, what would it look like? This is the question the city of Santa Clarita, California, asked itself in 2014 when it conducted a community needs assessment to decide what to include in its latest branch: the Saugus Library Center. More than 1,500 residents filled out surveys, and 300 participated in community meetings. What they found may surprise you. In addition to wanting things like "comfortable seating, a children's library, a café, a quiet study area, more books, free Wi-Fi, [and] a family events center," the community also asked for "a place for fitness and exercise." Indeed, 47.2 percent of survey respondents said they wanted to see "Exercise/Fitness classes" in the new Saugus Library Center, making it the fourth most popular response, behind "Free Wi-Fi," "Books," and "Family Events" (Santa Clarita Library 2017).

Similarly, in La Crosse Wisconsin, a community-needs survey for a branch library found that one-third of survey respondents wished to see "exercise and sports programs" at the new library location. As such, the space is being designed with "exercise areas" in mind (Vian 2019). And in the small town of West Point, Iowa, a community-needs survey conducted in 2018 to determine future directions for adult programming found that "it was equally divided between those wanting games and those wanting some type of exercise program," library director Dara Sanders told a local reporter (Delaney 2019).

In fact, the trend of colocating opportunities that involve libraries has been building for some time. One of the newest branches of the San Antonio Public Library, in Texas, is colocated within a YMCA fitness center, and other branches have outdoor exercise equipment installed around them (see Lenstra 2019a). In Alberta, Canada, one of the newest locations of the Calgary Library is within what has been described as the world's biggest YMCA. Shannon Doram, president and CEO of YMCA Calgary, said the facility "was designed very intentionally to give people opportunities not only for physical wellness but for the spiritual, social, and emotional wellness that comes with other activities, like the arts" (Getaneh 2018).

Some libraries work so extensively with the YMCA that they have actually codesigned new spaces. In Summerville, South Carolina, the Berkeley County Public Library System signed a twenty-year agreement with the Cane Bay YMCA to host a library branch *inside* the Y. According to planners, this new YMCA facility, which opened in late spring 2019, is the first YMCA building in the country that was designed from the beginning to have a library inside of it. The process of building the new YMCA-library was highly collaborative, with library staff and the YMCA working together on everything from color schemes to carpeting choices within the facility. According to Paul Stoney, president and CEO of the YMCA of Greater Charleston and Cane Bay Family YMCA, the idea of building a library into a YMCA will promote "the overall goal of healthy living—which is spirit, mind and body" (quoted in Bonala 2019). That sounds like a whole-person librarianship to me!

Similarly, in London, Ontario, the Bostwick Community Centre, which opened in November 2018, includes both a YMCA and a branch of the London Public Library. Chief Librarian Susanna Hubbard Krimmer said they are "excited to be able to provide a space for our community that forges stronger social connections, that makes it easy and fun for those of every age and ability to stay healthy and to learn new things" (quoted in City of London 2018).

Meanwhile, in the nation of Singapore, a new type of public library opened on February 4, 2018. Called Heartbeat@Bedok, the facility brings together a "sports centre, public library, community club, polyclinic and senior care centre under one roof" (Bei Yi 2018). Prime Minister Lee Hsien Loong said that bringing these entities together in one facility will enable the hub to become a "national innovation laboratory" (ibid.) to pilot new services, which could include telemedicine and the pairing of workout data with health statistics.

Back in Santa Clarita, California, the city is committed to meeting community needs by creating a space for exercise and fitness in its newest library branch, which is scheduled to open to the public in 2020. The concept for the new library is that it will be a "multi-generational family destination and gathering place for all Santa Clarita residents [and a] vibrant community hub with unique indoor and outdoor spaces. A place where learning, exploration, imagination and play can happen simultaneously in the same area."

Architect Traci Lesneski (2017) talks about "encouraging activity in today's libraries. . . . The next frontier in creating buildings that support human health is encouraging more movement." She presents examples of public librarians who deliberately create places that enable and support physical activity, including one who marked "off a five-minute 'trail' through the building" (ibid.) to encourage physical activity.

Librarians are also working to create communal spaces that facilitate shared engagement in physical activities. For instance, Bellingham Public Library, in Washington, removed two book stacks from its main room to create what it calls the "SkillShare," an open place where community members share their skills (Bellingham Public Library 2017). Among other things, the SkillShare hosts regular tai chi sessions.

Making Space for Movement via the Makerspace Ethos

You may not be able to completely redesign your library, but you may be able to make space for movement by embracing the makerspace ethos. In a curriculum plan entitled *Learning through Movement: Applying Exercise Education and Movement Activities in a Library Setting*, North Carolina school librarian Deborah Yu-Yuk Jung states that the makerspace movement creates opportunities for libraries to become more active play spaces: "As librarians begin to turn towards a learning commons and/or MakerSpace environment for learning, we need to provide for areas of active learning. This means not only incorporating technology and re-designing facilities for flexible grouping, social learning, and increased noise, but also providing areas for safe movement" (Yu-Yuk Jung 2015).

Part of the rationale for the makerspace movement in libraries has been to support a variety of learning styles and formats. As Jung points out, however, we have yet to fully integrate learning through our bodies, through movement—that is, kinesthetic learning—into our makerspaces.

Nonetheless, one of the more unexpected findings from my research has been that more and more librarians *are*, in fact, integrating physical activity into their makerspace activities, literally making spaces for movement. We can learn from these early adopters to reimagine our library spaces. In spring 2019 the Santa Maria Public Library, in California, started a "Bike Kitchen" program focused on providing access to supplies and expertise needed to assemble and repair bicycles. This has become a popular program model in other California libraries, with similar initiatives in Oakland and in San Diego. The Oakland program extends the initiative beyond bike repair and includes bike decoration. Participants are invited to customize their bicycles in creative, personal ways, and the library has a space dedicated to this program.

Other libraries apply this model to skateboarding. Since 2017 the Aldine Branch of the Harris County Public Library in Texas has sponsored an annual skateboarding program that takes students' love of sports and design and blends them together. Youth create their own skateboards, which they design themselves, and then learn how to use them at a local skate park. This collaborative program involves the library working with the local YMCA and the county parks department.

Libraries also empower patrons to make the library into a space for movement. At the Waterford Public Library, in Wisconsin, librarians developed a Teen Mini-Golf program in which participants created their own golf course using supplies like foam noodles, book discards, tape, and paper rolls, and they then played a couple of rounds on the course they made in the library. They have also done this program at the Cumberland County Library, in Fayetteville, North Carolina.

Finally, we see makerspaces and movement coming together in initiatives focused on making things through movement. A Dutch designer developed the Cycle Knitter, a contraption that knits a scarf using the energy generated from pedaling a stationary bicycle. Similarly, at the Cowbridge Library, in the United Kingdom, the library sponsored a paint-spinning program in which paint poured into a drum took on different shapes based on the speed at which one pedaled an attached stationary bike.

Spaces to Move in Academic and School Libraries

To help stressed-out students relax, unwind, and get a little exercise in, school and academic libraries are also offering spaces for movement. DeClercq and Cranz (2014) share how the University of California–Berkeley librarians work with architecture students to identify how library spaces could support physical activity. They conclude that academic libraries should strive to have "a mix of furniture options that together welcome a variety of healthy postures," as well as "rooms where students can stretch," and other "opportunities to introduce physical activity into library settings."

Toward this end, librarians elsewhere have installed FitDesk study bikes and Desk Treadmills, while others have created walking routes that encourage students to get up and go for a walk in the library. At Walsh University in Ohio, librarians worked with University Wellness to create laminated guides that were placed on tables throughout the library and also attached to the walls. These guides show easy exercises, such as body weight lunges, that can be done in the library.

Academic libraries also increasingly offer spaces for meditation and movement. In fall 2018, McGill University in Montreal unveiled its new "Tranquility Zone." In addition to relaxing seating and meditation spaces, the Zone includes stability balls, foam rollers, yoga blocks, and trigger-point massage balls, suggesting the purpose of the room encompasses both stillness and movement. Similar purposes can be discerned in the University of Toronto library's Reflection Room. According to the library's website, as well as the flyer posted on the physical entrance to the room, acceptable "activities welcome in the room" include "prayer, meditation, yoga, [and] mindfulness."

Biking Around in the School Library

On September 17, 2018, the Alliance for a Healthier Generation announced its annual "America's Healthiest Schools" list. On the list was J. Wilbur Haley Elementary in Fort Wayne, Indiana. The school received accolades for, among other things, "adding stationary exercise bikes at the Haley Elementary Library," where, according to the school, reading while biking "helps increase oxygen to the brain and it actually helps with comprehension" (Brantley 2018).

Far from an outlier activity, pedaling in the school library has become a common sight across the country. At Falls Church High School, in Virginia, the library has had four recumbent bikes since October 2013. It all started when librarian Laura Potocki wrote a Healthy Kids grant to fund the purchase and installation of the machines (Taylor 2014). The bikes anchor a corner of the library devoted to health and fitness. The nook also includes books and magazines that highlight health and wellness, and Potocki reports that the response she has gotten from her community has been overwhelming. Libraries are increasingly becoming places to exercise both your mind and your body.

Bikes at the library are part of how school libraries serve the whole student. As Jill Slapnik, from Batesburg-Leesville Middle School, in South Carolina, expressed it for a DonorsChoose campaign, "In addition to having makerspace activities, like games, puzzles, STEM materials, robots, to engage students in the library, we want FitDesk exercise bikes to get students moving and further activate their learning" (Slapnik 2018). Like makerspaces, exercising at the library represents a new and exciting way librarians positively impact student learning and student success.

Getting Started with Bikes

When librarians decide to bring bikes to the library, a first step is figuring out how to fund them. Three common sources of funding are crowdsourcing, grants, and internal partnerships. In Saginaw, Texas, Lori Wallis, librarian at Willow Creek Elementary School, submitted to DonorsChoose.org her idea for "Reading + Peddling = Smarter, More Active Kids" (Wallis 2016). Less than a month later, the project was fully funded. The total cost was less than $1,000. She decided to get pedal stations rather than full stationary bicycles because of cost and space constraints at her library. The setup is simple: She puts five chairs against the wall (for stability), and then the pedalers go in front of the chairs. Even though the pedalers cost less than $200 each, they have held up. Wallis made sure to buy "something that is going to last" (phone interview, October 16, 2018).

Betsy Long, the librarian at Doby's Mill Elementary in Lugoff, South Carolina, agrees that it is important to get quality equipment. She initially bought two inexpensive, adult-sized bike desks in 2017, but she found that although they worked somewhat well for the older kids, they were too big for many, and they also suffered a lot of wear and tear. She then identified a local company called Kinesthetic Classroom that specializes in youth-focused physical activity materials, such as recumbent bikes designed for elementary school–aged children. Long said that these materials are "sturdy, safe, and easy to use." They are also expensive, but "as the old adage goes . . . you get what you pay for" (email correspondence, October 11, 2018). To finance the new bikes, Long wrote grants to local charity organizations and used some book fair revenue to purchase four bike desks.

Other school districts have gone all in. In Kansas, the Maize Unified School District 266 received $20,000 from the Kansas Health Foundation, to which the district added an additional $4,700, to purchase twenty-six recumbent bikes that it installed in libraries district-wide. Now each elementary school media center in the district has two Schwinn recumbent bikes and two mini cycles (Maize Unified School District 266 2018). See below for more information on selecting and arranging library bikes.

Building Excitement and Rationale

To get your administration on board with the idea of biking, it can help to demonstrate the potential of this new addition to the library. That's exactly what John F. Parker Middle School librarian Ina Collins did in Massachusetts. Collins discovered there were some unused stationary bikes tucked away in an upstairs storage closet that was used by the athletics department. She convinced the department to move the bikes into the library, and after the administration saw how successful the bikes were, they agreed to purchase seven brand-new LK500IC stationary bikes, which are much quieter. The bikes pull in not only students but teachers as well (Deschenes 2018).

In New Jersey, Clearview Regional High School librarian Arlen Kimmelman did something similar in 2016. She said she wasn't sure if her administration would get behind her idea, so she personally raised funds through a GoFundMe campaign to purchase four bikes, which she then donated to the school district. She said, "I didn't want the district to have to deal with the money. . . . All I needed was permission to donate bikes" (email correspondence, October 4, 2018). In a presentation she made to other school librarians on the program, Kimmelman, a past president of the New Jersey Association of School Librarians, said this of her approach of donating the bikes: "Ask for forgiveness instead of permission" (Kimmelman 2017).

She added, "Stationary bicycles are an appropriate way to use the available space in a positive, forward-thinking, and multieducational manner." However, the bikes did not come assembled, so Kimmelman, always looking to tick multiple boxes, was also able to tie the bikes into the New Jersey learning standards for architecture and construction, which focus on being able to read, interpret, and use technical drawings, documents, and specifications to plan a project. This enabled her to turn to the campus robotics club to put the bikes together and help maintain them.

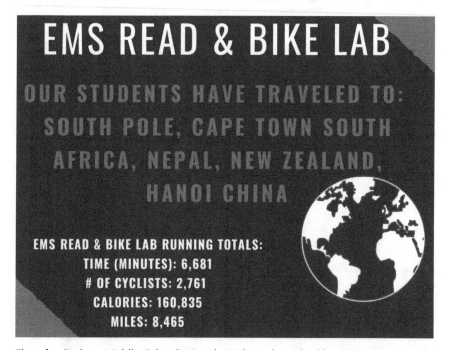

Flyer for Eudora Middle School's Read & Bike Lab in the library. Reprinted with permission from the Eudora Schools Foundation.

Introducing and Integrating Bikes

Once your bikes arrive, you may find that your students do not initially understand how best to utilize them. That is what Lori Wallis discovered: some students did not realize they had to adjust the resistance and would go "pedaling a mile a minute." Others forgot to tie their shoes: She has twice had to cut shoelaces off because they got caught around the pedals. She now gives students mini lessons on the pedalers before the students start using them. Wallis also found that reading a book on the bikes does not make sense for all students. Some get dizzy, and others cannot concentrate while pedaling. To enable those students to use the pedalers to full advantage, she also offers audiobooks. She said, "When they move and have the tablet with the headphones, they can focus more on the content," than they would by simply listening while sitting still.

In addition to having bikes available, some librarians have found fun ways to mobilize the communities around them. In Eudora, Kansas, a middle school librarian teamed up with the athletics department and the district's foundation to bring twelve stationary bikes to a room in the library that is now known as the Read & Ride Lab. The school keeps track of how many "miles" students bike in the lab and releases fun graphics on a regular basis to keep people motivated and excited. In fact, the school got so excited about the bikes that they were featured on the school's landing webpage: https://www.eudoraschools.org/Domain/9. The Eudora Schools Foundation also highlighted the bikes on the front cover of its 2016 annual report. The Read & Ride Lab got so much attention that U.S. representative Lynn Jenkins stopped by to visit in person.

Exercising Inclusivity

Virtually everyone I talked to about bikes in the library told me that bikes have had a large impact on special-needs students. In New Jersey, Kimmelman found that the bikes have been especially popular with "our special education students, who find the bikes enable them to focus, burn off extra energy, distract from anger, do what others are doing, and be seen doing something easy or successfully instead of being watched struggling to read." She also said that sometimes a guidance counselor will bring an anxious student down to the library to use the bike to relax.

Wallis said that one of the initial impetuses for bringing bikes to her library was to make it a more inclusive space. She noticed students who not feel comfortable in the traditional recess environment and instead opted to stay in the library during recess. "Just being outside at recess was just way too much for them. But I don't want them to not be moving," she said. The bikes enabled these students to get exercise without having to negotiate the fraught terrain of the recess environment.

In Frisco, Texas, high school librarian Ashley Hill also found (as explained on her DonorsChoose site) that the bikes have a positive influence on students who may otherwise be overly disruptive. She writes, "The FitDesks are beneficial for students who sometimes might get in trouble during class for being too rowdy or disruptive. The FitDesks allow these students to get their energy out in a constructive and positive way" (2016).

Bikes can also pull new users into your library. In Wilmington, North Carolina, New Hanover High School librarian Melissa George teamed up with the district's healthful living coordinator to bring bikes to the library. She found that the bikes especially appealed to boys who previously did not want to use the library. In a local news report, Principal James McAdams said he was "enthusiastic to bring the bikes into the library. Students now have the opportunity to stretch their muscles while also stretching their minds as they read and ride on the stationary bikes" (Thompson 2015).

Furthermore, some students may carry around a lot of stress throughout the day, which pedaling can help them release. In Fulshear, Texas, Leamon Junior High librarian Katie Poland shared in her DonorsChoose documentation that in her community she sees students with a lot of "extra energy, anxiety, and frustration" because of what is happening in their lives outside of school. The bikes help her, and a growing contingent of librarians across the country, "make the library a place where students can collaborate and learn, but also have a place of fun and relaxation" (Poland 2018).

Space and Equipment Considerations

There are now many varieties of exercise bikes available. They range from under-the-desk pedalers to full-sized recumbent bikes, with prices that range from less than $100 to more than $4,000. What's right for you and your library will depend on the age ranges you serve and the budget you have available.

An important consideration is where to put the bikes. Pedal bikes are small and can easily be moved. If you're in a situation where space is a concern, an under-the-desk pedaler or elliptical may be your best option. One downside to pedalers is that they do not have attached desks or chairs, which means that they are less self-contained as a unit. The larger recumbent bikes and FitDesks have more stability and require less setup.

Libraries: Spaces for Cooking

From Philadelphia, Pennsylvania, to Columbia, South Carolina, public libraries are installing kitchens and kitchenettes for cooking programs. In Forsyth County, North Carolina, the new central library location opened in fall 2017 with a commercial-grade demonstration kitchen designed to support cooking programs on a regular basis. At the national level, the library that has developed this idea to the greatest degree has been the Free Library of Philadelphia, which since June 2014 has been "revolutionizing the way Philadelphians think about food, nutrition, and literacy" through its Culinary Literacy Center, "the first kitchen-classroom in a public library in the United States of America" (Free Library of Philadelphia 2017).

What kind of spaces could you develop to support healthy cooking programs? Here are three options you may consider: commercial grade kitchens, mobile kitchens, and kitchenettes.

Commercial-Grade Kitchen

This is by far the most elaborate model but definitely something to consider if you're thinking about major renovations and/or a new library. In Burke County, North Carolina, nestled in the foothills of the Appalachian Mountains, library director Jim Wilson has made a commitment to installing kitchens in *every* branch of his library system whenever major renovations occur. They have already installed a demonstration kitchen in the newly renovated C. B Hildebrand branch of the library. He said, "That's not necessarily something that most libraries would have, but we felt like that health and wellness component is an important one for us. . . . That area is used quite a bit." Danielle Townsend, the adult program coordinator for the library, added that "if Morganton [the library's main branch] gets a demonstration kitchen, I will be able to offer programs on foods from other countries, healthy meals and snacks, cooking for one, and holiday cooking, among others" (Gercken 2019).

There is no one right way to develop a kitchen in a library. Work with your architects and make sure that you've consulted with your local health department about regulations for public food spaces.

Mobile Kitchen

The next option to consider is a mobile kitchen. These range from incorporating cooking equipment into your bookmobile to purchasing mobile kitchens that can be used for pop-up outreach and in-library programs. In addition to the Charlie Cart model discussed in the previous chapter, other libraries, particularly in urban areas, have worked with partners to develop mobile kitchens for cooking programs. The Camden County Library System, in New Jersey, uses a mobile kitchen in its Books and Cooks program. The library transports the kitchen to its eight neighborhood libraries and other community locations to demonstrate cooking techniques and recipes (Ewan 2018). The San Francisco Public Library takes its Biblio Bistro out to farmers markets and library branches for programming.

Kitchen in a Box and Mobile Food Services

Finally, some libraries have developed supplies they can use to convert their meeting rooms (or any room, really) into pop-up kitchens. If your budget is tight, the only things you really need are a table, an outlet, running water, and the most basic cooking tools. Try to boil down your supply list to what can fit inside a large, lidded plastic bin so that it can be moved around easily and stowed away when not in use. Keep a checklist of all the contents to make sure things don't go missing. You can outfit a kitchen in a box for $100, and partners may be willing to front the funds needed to get started.

Spaces to Distribute Food

In addition to creating spaces to teach cooking, libraries create spaces to distribute food. Public libraries in Richland, South Carolina, and High Point, North Carolina, started community farmers markets where none existed previously (Phillips, Hambright-Belue, and Green 2018). A library in Philadelphia started a farmers market but with the unique twist that fresh produce would be distributed at no cost. The Fresh for All free farmers market, run by Philabundance in partnership with the Lillian Marrero Library, distributes fresh produce to low-income residents of a North Philadelphia neighborhood every Wednesday afternoon (Neil 2018).

Other libraries adopt the "Little Free Pantry" program model to create food distribution sites. Inspired by the Little Free Library movement, food justice activists started developing micro food pantries where people could take and leave food as they wished. A library in Sylvan Lake, Canada, offers this service, and a librarian there said she developed it after seeing similar little free pantries offered at U.S. public libraries (Vaughan 2016). Sometimes these programs operate without affiliation with the Little Free Pantry movement. For instance, in the small community of Clive, Iowa, the library has what it calls a "Veggie Exchange," which consists of nothing more than a picnic table at the library where community members who garden are invited to leave excess produce for others who wish to have it. In a news story, librarians from Clive said that they "went to a conference, and heard other libraries were doing it" (Beckman 2018) and decided to try it at their library. Try it out at your library!

New Collections

On May 16, 2019, *Money* magazine published what may be the most comprehensive inventory of all the different objects that libraries now check out to patrons. The list of "200 Things Libraries Will Let You Check Out for Free"

(Glum 2019) includes the following supplies that can be used to increase healthy living through food and physical activity:

1. Air fryer
2. Bicycles
3. Bike locks
4. Birding journal
5. Blood pressure monitor
6. Bocce ball
7. Bounce house
8. Bundt pans
9. Butter churn
10. Cake pans
11. Cake pop maker
12. Camping tent
13. Canning kit
14. Cheese warmer
15. Coffee grinder
16. Cookie cutters
17. Cookie press
18. Cooler
19. Cornhole (a.k.a. bean bags)
20. Crockpot
21. Croquet set
22. Disc golf
23. Doughnut maker
24. Fishing pole
25. Flour mill
26. Food dehydrator
27. Food grinder/ sausage stuffer
28. French press
29. Giant Connect Four
30. Giant Jenga
31. Golf range finder
32. GoPro
33. Handbells/ deskbells
34. Hand blender
35. Hula hoop
36. Ice cream maker
37. Instant Pot
38. Juicer
39. Knife sharpener
40. Lawn checkers
41. Lawn darts
42. Lawn mower
43. Leaf blower
44. Mochi maker
45. Panini maker
46. Pasta machine
47. Pedometer
48. Pickleball
49. Popcorn machine
50. Raclette maker
51. Rapid egg cooker
52. Resistance bands
53. Seeds
54. Slackline set
55. Snowshoes
56. Sous vide
57. Spices
58. Spiralizer
59. Stand mixer
60. Tennis racket
61. Tortilla press
62. Vitamix
63. Volleyball set
64. Waffle maker
65. Wheelbarrow
66. Yoga mat
67. Yogurt maker

Fully one-third of the objects mentioned in the article support healthy living practices, ranging from daily fitness routines to gardening to outdoor recreation to experimentation in the kitchen. The article includes citations, so if you want to dig deeper, pull it up and check out what's available.

I'll forgive the authors for overlooking one object that is growing in popularity in some libraries located near bodies of water: kayaks! As the *Washington Post* reports, "In the recreation-oriented community of Payson, Utah, the library lends paddleboards and kayaks, including life jackets and car-attachment straps, as well as snowshoes" (Daily 2018). You can also snag a kayak at two different libraries in Michigan: the Kent District Library, based in Grand Rapids, and the Tamarack District Library. Foldable kayaks are also available for checkout at the Westport Library, in Connecticut. Idaho's

Clearwater County Free Library District is also considering getting some kayaks and paddleboards to check out (Morgan 2019).

Providing a comprehensive overview of this rapidly developing trend is far, far beyond the scope of this book. Here we'll just take a look at a few examples of libraries circulating objects to support healthy living practices and leave you with the message that libraries today can check out pretty much anything, including passes to facilities like gyms, rock-climbing walls, parks, and more. Make sure you communicate this message to your partners so they realize that healthy living at the library can involve both programs *and* collections.

Indeed, most innovative libraries find ways to *integrate* collections and programming. A perfect example of this comes from two libraries in southern Alberta, which are connected by one librarian, Lisa Weekes. First, at the Lethbridge Public Library, which serves Alberta's fourth-largest city, and then at the Chinook Arch Regional Library System, which serves rural libraries throughout southwest Alberta, Weekes has championed the integration of the library of things with programs around physical activity. Let's see how she and the rest of the staff at these two libraries did it (and how you can too).

Around 2014 the Lethbridge Public Library Physical Literacy project began, when librarians like Weekes and others started working with community organizations on how to increase opportunities for healthy living. In the library's community needs assessment, they noticed many community organizations focused on health and wellness. A kinesiology professor at the University of Lethbridge showed the library there was a "free play" gap in Lethbridge. There were plenty of organized sporting opportunities but not enough opportunities for people to get together and engage in active, semistructured play (Weekes and Longair 2016). This professor introduced the concept of physical literacy to the library. Physical literacy is a foundational skill in everyone's lives, enabling individuals to move with competence and confidence and thus to want to move more—including getting out and visiting the library.

After learning more about this topic, and in collaboration with partners, the library invested $2,500 in 2015 to get started on a pilot project. The project's goals were to

- Encourage physical activity through physical literacy kits
- Integrate local libraries with the city's recreational spaces
- Provide accessible equipment and instruction to allow children, youth, and families to be outdoors and physically active (Weekes and Longair 2016)

Because Lethbridge, like most cities, has many complementary organizations, it was important for the library to supplement, not replace or re-create, work already being done. In order to supplement activities, the library offered to provide a circulating collection of outdoor sports kits that encouraged free play.

The kits are "low-tech" and easy to use. Items are kept in large Ziploc bags cataloged as a kit; each item is barcoded. Each kit contains an instruction booklet that in very basic terms outlines how to use the equipment. The instruction booklets also contain a contents page with the barcode, and a first-time-user survey that gets returned to the library. The kits are kept in a big Rubbermaid tote and circulate like regular items.

Library staff received training from the partners on how to integrate the physical literacy kits into existing programming. New programming has also been created based on community feedback. For example, the Bookmobile is now the starting point for a walking club: Patrons can borrow walking poles to use and keep track of their progress. During the winter, a program called Move and Play is run for preschoolers to participate in structured physical activities. This is followed by free-play activities using items from the physical literacy collections. Even the ESL Storytime has physical literacy components; for example, name and vocabulary games are played using a ball. The programmer stated that tossing the ball back and forth broke down the intimidation of speaking in a group.

Patrons can borrow everything from basketballs, baseball kits, soccer balls, skipping ropes, horseshoes and lawn darts, pickleball, Hi-Lo scoopball, beach volleyball equipment, and even rubber chickens and rubber pigs: all motivational throwing tools. These supplies are also used in ongoing library programming for all ages.

A few years later, Weekes had the opportunity to join the Chinook Arch Regional Library System as their manager of partnerships and community development. One of her first initiatives was to replicate the work she did in Lethbridge in the context of this large, mostly rural library system. Taking things out into rural areas quickly illustrated vast differences in infrastructure. In Lethbridge, there were ample opportunities to engage in organized sports and physical activity. Not so out in the country: Weekes explained to me that in small towns during the long, cold, dark Canadian winters, "You can only go to McDonald's Fun Palace so many times before you start to lose your mind." In many communities, *there are no other options*.

So Weekes applied what she learned in Lethbridge to this very different context. In fall 2017, Lisa and her library team successfully applied for a $7,500 grant from the Henry S. Varley Fund for Rural Life at the Community Foundation of Lethbridge and Southwestern Alberta to develop "recreational and programming opportunities at the region's 33 member libraries." They purchased "giant checkers, parachutes, juggling scarves, mini golf and other physical literacy games." The grant also helped the library hire a part-time staff member who could go around the region and help librarians learn how to offer active play programs with the new collections. Unlike in the city of Lethbridge, where the objects could be checked out directly by patrons, in Chinook Arch the "patrons" are the member libraries, who borrow the supplies to offer programs and special events at and around their libraries.

The initiative has been hugely successful, so much so that in November 2018, Lisa and her team won Alberta's ChooseWell Healthy Community Award, which is equivalent to winning an award from a state parks and recreation association in the states. The press release announcing the award states,

> What do a library system and a fitness resource centre have in common? The answer that may spring to mind is "nothing," but the successful partnership between Chinook Arch and Lethbridge College Be Fit for Life (BFFL) proves otherwise. These two organizations share a passion for bringing active living opportunities to as many people as possible. . . . "As community hubs for activity and information, libraries strive to serve their communities to the best of their ability," says Lisa Weekes, Manager of Partnerships and Community Development for Chinook Arch. "It is through unique collaborations that libraries are able to offer a wider variety of programming than they could on their own. The power of partnerships never fails to amaze me. Together we were able to offer what neither organization could on its own."

Lessons Learned

- Weave whatever objects you circulate into your programs; don't just develop a collection of objects and leave it at that. Whether it's a sous vide or a kayak, find ways to integrate your collection into public programs.
- Partnerships, partnerships, partnerships: they make or break a successful initiative. You may find that partners literally have stuff lying around and are waiting for someone like you to knock on their door. I've heard that story over and over again. Get out there, and get the word out that you're interested in doing this work.

Checking Out Health at the Academic Library

Academic libraries also increasingly check out healthy living objects. Merrimack College's McQuade Library, in Massachusetts, started "a holistic mindfulness initiative" that included, among other things, purchasing four exercise bicycles "for students to take an active and mindful break from their studies" and assembling kits that students could check out for physically active pursuits like yoga and gardening (Eberle 2018). Similarly, the medical library at East Tennessee State University (2018) embraced this trend by purchasing twenty yoga mats and four bicycles that could be checked out from the library. In addition, "the library basement includes a room with several spin bikes and hand weights for in-library use." The library's website states, "These items are

Banner for the Active Terp Brain Breaks collection at the University of Maryland libraries.

provided as part of the library's commitment to supporting our students, faculty, and staff as whole people" (East Tennessee State University 2018).

In Virginia, Roanoke College developed a bike library where, as of 2016, there had been 275 check-outs per bike per year between 2010 and 2016. According to the librarians, the bikes are constantly in use during periods of good weather (Vilelle 2017). Academic libraries also check out bicycles at the

University of Georgia; East Tennessee State University; Keene State College, in New Hampshire; and McMaster University, in Hamilton, Ontario; among other locations (Lenstra 2018a) In addition, at Meredith College (Allen 2017) in Raleigh, North Carolina, and at the University of Maryland, libraries check out a variety of sports and fitness equipment for students to use (Maryland Today Staff 2018). Discussing law libraries, Aiken, Cadmus, and Shapiro (2012) write that "it is also not unusual at the law libraries at Yale or Cornell to find non-traditional items available for check out. Patrons can borrow, for example, bicycles, soccer balls, soccer goals," suggesting these types of collections are becoming increasingly common in law libraries.

Exercises

1. How could you integrate healthy living into your library's spaces and collections?
2. Are there other initiatives in your community that you could work with to develop these collections and spaces (e.g., bike-shares, seed libraries, tool libraries, etc.)? What are they?

13

Take Your
Programs Outside

When I first started researching this topic, a refrain I heard again and again was "I'd *love* to do this at my library, but we just don't have the space for it." Well, I'm here to tell you that you can solve this problem by taking your programs outside! Don't have space for tai chi? Do tai chi on the library lawn or at a nearby park. Want to get kids moving and reading? Do a StoryWalk®. Looking to educate your community on food systems and get some free produce for your cooking classes? Start a garden, either on your library's greenspace or at a nearby open lot.

In addition to solving space issues, doing outdoor programming has the benefit of extending access to nature and greenspaces, which medical researchers have identified as crucial to our health. The growth of movements like ParkRX, Walk with a Doc, nature therapy, and the National Recreation and Park Association's Health and Wellness initiative all testify to the fact that one of the best things we can do for our health is spend time outside. Time outside is even better spent if we're being active, and the best is when we're growing some fresh food together with our friends at the library garden.

Librarians have done their part to unlock the health benefits of spending time outside by organizing programs like StoryWalk® for children and families, poetry walks for adults, walking book clubs, community bike rides, hikes, snowshoe adventures, hands-on gardening, and just taking kids, families, and adults of all ages on trips to farms, orchards, lakes, and local, state, and national parks. We've also started circulating hiking backpacks and other equipment, like fishing gear, kayaks, snowshoes, birding kits, and more. Get inspired to go outside by one of the national leaders of this trend, the San Francisco Public Library, which now makes "experiences in nature" **one of the three pillars of its summer programming,** alongside "reading enjoyment" and "STEM learning." Learn more at https://sfpl.org/?pg=2001098901. Once you start programming outside, you won't want to come back inside.

Catch up to San Francisco by starting small with a StoryWalk®. According to my research, the most common way librarians take their programs outside is through StoryWalk® programs, followed closely by hands-on gardening and outdoor movement programs. In fact, of the 1,157 public libraries that filled out my Let's Move in Libraries survey, 303 said they had done outdoor Story-Walk® programs, 246 said they had done outdoor gardening programs, and 90 said they had done both (Lenstra 2019e). In addition, 281 stated they had offered outdoor walking, hiking, bicycling, and/or running programs. In this chapter, we'll take a look at these programs and provide the information you need to take *your* programs outside.

StoryWalk®: The Perfect Way to Get Families and All Ages Outside

Hundreds of librarians have embraced the StoryWalk® movement, which has spread throughout the United States and beyond. The Vermont public library where it originated reports that a StoryWalk® has been installed in all fifty states and twelve countries.

What is a StoryWalk® and why does it carry a registered trademark? The StoryWalk® concept was created in 2007 by Anne Ferguson of Montpelier, Vermont, with the help of Rachel Senechal of the Kellogg-Hubbard Library and the Vermont Bicycle & Pedestrian Coalition. Basically, Anne Ferguson focused a huge amount of her time working out the legal issues associated with taking apart books so that you can display their pages along walking trails. She registered the idea with a trademark so that StoryWalks are only used for "educational, noncommercial projects consistent with the StoryWalk® Project mission to promote literacy" (Ferguson 2017). Think of it as a creative commons license in which only noncommercial uses are authorized. All you have to do is credit Anne Ferguson for coming up with the idea, and you're good to go! Learn more at the project's website: https://www.kellogghubbard.org/storywalk.

The original impetus of the first StoryWalk® was to increase healthy living among Americans. Anne Ferguson writes: "I was working as a chronic disease prevention specialist at the time and knew that I wanted to create something different, fun, and interesting. I had tried some different approaches involving children but found that the parents stood around chatting while the children were physically active. I knew I wanted to create something where the parents had to be as active as the children. Active parents have active children and physical activity is a key component to chronic disease prevention" (Ferguson 2019). This idea inspired Ferguson to create the StoryWalk® concept, which gets whole families up and moving and reading together.

This program model has evolved over the years. Initially conceived of as a temporary installation, with the different pages of the story laminated and posted like political yard signs, some libraries now have permanent, weather-proof StoryWalk® installations that can be opened, to rotate the stories on a regular basis. Others post pages in storefront windows to create walking routes through business districts.

In Burke County, North Carolina, the library set up a temporary StoryWalk® along a greenway, which was so successful that in 2018 the library installed a permanent StoryWalk® installation at the same location. Library director Jim Wilson said the StoryWalk® represents "a unique and wonderful opportunity for local families to not only read and discover the wonderful stories found in books, but also walk a quarter mile on our beautiful greenway" (Gercken 2018).

Further evidence of how embedded the StoryWalk® concept has become in the public library profession is the fact that at least two vendors now specialize in selling these permanent StoryWalk® installations to librarians, and at least one library in New York has hired a StoryWalk® project manager to organize these programs on an ongoing basis (Lenstra and Carlos 2019).

In addition, although a StoryWalk® typically consists of a deconstructed children's book posted in a park, some libraries have partnered with downtown businesses to create storefront StoryWalks. In Lewes, Delaware, and Boone, North Carolina, downtown businesses agree to post different pages of a StoryWalk® in their store windows. In Boston, a branch of the public library system created a StoryWalk® spread throughout the Latin Quarter of the city to celebrate Latinx heritage month (see Lenstra and Carlos 2019).

A common partner in developing StoryWalk® programming is parks and recreation departments. The assistant director of the Norwalk Public Library, in Ohio, called partnering with her parks and recreation department on StoryWalk® programming a "win-win" (Ashby 2018). This short video from the Stillwater Public Library in Oklahoma explains what this program entails and how to get started building one in a park: https://www.youtube.com/watch?v=Lrucs7NE9C8.

Over the past three years, I have been systematically collecting online resources on healthy living programs in libraries. I've collected ninety-four articles on walking programs and, of those, forty-five (48 percent) focused on StoryWalk® programs, suggesting this type of program is the most (or among the most) common type of walking program that public libraries are developing (Lenstra and Carlos 2019).

Spontaneously, librarians across the country have realized that scouts make the perfect partners for these endeavors! In order to achieve the highest rank possible, both Boy Scouts and Girl Scouts have to undertake large, service-oriented projects. In Illinois, Bethany Pohlman decided to work for the Girl Scout's top honor, the Gold Award, by teaming up with the Jacksonville Public Library and the YMCA to install a StoryWalk® along a one-mile walking trail on the YMCA grounds. She said,

> As a child I spent many years going to babysitting, play group, swimming
> lessons, working out and practicing cross country on the running trail and
> I loved going to the library and reading the books. . . . When I was looking
> for a project I talked to my mom, who works at the library and she had just
> read about this StoryWalk®. I thought what a great way to combine the love
> of reading with the outdoors. (Lenstra 2019d)

This story has played out over and over again all across the country. You can
find very similar stories of public libraries teaming up with scouts to build permanent StoryWalks in New York, Washington, New Hampshire, Connecticut,
Indiana, Tennessee, Massachusetts, Michigan, Florida, and Wisconsin (see
Lenstra 2019d).

How can you bring this partnership to your library? The first step is to get
the idea into the heads of local Scouts. Try to meet with local Scout leaders to
share the idea with them, and also use some of the articles in this blog to illustrate that Scouts are already doing this work successfully across the country.
Second, see this project as a partnership, not as a service project. To do this
work successfully, you'll have to coordinate with the site where the StoryWalk®
will be based, ensuring that they approve of the placement of all the signs.
You'll also want to work closely with your partners to ensure the design will
work for your library. Most permanent StoryWalk® change titles every month,
or even every other week. Make sure you're prepared to keep the stories fresh
so that the project is sustained after the initial investment of time and resources
by the Scout. Finally, start building up a collection of StoryWalk® titles you
can use in your display. Some good places to look for inspiration include (1)
The official StoryWalk® website and (2) "Reader's Advisory: StoryWalk Titles!"
written by the Central Minnesota Libraries Exchange: https://cmle.org/2017
/03/28/readers-advisory-storywalk-titles.

An alternative model would be to purchase StoryWalk® titles from vendors
such as Curiosity City or Barking Dog Exhibits. Or, if you're really creative,
you could even use your makerspace to make your StoryWalk®. In Maryland,
the Laurel branch of the Prince George's County Library adapted this model
by adding making activities to it. Young patrons used TinkerCad and a Mak-
erbot 3-D printer to create their own tactile StoryWalk® (Scott-Martin 2018).
In other words, rather than walking along a StoryWalk® created for them,
here youth made their own StoryWalk®. Similarly, at the Albert Wisner Public
Library, in Warwick, New York, the library decided to feature artwork made
by local seventh-graders in its StoryWalk® installation as opposed to the traditional use of a published book (Warwick Valley Central School District 2018).

Finally, as we've said time and time again in this book, why should kids have
all the fun? Some libraries have developed poetry walks, which are designed
for older readers and for adults. Poetry walks have been developed through

collaborations between public libraries and state and national parks in New England and in Washington state. One Massachusetts library teamed up with an adult education project to feature the voices of adult literacy learners in a downtown poetry walk. The Greenfield Public Library in Massachusetts posted poems created by adults enrolled in a local HiSET (High School Equivalency Test), in downtown business windows. Francesca Passiglia, assistant head of borrower services at the library, said she is excited about this partnership. "We'd love to keep doing it every year with the Literacy Project," Passiglia said. "We're always trying to make these types of community connections" (Fritz 2019). The library sponsors a poetry walk during the Greenfield Winter Carnival, as well. "We took it slow this first time around," she said. "There was no pressure on anyone. We just wanted students to enjoy themselves. It's so moving to see them put so much into writing or choosing poems" (Fritz 2019).

Similarly, the North Olympic Library System in Washington partnered with the nearby Olympic National Park for a variety of programs, including a poetry walk mounted on local trails, with the poems changing every spring, as well as poetry hikes, storytimes in the park, and an Explore Olympic backpack that includes a free entrance pass.

As the above examples suggest, the programming possibilities within the concept of the StoryWalk® are seemingly endless. The model of the StoryWalk® is, in essence, the idea that stories are not only experiences in books and in stillness but can be experienced in motion, combined with movement. This is indeed the idea of libraries for the whole person: mind, body, and nature. What could be better?

Hands-On Gardening

The second most common form of outdoor, healthy living programming is gardening. There are lots of ways that gardening and librarianship intersect, as a recently published book on this topic illustrates (Banks and Mediavilla 2019), but here we are primarily concerned with *immersive, hands-on gardening*, in which adults and youth, to the best of their abilities and with adaptive modifications as needed, get moving, get weeding, and get their hands dirty, all while growing healthy, nutritious food that can be used in everything from healthy dishes served up in the library café to cooking classes to food bank donations, or just taken home and gobbled up!

In spring 2006 in Goldsboro, North Carolina, then children's librarian Shorlette Ammons approached her director with the idea of creating a community garden on the greenspace owned by the library. The director admitted she had misgivings and asked, "What does that have to do with the library?" (Lenstra 2019e). But Ammons persisted and eventually convinced her boss the garden was a good idea. She documented every success along the way, and in summer

2008 the library received a $3,000 grant from the American Library Association to expand the garden for summer reading programming.

Over the years the library has struggled with vandalism and with maintaining momentum, including one summer in which someone knocked over all the sunflowers. But the community rallied behind the library, and thirteen years later the "library garden plows ahead" (Moore 2018) as a local reporter puts it. Every summer, children tend the garden, pulling weeds, planting seeds, and gaining an understanding of the food chain. The library also invites guests to talk about things like worms and beekeeping. The special programs change every year, but one consistent element has been the bumper crop harvest. Most of the produce grown goes to the children who participate, and anything that's leftover is put out in front of the circulation desk for anyone to take.

After starting the garden, Shorlette decided to take her passion for food justice to the national level. She now works as the community food systems outreach coordinator for the North Carolina State Extension. There, she focuses on the engagement of "southern women of color" in food systems (Herring 2013).

Hands-on gardening programs at libraries don't just develop overnight. Pace yourself and start out with some more informational gardening programs so that you build your partnership network, and "grow" from there. Invite a local Master Gardener to come lead a class. If you don't know how to find a Master Gardener, reach out to your local Extension agent (see the previous chapter): The Master Gardener program is an initiative of the USDA's Cooperative Extension System. Some libraries have gone further. In Akron, Ohio, the library partnered with Let's Grow Akron and the Ohio State University Extension to offer a "Community Garden Leadership Training" course at the library, which focused on preparing community members to develop and sustain more community gardens (Chatfield 2018). A similar program was offered at the High Point Public Library, in North Carolina, in February 2019.

The partnerships you build through these indoor gardening programs can develop into full-fledged outdoor library gardens. That is what happened at Dunn Public Library, in Harnett County, North Carolina. There, community partnerships led to a small demonstration garden that was built in cooperation with the local Extension Service and Master Gardeners. They are growing tomatoes, eggplant, cucumbers, green beans, and squash, and trying to use the theme of "Southern Staples" to involve kids in the gardening as much as possible.

Hands-on gardening is a wonderful multipurpose program. In addition to improving health, gardening can also be used to educate on the environment, STEM topics, and more. According to the University of Colorado, gardening has lifelong benefits, such as developing positive social and emotional skills among children, promoting healthy eating and nutrition, increasing science achievement and improving attitudes toward learning about science, and increasing design skills and environmental stewardship awareness. And gardening can be especially impactful among special populations for which it can have great therapeutic value (University of Colorado 2011).

Gardening is also a wonderful intergenerational activity that can be used to build bridges among people of many different backgrounds. Culinary heritage can also anchor the garden. Invite some of your community elders to share their experiences gardening and cooking as part of the program. As part of research she conducted in the doctoral program at the School of Information Sciences at the University of North Carolina–Chapel Hill, Mary Wilkins Jordan (now executive director at Central Minnesota Libraries Exchange) researched the spread of community gardening within American public libraries (Jordan 2013). She found that libraries start gardens for different reasons, some having to do with food insecurity, but others having to do with extending access to, and engagement in, nature, as well as promoting ecological awareness and knowledge of scientific processes in the environment and in food systems.

Other library garden programs seek to combine gardening with the library café. A public library in Alabama collaborated with the local school district to develop a program that trained cognitively impaired adolescents and adults to prepare and serve food in the library café. The produce for the café was grown in the library garden (Nicholson 2017). There is really no wrong way to garden at your library.

Hiking, Biking, Running, Walking, and More

In addition to StoryWalk® and immersive gardening programs, the third way libraries get our bodies engaged in healthy outdoor activities is through hiking, biking, running, and walking programs. In truth, this list could be expanded to include snowshoeing and other forms of ambulation, such as using wheelchairs. The basic idea here is to focus on how you can get people moving outside and engaged in nature and neighborhoods.

Get Walking and Hiking, with the Help of Your Local Library

Many state and national parks, as well as local arboretums, now provide libraries with park passes and backpacks that can be checked out to encourage healthy active outdoor activities. Some states, such as Missouri, also provide libraries with other equipment, such as fishing gear, that they circulate to encourage active lifestyles among their patrons. A growing number of libraries use this equipment for programming, such as the Henrico County Library, in Virginia, which uses the nature backpacks provided to it for birding and other

During Summer Reading at the High Point Public Library in North Carolina, every Thursday features the Children's Garden Club, which utilizes this Teaching Garden, located behind the public library.

outdoor activities. Learn more at http://letsmovelibraries.org/get-outside-via -non-traditional-library-collections.

Other libraries weave together technology and walking. In North Carolina, the Farmville Public Library partnered with Dr. Mary Grace Flaherty, from the University of North Carolina at Chapel Hill, for a Get Walking at Your Library program. This program involved circulating pedometers from the library and having participants fill out a health assessment tool when they returned the devices. This collaboration inspired the librarian to take a more active role in promoting walking. After the collaboration ended, the librarian partnered with the local parks and recreation department to develop a Farmville Moves program, in which participants train together to complete their first 5K race together. The library provides health and exercise books as well as health and wellness professionals, who give short talks about staying healthy and exercising safely (Flaherty and Miller 2016).

Libraries also develop recurring walking programs. Two examples illustrate the types of large-scale efforts you could work toward in your region. Public libraries in Fife, Scotland, developed the Walk ON program in the mid-2010s. From 2017 to 2018, 113 walks with 1187 participants took place across the 34 public libraries in this library system located north of Edinburgh, and 25 library staff have been trained as health walk leaders, with some also receiving additional training as dementia-friendly walk leaders. The library also offers Buggy Walks for individuals with strollers. According to organizers, "walks progress at the pace of the least able walker and since some group members use mobility aids, it's important each walking route is planned to make sure they are accessible." The Walk ON program explicitly focuses on increasing walkable neighborhoods. One librarian stated, "We've aimed to change attitudes towards walking by showing the variety of easily accessible walk routes in our communities," and the program "encourage[s] regular walking and reduced car use" (Stewart 2019).

A similar initiative emerged in the Pittsburgh, Pennsylvania, area in 2008. There, the Allegheny County Library Association helped their forty-six member libraries offer Wise Walk programs. According to the Carnegie Library of Pittsburgh, a Wise Walk is a librarian-led one- to two-mile walk around the neighborhood, geared toward those aged fifty and older. While comprehensive statistics are not available, one participating library reports that over the years, registration has varied from ten to thirty in this ten-week program offered twice a year, in the spring and fall.

Other librarians develop walking programs by themselves, without a larger structure like the Walk ON or Wise Walk program model to follow. In Arkansas, staff from the Dee Brown Public Library decided to lead walking programs in an adjacent park. One librarian said, "Walkers often tell me [the librarian] they didn't know it [the park] was here until they joined our walking group" (see the story "A Shared Journey to Better Health at the Dee Brown Library" in chapter 5). In Maitland, Florida, librarians developed several measured trails that originated from the library, for a weekly Maitland Walks club.

Sometimes these programs have ancillary purposes beyond walking. One great idea is to organize a program around trash pickup. In Massachusetts, the Oak Bluffs Public Library organized a Community Walk and Clean-Up day in which members of the community picked up trash as they walked around the neighborhood around the library. Librarian Carolina Cooney said she intends to make this a monthly program. Still, others combine bookmobile services with walking.

You can also do these programs wherever your bookmobile stops. In Lethbridge, Alberta, the bookmobile is the starting point for a walking club where patrons can borrow walking poles from the library if they need them. The library in Helena, Montana, hosts a monthly walking group when the book-mobile visits a rural park.

Why do librarians develop these programs? One answer to this question comes from Eureka, Illinois, where library director Ann Reeves said that she developed the Roaming Readers Walking Club, which meets weekly at the library for a thirty-minute walk, because "in a larger community, there might be better options (for a public fitness program) . . . but we don't have a community center. We are the community center. If we can provide these services, it helps us and it helps the town" (Swiech 2015). This quote illustrates the idea discussed in the introduction, namely that Americans increasingly expect public libraries to fill in gaps in social services, providing things that otherwise would be inaccessible in local communities.

These programs typically depend upon community partnerships. In Eureka, Illinois, the library teamed up with the local school to use their track. Other common partners include walking and running groups, health professionals, and urban planners. In Ohio, the Worch Memorial Library partnered with a local Volkssport Association chapter for a walking event. In Sacramento, California, librarians partnered with Downtown Grid Sacramento; the library distributed walking maps of downtown and the library's book club created a guided tour of downtown to visit those places. Partnerships can also include national organizations. Librarians in Denver, Colorado and Paris, Texas, have teamed up with the national nonprofit Walk with a Doc to offer programs in which patrons walk with doctors and other medical professionals. Find out if this program is available in your area—and if not, think about starting one—at https://walkwithadoc.org.

These partnerships are not restricted to urban areas. In the rural, primarily indigenous community of Utqiagvik in far northern Alaska, public librarians partner with a variety of entities to offer "summer lagoon walks" every year. Youth participants go walking with local experts, who educate them about the ecology, culture, and environment of the community as they walk together. In the small town of Woodstock, New Brunswick, librarians partner with a local running club, and the club hosts their monthly meetings at the library. The library provides the running club with space and access to running books and periodicals, and the running group encourages patrons of the library to join them on their fun runs, which start and end at the library. According to the librarian, "No one gets left behind, and all ages and genders turn out, from parents with their kiddos in strollers to some slow-moving elderly walkers that come 15 minutes early to get a head-start" (Carson 2016).

Finally, the library in the small town of Irvine, Kentucky, partners with its local hospital and health department for a variety of walking programs. One of these is a walking club that meets Tuesday evenings for a thirty-minute walk in downtown Irvine. Devices are available to record resting and active heart rates before and after the walk. Given that the library serves a rural area, the library also encourages bookmobile patrons who cannot make it to the library to use a pedometer or step-counting app to track steps. The library also works with partners to turn Irvine into a Kentucky Trail Town by working to increase trails and greenways throughout the county.

Want to start a walking club? I recommend the free online resource released in summer 2019 by the National Institutes of Health on how to start these clubs. Although not written explicitly for libraries, the lessons it contains are broadly applicable: https://go4life.nia.nih.gov/walking-clubs.

Get Running with Your Local Librarian

Why stop at walking? Many libraries now also offer running programs. At Rye Public Library, in New Hampshire, the library director organized a reading and running program in which members discussed sections of Chris McDougall's Born to Run before heading out on a group run together (Richmond 2012). The librarian received inquiries about the idea from other libraries in the region, and the model has since spread to other places in the nation.

The other main way that libraries get people running is by offering Couch-to-5K programs, which at least a few dozen libraries across the United States have done over the last decade. In some places, this program has been so successful that it has become a recurring program offered every year in early summer. This is the case at the Stickney-Forest View Public Library District, in Illinois. What is great about this program is that it can also double as a staff wellness initiative. Libraries that offer this program report that staff enjoys the opportunity to try out running (or maintain running as a healthy habit) while bringing their community members along for the activity.

Let's see how it works at a library in Massachusetts. This story comes from the first time the library offered this program in 2018. (Staff found it was so successful that they did it again in 2019, and plan to keep doing it!) The Shrewsbury Couch-to-5K Runners Group and Workshop was organized by Shrewsbury Public Library. The program started because reference librarian Caitlin McKeon Staples was interested in getting into running, and she thought, Why do it alone? I can do this as a library program.

Staples and staff reached out to a local running store (Marathon Sports). The store was thrilled to work with the library on this free program and donated their staff time, gift certificates, and more. To make the program as unintimidating as possible to those new to running, Staples identified a casual 5K that only cost five dollars to enter, and her Friends of the Library paid registration fees for participants. The program was open to thirty participants. To incentivize participation, the library created a punch card with a message: "Come to at least two-thirds of the runs and you enter a raffle for prizes paid for by the Friends of the Library."

With the running store, the library organized three group runs a week, with different library staff joining the groups on different days. The running store and library provided waivers of liability that all participants signed. In the end, eight individuals completed the entire program during 2018, and in 2019 the program expanded, with over a dozen doing the whole program.

Staples was "very happy with that number since the program was such a huge commitment. The best thing (apart from now being able to run, myself) was seeing the accomplishment of participants in the group. Everyone was so happy. It was one of the most positive programs I have been involved in" (Lenstra 2018g).

One thing Staples learned was that prizes don't really matter; she said, "Most of the participants didn't care one way or the other if they got a prize. The real prize for them was succeeding in the program." So in the second year, they got rid of that part of the program, which simplified the offering immensely. Furthermore, in addition to a new, successful program, the Shrewsbury Public Library now has new community partners it can turn to for this or other health programs in the future.

Running and Reading with the Rye Public Library

Andy Richmond, Director, Rye Public Library

In 2012 we developed Running and Reading, a six-week program reading and discussing Chris McDougall's 2009 book *Born to Run*. In that pilot program, six group members met to discuss the best-selling book in sections, took group training runs after each session, and participated in a 5K road race as our finale.

During that summer's Olympic Games in London I learned about the inclusion of fine arts in competition alongside athletics in the original Olympiads. Understanding this precedent helped push me over the edge to try out an earlier idea I'd had. The Greeks recognized that mind and body were of equal importance for overall fitness and health. They included their finest poets and painters in competition alongside pentathletes. Even in modern Olympic competitions between 1912 and 1952, medals were awarded for sport-themed painting, sculpture, literature, architecture, and music. With Running and Reading, I planned to incorporate a physical activity with a book discussion—using the book as motivation and inspiration to read and run.

Working backward from a popular local 5K race in early October, I developed a six-week, six-session book discussion and running program. Having already read *Born to Run*, I knew the book had plenty of discussion appeal and would be a great vehicle around which to develop an activity-based reading group. Using our legal database, I put together a release form and

running and reading

Tuesdays at 6:00 –7:00 pm from Tuesday, July 23rd through Tuesday, August 13 here at R.P.L.!

Want to tune up your running or get ready for a road race, and read a fascinating running book with new friends?

Join us for this four-week program at Rye Public Library! This session we'll read and discuss *Running To The Edge* by Matthew Futterman.   Already signed up for Saunders 10K on August 15th? Join us to run some lighter mileage in style! This program is for those who are running regularly already, but are looking for a good book and a fun training opportunity. We will have expert guests to help along the way.

Come dressed to run!

Books will be provided. Liability waiver required. Sign up at circulation desk

Rye Public Library Running and Reading Group flyer. Reprinted with permission from Andrew Richmond.

opened the group to any readers and runners who were already doing some mileage (I consciously did not intend a complete training program for non-runners in this first go-round). I also had to break the book into six sections, developing questions relative to each.

I piped the program through our social media channels, created a web presence, and started to see sign-ups. Ultimately, six regular members took the bait and set out on our adventure. We shared a lot through the sessions between running, reading, sampling shoes and foods, and ultimately racing on a seaside five-kilometer course.

There was a sense of fun and adventure inherent in the group. I think we all knew we were part of something unique. One young man who joined us commented that he had never finished a run *at the library* before(!) (or been as captivated by any book in recent years). Our inaugural group enjoyed a bonding growth experience along with a great book. Members either joined both the discussion and the run or only a part of the meeting, as their schedules allowed. We developed a wiki to allow for remote contributions, to accommodate multiple schedules. Inspired by *Born to Run* during the course of the program, we all (independently, and unplanned) took a barefoot run, together tried the storied chia seed, and all found inspiration for our exercise. One member ran a marathon during the six weeks of the program, while others nervously prepared for their first race. We had fun, learned, and enjoyed our journey through *Born to Run* and the buildup to our 5K challenge.

In the years following that pilot program, Rye Public Library (RPL) has built on the model and repeated the running theme with other books, as well as trying a different pairing of activity and literature.

Since using the remarkably popular *Born to Run* as a ringer title for our first session, we have explored other fine options in running literature as inspiration. A brand-new book for spring 2012—*Run the World*, by Becky Wade—was our vehicle for that year's session. Similarly, the book was sectioned into discussion segments, and questions were developed to consider each stave. In this instance, I was able to contact Becky and arrange a Skype session as our final meeting! The interaction with the author truly made that session memorably fulfilling.

Over an ensuing winter period, I followed another avenue of personal interest to create a program called Vertical Volumes. This was a "climbing and reading" session discussing the book *Touching the Void*, by Joe Simpson, and visiting local rock-climbing gyms to learn and practice climbing techniques as we read and considered a gripping mountain adventure.

Back on the roads and trails, Naomi Benaron's book *Running the Rift* served as inspiration for another Running and Reading session. The African setting and narrative surrounding the Rwandan conflicts served as intense content for discussion. I still hope to visit Rwanda in the future for cultural and running and cycling adventures.

As a continuing theme, each Running and Reading session culminated in a specific local race available to any interested participants. The wiki communication format gave way to a weekly newsletter that kept participants up to date with the next reading sections, and shared cultural or informational asides to enhance that week's reading.

Our latest Running and Reading session will involve *Running to the Edge*, by Matthew Futterman, and will lead up to a renowned and venerable local 10K. In fact, I hope to entice the race promoter (also a local mystery author) to take part.

I have enjoyed excellent feedback and outcome-reporting on the Running and Reading programs. While the mission of cultivating both mind and body is not expressly stated in our library's vision, I believe offering this unique opportunity more fully meets our community service responsibilities. The success of our active reading group concept (along with the support of my trustees) has allowed me to actuate a personal philosophy of attending to both physical and cerebral needs while enhancing RPL's library service to the community in a truly holistic sense.

Supporting Outdoor Recreation during the Winter

A big concern I hear from librarians is that outdoor programs are fine when the weather is nice, but what about when the weather makes outdoor activities more daunting? As winter arrives in the Northern Hemisphere, days get shorter and colder. It can be a struggle to get outside and stay active. Libraries throughout North America find ways to help people stay active during the winter! In Maine, the Blue Hill Public Library held an event called How to Enjoy Winter. This event featured opportunities for folks to get out and be active. Among the several local organizations that gave short presentations about their resources and how folks can get active and involved in them, were Blue Hill Heritage Trust, Great Pond Mountain Trust, Maine Coast Heritage Trust, Downeast Audubon, Blue Hill Peninsula Nordic Ski Club, and Blue Hill Skating Club. They covered activities like walking, hiking, skiing, skating, snowshoeing, bird-watching, snowmobiling, and sledding (Blue Hill Public Library 2018).

Elsewhere, more and more libraries have started checking out snowshoes at the library. Thanks to a partnership with the Vermont Health Department, you can now check out snowshoes in forty-six public libraries there. Libraries in Spokane, Washington, as well as Dodge Center, Minnesota, also recently developed new snowshoe collections. These collections are also becoming widely available in parts of Canada.

Libraries also continue to host fun outdoor events during the winter months. In Woodstock, New Brunswick, the L. P. Fisher Public Library holds its annual Reindeer Run program in December, and has been known to make the front page of the local paper. In High Point, North Carolina, the library cosponsors the Jingle Jog 5K. And in Tennessee, the Friends of the Fairview Public Library host the annual Fernvale Freeze event on New Year's Day, in which brave participants take a plunge into an icy pool.

Even though it's cold out, libraries are still putting up outdoor StoryWalks in local parks to encourage reading and being active in nature during the winter. Some of these libraries are Westmont Public Library (Illinois), Jasper Public

Library (Indiana), Lewes Public Library (Delaware), and Carter County Public Library (Tennessee), where the local paper reported that a StoryWalk® had a "successful debut despite snow" (Thompson 2018). So don't let the weather get you down!

Creating Accessible Communities

Finally, library programs can focus on increasing active transportation through public programs. In the public-health literature on walkable communities, public libraries are framed as destinations that should be accessible by walking. In spring 2018 the U.S. Centers for Disease Control and Prevention (CDC) unveiled the "Connecting Routes + Destinations" campaign to increase physical activity. The campaign focuses on making it easier for people to walk, bike, and use a wheelchair throughout their communities. Public libraries—alongside schools, worksites, homes, grocery stores, and parks—are framed as key destinations to which walkable routes should be made. The message could not be clearer: policy makers want us to think about how we can make our libraries accessible for walkers, bikers, wheelchair users, and others. We can rise to this challenge by offering public programs that focus on increasing walking, bicycling, and engaging in other forms of nonmotorized transportation around our libraries.

Here are some program ideas you can emulate to answer this call to action. In April 2018, the St. Louis County Library, in Missouri, offered Walkability of Your Neighborhood programs. These programs were offered in partnership with two nonprofit organizations, the St. Louis County Older Resident Programs (CORP) and OASIS. The program was offered at three different branches and consisted of a one-mile guided walk with a representative from CORP. During the walk, the sidewalks and surrounding areas were assessed for pedestrian safety. Patrons filled out their walkability assessment forms, which were provided by CORP. At the end of the walk, everyone met back in the branch to discuss findings and how to improve pedestrian safety around the library.

In Lorain, Ohio, city engineers who were planning a community forum on how to make the city more bike- and pedestrian-friendly naturally turned to the library. A city engineer told a local reporter, "The library was chosen as a meeting location [for local bike/walk plan] because it always has a full bike rack, meaning it already is a destination for people already using Lorain streets to ride bicycles" (Payerchin 2019).

This didn't just happen. Anastasia Diamond-Ortiz, the chief executive officer of the library, has championed the cause of making Lorain a bike-friendly community for years and has ensured her library participates in bike events, initiatives, and dialogues. These efforts culminated in the Go Lorain Bike Share

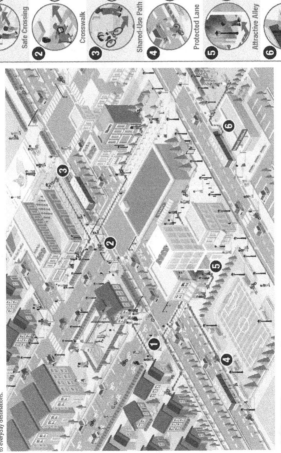

Connecting activity-friendly routes to everyday destinations, including libraries.

Program, the city's first bike-share, based in the public library, in collaboration with Lorain County Public Health, Lorain County Metro Parks and the Lorain County Community Action Agency. At the main branch, you can check out a bike with your library card. You can also check out a helmet and a bike lock.

Other libraries turn their attention to ensuring that people can get to them without having to drive a car. A few years ago, the public library in Palo Alto, California, became the first in the country to launch a Safe Routes to Libraries campaign. You may have heard of Safe Routes to Schools or the Walking School Bus, efforts to ensure that kids can walk to school safely. Well, some enterprising librarians are bringing this to libraries. Check out the map the librarians created, https://www.cityofpaloalto.org/civicax/filebank/documents/61836, and get the inspiration you need to organize safe routes to libraries in *your* community.

Making the map is just the beginning. The next step is to offer programs, led by library staff ideally, where you actually demonstrate the routes by walking or biking them with your community members. Since 2014 Misty Von Behren, deputy director of the Perry Public Library, in Iowa, has led a walking school bus program in her small town (pop. 7,702). On Fridays throughout the year, fifty to seventy elementary school–aged children walk from the town's high school to the elementary school, led by the public librarian and other volunteers that she coordinates. The program has been so successful that in 2017 Von Behren was asked to speak about it at a state conference for librarians, to encourage others to lead similar initiatives. In High Point, North Carolina, the library, in partnership with the local parks and recreation department, received a Community Change grant from the national organization America Walks to create maps of walkable and safe routes throughout the city, to be distributed at the library events and utilized for library programs.

Some librarians also work with partners to increase safe walking routes to their libraries. At least two libraries—one in Galion, Ohio, and another in Seymour, Indiana—participate in the national Walk [Your City] campaign. In these communities, librarians and others installed signs throughout town indicating how long it takes to walk to the library from different points. In Arkansas, the Springdale Library participated in the town's Safe Streets planning commission, with the commission's pilot project focused on linking "Springdale's revitalizing downtown area with the hospital and public library," such that one could walk or bike easily among these destinations. In San Antonio, Texas, the public library developed two walking paths on its land. Librarians said, "Library patrons visiting these libraries often express their appreciation of offering healthy exercise on the library grounds" (quoted in Lenstra and Carlos 2019, 9). A recent renovation of the public library in Wilmette, Illinois, included the installation of ADA-accessible walking pathways around the library.

You can also organize these programs around bicycling. In Brooklyn, San Jose, Washington, DC, Tucson, Arlington, and elsewhere, librarians offer annual events in which community members are invited to join library staff on a bike tour of a select number of branches throughout the cities. These events vividly show that you don't need a car to get to your library.

Exercises

1. Are there any greenspaces or parks near or around your library? What are some ways that you could utilize these spaces for outdoor programming? What partnerships would you need to make these outdoor programs successful?
2. Are there any community garden initiatives in your area? How could your library join or partner with these initiatives to increase access to gardening?
3. How accessible is your library for individuals who do not drive themselves there?
4. Are there things and programs you could do to increase accessibility of your library for bikers, walkers, wheelchair users, and others? Describe them.

14

Putting the Pieces Together into a Programming Plan

In the last five chapters, we've gone over five ways to add healthy living into your library's programming mix: (1) add it to existing programs, (2) embrace the power of play for all ages, (3) offer immersive cooking and fitness classes, (4) develop health-supporting collections and spaces, and (5) take your programs outside.

Using these five pieces, there are many ways librarians and their partners can support healthy eating and active living. What new, creative program will you develop in your community? Share back, and let's keep this conversation going!

To help you get started, let's return to the exercise with which we began part III:

1. Reflect on your library's mission, vision, and current assets.
   Now identify and write out **three potential programs** that you might wish to provide to support healthy living in the community you serve.
2. Reflect on the constellation of individuals and institutions in your community.
   Now identify and write out **three potential partners** that you might wish to work with to bring these programs to fruition.

Table 14.1 serves as an example, based on real-world programs I've seen in my work on this topic.

You don't have to fill in every box of this table. But do use this exercise to brainstorm for some ideas of where you want to prioritize. You could start with a partner or you could start with a particular program or you could just start with a general *type* of program you want to try out. There are benefits to all

TABLE 14.1   Play your healthy living programs

Program Type	Program Name	Program Partner
Add it to existing programs	Summer Reading Kickoff Party at the Park	Parks & Recreation Department
Embrace the power of play	Library Olympics	Campus Wellness
Immersive cooking/fitness	Namaste & Nosh	State library, Charlie Cart Project, local chefs, Extension agents
Collections and spaces	Read & Ride Bicycles	K–12 school athletics department/school district foundation
Take it outside	Library garden	Extension/gardening club

these approaches, and there really is no wrong way to do this. Having at least a general idea of what you want to do enables you to have constructive dialogue with your library team and with your partners about the particular directions in which you want to go, leaving space for creativity and innovation. On the other hand, if you're concerned about things getting too unwieldy, or if you're working on a tight timetable, having a tightly focused program plan can help.

If you want to keep things focused on literature, you may want to stay within the "Add it to existing programs" quadrant, maybe by adding some healthy eating or active living to your book clubs, or maybe you could think about going outside with a StoryWalk®. If you're comfortable branching out, think of the other sections. There is more than one way to promote healthy living at the library. Not everybody has to offer yoga classes. Move your way. Choose your plate. As I said at the beginning, this book is about finding *your way* to promote healthy living at *your* library. Nobody can do it but you!

15

Healthy Living across the Seasons: Ideas for Year-Round Healthy Living

I want to end part III with a season-by-season guide that can help you think of year-round healthy programming at your library.

Winter

- New Year, new you—Supporting healthy resolutions at the library
- Staying active outside—Snowshoeing, and more
- Break out of cabin fever with a family dance party—Noon Year's Eve, and more
- Hot dishes for cool nights—Salsa making at the library

Spring

- Getting your garden ready
- Intro to seed sharing
- Bike maintenance 101 (with a bike tour of your library branches)
- Spring break fun!

Summer

- Summer meals and more at the library
- Check out nature with a park pass and a birding backpack (and accompanying programs)
- Introduction to farmers markets (how they work and how to make the most of them)
- Cool dishes for hot nights—Intro to smoothies, juicing, and blenders

Fall

- Safe routes to schools (and libraries)—Take the lead in promoting active transportation
- StoryWalk® in the park
- Putting your garden to bed for the season
- Cooking with the three sisters (corn, beans, and squash)

Part IV

Sustaining Healthy Living at the Library

16

Assessing and Communicating the Impacts You've Made

We all know that healthy living is a lifelong pursuit, and since libraries are all about lifelong learning, supporting healthy living in libraries is a perfect fit. In parts I through III, we've discussed how to start and offer healthy living programs, and now we'll shift to sustaining this programming area, making it an integral aspect of your library's identity.

We'll start by going over how to assess programs to make sure you're achieving your (and your partners') goals, and how to course-correct as necessary, before we end with administrative topics like planning, funding, and formalizing the partnerships that undergird all truly successful healthy living at the library programs.

The four interlocking facets of program assessment are:

1. Needs assessment: What does our community need?
2. Patron satisfaction: What should we do better?
3. Outputs: How much did we do?
4. Outcomes: What good did we do?

Finding out community needs for healthy living programming should not be something librarians have to do on their own. Let's pick the brains of the experts in our local health departments, hospitals, park and recreation departments, and campus wellness and athletics departments, rather than reinvent the wheel. We're going to focus on the last three dimensions of program assessment in this chapter. I'm advocating for folding "needs assessment" into partnership planning (see part II).

Nonetheless, before we get into this topic, let's take a look, for example, at how the Nashville Public Library, in Tennessee, has made assessment part of its healthy living programming.

Program Assessment at the Nashville Public Library

Since 2015 the Nashville Public Library has made healthy living a core part of its programming, offering, according to its 2017–2018 annual report, in one year 1,952 healthy living programs to more than 25,000 Nashvillians. Programs included "nutrition seminars . . . casual cooking clubs . . . and weekly yoga classes" (Nashville Public Library Foundation 2018, 29). The goal of Be Well at NPL is to provide "free wellness programming at library branch locations, and connect you to trusted health resources found online, in our stacks, and in the community" (Nashville Public Library 2019). The reason for these programs is that Nashville is ranked forty-fifth in community fitness among the fifty largest U.S. metro areas, and Tennessee ranks forty-fifth overall among all states (Roth 2018).

While the library was developing Be Well at NPL, it hired Elizabeth Roth, a public health professional. Part of Roth's job involved creating assessment tools. She developed (and tested) surveys, logic models, and more. Some of the tools she and the library created are shown below. Use these to inspire your own efforts.

As part of the early development of Be Well at NPL, Elizabeth and the NPL staff needed to figure out what people wanted. As such, they developed a tool that was both used in oral interviews and printed for patrons to fill out and return to library staff. You could use this as a model for your own needs assessment. It doesn't have to be overly complicated but could help you test the waters before you invest time, energy, and money into something new. The library found people wanted to try a variety of things, so the library developed the partnerships needed to bring bike rodeos, yoga classes, community gardens, seed exchanges, health fairs, and more to the library. They even installed a small climbing wall, which they called the crawl wall, in the children's area of the downtown library, in order to get kids experimenting with active play in the library. Learn more at https://www.tennessean .com/story/life/shopping/ms-cheap/2015/11/27/renovation-rejuvenates -childrens-library/76302730.

Please **circle** the health programs that you or a family member would like to attend at the library.

Food/Garden	Physical Activity	Emotional Health
• meals on a budget	• yoga	• meditation
• healthy meals for kids	• Zumba	• stress reduction
• composting	• dancing	• healing music
• reading food labels	• kids fitness	• counseling session
• reduce sugar	• walking group	• relaxation crafts
• home gardening	• learn to ride a bike	• support group
• what is organic?	• hula hooping	• energy healing
• vegetarian eating	• martial arts	• singing

When developing assessment tools, it can be helpful to see multiple examples that you can weave together to create something unique for your community. An alternative approach to a community needs assessment for healthy living programming took place in the summer of 2014 in St. Louis, Missouri. There, librarians from the Washington University School of Medicine teamed up with public librarians to survey 517 library patrons around their preferences for healthy living programs. The options they gave people, which they organized into Topics and Demonstrations, are shown below. They are listed in the order of preference given by survey respondents, which means that "exercise" was the most desired topic for programs and "stress relief" was the most desired demonstration. It is no surprise that the three most desired topics are the subject of this book: exercise, nutrition, and food (Adapted from Engeszer et al. 2016).

Topics

1. Exercise
2. Budget-friendly nutrition
3. Food myths and safe dieting

4. Mental health
5. Sexually transmitted diseases
6. Alcohol use and abuse
7. Obesity
8. Sleep issues
9. Health insurance
10. Diabetes

Demonstrations

1. Stress relief
2. Healthy cooking: quick meals
3. Healthy cooking: budget-friendly nutrition
4. Healthy cooking: local foods
5. Tai chi/balance exercises
6. Yoga
7. Cooking for diabetes
8. Low-impact exercise
9. Acupuncture/pain relief
10. Healthy cooking: other foods

Next, returning to Nashville Public Library, to measure the impacts of all of these programs, the library developed a simple, one-page survey, available in both English and Spanish.

Library Branch: _____ Program: _____

Your completion of this survey allows us to keep offering free programs. Thank you!

1. **Is this your first time attending a Be Well at NPL program?**

   Yes   No   Not sure

   BeWell At NPL
   LEARN • GROW • THRIVE

2. **How satisfied were you with this program?**

1	2	3	4	5

3. **I feel more confident about what I just learned today.**

1	2	3	4	5
Strongly Disagree	Disagree	Neutral	Agree	Strongly Agree

4. **I intend to make a health change based on what I learned today.**

1	2	3	4	5
Strongly Disagree	Disagree	Neutral	Agree	Strongly Agree

   If so, what health change? (optional)_____

5. **I intend to return for future health programs at the library.**

1	2	3	4	5
Strongly Disagree	Disagree	Neutral	Agree	Strongly Agree

6. **Which of the reasons below affected your decision to attend this health program: (Check all that apply)**

   ☐ It was free   ☐ The environment was safe
   ☐ The location was convenient   ☐ The staff was welcoming
                    ☐ None of these affected my decision

7. **Do you have a Nashville Public Library Card?**

   Yes   No   I just got one

   NIH ⟩ NLM ⟩ NNLM
   All of Us
   RESEARCH PROGRAM

8. **What is your zip code?** _____

9. **Suggestions for future health programs at the library?**

   the HCA Foundation.
   Serve · Lead · Support

   _____

Assessment surveys used for Be Well at NPL (Nashville Public Library programs), English. Reprinted with permission from Nashville Public Library.

Library Branch: _____   Program: _____

Su respuesta a esta encuesta nos permite ofrecer más clases gratuitas. ¡Gracias!

1. ¿Esta es la primera vez que asiste a un programa de salud en la biblioteca?

Sí	No	No estoy seguro

2. ¿Cuán satisfecho estuvo con el programa hoy?

1	2	3	4	5

3. Me siento más seguro de lo aprendí hoy.

1	2	3	4	5
Totalmente en Desacuerdo	En Desacuerdo	No Opina	De Acuerdo	Totalmente de Acuerdo

4. Tengo la intención de hacer un cambio de salud basado en lo que aprendí hoy.

1	2	3	4	5
Totalmente en Desacuerdo	En Desacuerdo	No Opina	De Acuerdo	Totalmente de Acuerdo

¿Qué cambio? (opcional) _____

5. Tengo la intención de ir a más programas de salud en la biblioteca en el futuro.

1	2	3	4	5
Totalmente en Desacuerdo	En Desacuerdo	No Opina	De Acuerdo	Totalmente de Acuerdo

6. ¿Cuáles cosas afectaron su decisión de asistir a este programa de salud?
(Marqué todas la que apliquen)

☐ Fue gratuito   ☐ Me siento seguro
☐ La ubicación fue conveniente   ☐ La bienvenida de los empleados
              ☐ Nada afectado mi decisión

7. ¿Tiene una tarjeta de la biblioteca pública de Nashville?

Sí	No	Apliqué por una hoy

8. Código postal: _____

9. ¿Qué son sus recomendaciones por otros programas de salud en la biblioteca?
_____

NIH〉NLM〉NNLM
All of **Us**
RESEARCH PROGRAM

the HCA Foundation.
Serve · Lead · Support

Assessment surveys used for Be Well at NPL (Nashville Public Library Programs), Spanish. Reprinted with permission from Nashville Public Library.

With this data, the library found, between 2017 and 2018, that 81 percent of the more than twenty-five thousand program participants indicated they would make a health change based on participating in a program. And 97 percent said that the classes being free, welcoming, and conveniently located affected their decision to attend (Nashville Public Library Foundation 2018, 29). Furthermore, the library also discovered that more than half of participants have attended more than one Be Well at NPL program, 95 percent were satisfied or very satisfied with the program, and 97 percent were likely to return to the library for wellness programs (Roth 2018).

But data is only as good as what you do with it. Finally, the library put the pieces together by developing a logic model. The 2018 Logic Model figure shows the type of benchmarks the library strives to achieve in a given year for its Be Well at NPL programs. Similar logic models have been deployed every year of the initiative, and the library has consistently met or exceeded most of the goals set for itself.

Finally, assessment at Be Well at NPL goes beyond numbers. Stories and photographs are extremely powerful. They convey meaning, creating a common narrative about what the library is doing through its programs. Take a look at some of the images created by Nashville Public Library to showcase

Inputs	Processes	Service Outputs	Goals	Actual	Program Outcomes	Goals	Actual
Qualified staff	Onsite library wellness programs	# of programs at system-wide	1,900		Indicate they are satisfied or very satisfied with the program they attended	90%	
Program incentives	Outreach library wellness programs	• Nutrition	300				
		• Physical Activity	900		Indicate they will return for other Be Well programs	85%	
Programmer fees	Health displays	• Mental Health	250				
		• Tobacco	20		Indicate they have attended more than one Be Well program	55%	
Program supplies	Survey collection	# attendance	22,000				
	Online content contribution	• Nutrition	3,500				
Equipment		• Physical Activity	10,000		Indicate they intend to make a health change based on what they learned today	75%	
Marketing and Communication	Library card sign-ups	• Mental Health	2,500				
		• Tobacco	100		Indicate that Be Well programs are accessible	90%	
Travel and Training		# of programs target	1,100				
		# attendance target	11,000		Be Well homepage survey respondents will indicate that they feel more knowledgeable about their personal health	75%	
Collections Development		# completed satisfaction surveys	400				
		# new partnerships	20		Be Well homepage survey respondents will indicate that they intend to use the library again as a source of health information	85%	
		# titles added to collection BCBST grant funded	50				
		# displays	4		Programmers had their expectations met	75%	
Logic Model 2018	Nashville Public Library BeWell At NPL	# library card sign-ups	50				
		# unique Be Well homepage visitors	2,000				

2018 Logic Model for Be Well at NPL. Reprinted with permission from Nashville Public Library.

their healthy eating and active living programs by searching for the hashtag #BeWellAtNPL on Twitter and Instagram. These images tell you something important about the impacts these programs have, in ways numbers alone cannot. Or consider this story collected by the library, and used in its reports and promotional materials:

> For 89-year-old Dean Stevens, the free yoga class she attends weekly at the library has given her a newfound stability she says her peers are often lacking. "So many of my friends are falling," she explains. "I almost fell in the strawberry patch the other day, but because I have better flexibility and control over my body, I was able to recover. And that's because of yoga."

For the full story and accompanying photos, see https://bettertennessee.com /library-partners-to-provide-community-free-health-activities.

In the course of collecting these data, stories, and photographs, the library also made changes to its offerings. They found that yoga programs were especially popular: at one point you could go to a free yoga class six days of the week at different libraries throughout Nashville, so they adapted the Be Well at NPL logo, replacing a figure of a person running with an image of a person in yoga's lotus pose. Learn more about Be Well at NPL at https://library.nashville .org/event/be-well-npl.

Assessment Tools for Project Outcome(s) and More

Since the pioneering efforts of Nashville Public Library, even more tools have become available to help librarians assess healthy living programs. In April 2019 the Public Library Association released a new tool kit focused on assessing health programs in libraries. Learn more at https://www.projectoutcome .org.

In addition, OCLC/WebJunction, as part of its Health Happens in Libraries initiative, has also developed an easy-to-use assessment tool. Learn more at https://www.webjunction.org/documents/webjunction/community-health -program-worksheet.html.

Of the two, the WebJunction one is simpler, so let's look at that one first. You could use this form for focus groups, for interviews, or even print it on a piece of paper (or put it on your website) to get input from your community.

Health Happens in Libraries Feedback Questionnaire
(via Morris 2016)

1. How did the activities and resources from today's event help you achieve your health and wellness goals?

2. How did you hear about today's event?
3. Why did you choose to attend today's event?
4. Would you recommend this event to a friend, family member, or colleague?
5. What other health-related topics or activities would you like to see the library address in future events or programs?

The other tool that has become increasingly employed to assess healthy living programming is the Public Library Association's Project Outcome health survey. Project Outcome focuses on enabling librarians to better assess the outcomes of programs, and not just how many people came. Hundreds of libraries are now using these free tools for data analysis to evaluate their programs, communicate impacts, and apply for funding.

In a nutshell, with the Project Outcome health survey you can determine if participants' lives are healthier as a result of your library's programs. For instance, if you're doing yoga at your library, you could use the health survey to show that 92 percent feel more confident using yoga to de-stress as a result of your program. This information, of course, helps immeasurably when making the case for continued funding and development of this programming area.

What's especially cool is that now that this resource exists, the library assessment hive mind can really develop. It isn't just a single library assessing their programs in isolation. It's the entire nation (and beyond) showing the collective impact of *all* healthy living programs in libraries.

And there are signs the survey is really filling a need. Just during the first month of its release, forty-five different surveys were created and 211 patron responses were collected for everything from healthy cooking classes to exercise programs to chronic disease management sessions (Plagman 2019).

The health survey has three levels: **immediate** (to distribute right after the program), **follow-up** (for people to fill out a few days or weeks later), and **additional questions** that can be used as you see fit.

Immediate Survey

(*Note that you are welcome to adapt as needed*)

For questions 1–4, options include "Strongly Disagree, Disagree, Neither, Agree, Strongly Agree, and N/A"

1. You feel more knowledgeable about the health topic presented.
2. You feel more confident about taking care of your or your family's health.
3. You intend to apply what you learned to adopt or maintain a healthier lifestyle.
4. You are more aware of health-related resources and services provided by the library.

5. What did you like most about the program?
6. What could the library do to better assist you in learning more about being healthy?

Follow-Up Survey

As a result of participating in the library's health program:

1. I learned new ways to do the following for my or my family's health
   [ ] Talk to a healthcare provider, [ ] Eat better, [ ] Exercise, [ ] Find health information, [ ] Take care of mental well-being, [ ] Other (fill in) _____
2. I'm better able to take care of my or family's health (Yes/No).
3. I changed at least one health-related behavior (Yes/No).
4. I checked out a book, attended another program, or used another library service or resource (Yes/No).
5. What did you like most about this program or service?
6. What could the library do to help you continue to learn more about being healthy?

Additional Questions That Can Be Added

7. I learned about a new online health information resource
8. I now use or plan to use my library as a health information resource
9. When I have a health-related question, I feel confident that staff at my library can show me where to find the answer.

This survey is a free resource. If your library is not yet using Project Outcome, I highly recommend it. There is a bit of a learning curve, especially with the data dashboard, but after you've cleared that hurdle, the potential is incredible!

Regardless of what tool (or tools) you use for program assessment, here are a few general tips:

1. Explain the *why* and *how* before asking patrons to complete a survey.
2. For low literacy patrons . . .
   a. Read survey questions aloud.
   b. Walk through questions one at a time.
   c. Explain the Likert scale before you administer (i.e., from "strongly disagree" to "strongly agree")
3. Keep it anonymous.
   a. Don't add any personal information questions to the survey (name, email, library card number).
   b. Have a volunteer collect the surveys, if possible.

    c. Have an anonymous drop-box for completed surveys.

    d. Use online surveys if the program includes technology (laptops, iPads)

4. Stay on time.

    a. Account for surveying time when planning: make it a part of the program.

    b. Don't keep patrons longer than you've promised.

Let's put the pieces together by seeing how program assessment works in action. In 2013, and with the financial support of the U.S. Institute of Museum and Library Services via the Oklahoma Department of Libraries, the Miami Public Library, in Miami, Oklahoma (pop. 13,570) started a health literacy project. Programs developed included an immersive children's garden, in which youth grew fresh produce and learned how to cook with it; yoga classes; diabetes prevention classes; and more. To assess the programming, the library used Project Outcome. In the 2017–2018 financial year, of the 711 patrons who attended healthy living programs, 694 strongly agreed or agreed that they learned something new by participating, 679 felt confident in using what they learned, 679 said they were likely to apply what they learned, 646 said they were more aware of library services and resources because of the program, and 637 said they were more likely to use other library services and resources because of the program. Based on these evidence-based impacts, the Miami Public Library is now widely seen in the local community as a trusted and vital partner in all efforts focused on improving community health. Learn more at https://www.webjunction.org /events/webjunction/health-literacy-begins-at-your-library.html.

Now, this data was collected *before* Project Outcome released its health survey. With the new health survey, which could be used in conjunction with the "Education/Lifelong Learning" survey from which these responses are based, you can get even finer-grained data on the health outcomes that result from your programs. The key is to make assessment part of your normal programming workflow. This takes time, so don't fret if it isn't completely seamless the first time out. You may need to try out some different things to find a model that will work well for you and your library team.

Exercises

1. When you think of program assessment, what comes to mind? (If you answered, "counting the number of participants," you're not alone!)

2. Could you or members of your library team try out some of the tools mentioned in this chapter at the end of an upcoming program? (The more experience you build up doing assessment, the easier and more routine it will become.) Which tools will you start with, and why?

3. When you and your library team make decisions about future programs and initiatives, what data and other information will you utilize in that decision-making process?

Building and Maintaining the Momentum

Once you start supporting healthy living at your library, you will see ripple effects. Impacts go beyond what happens in the programs itself. In the best cases, libraries become seen for what they are, or could be: Vital community hubs able and ready to step up to support lifelong learning about healthy living through fun, community-building programs. You know you're doing it right when the health department or campus wellness office calls you up to propose a collaborative program.

In this chapter, we'll conclude the book by looking at the big-picture planning needed to achieve this goal. We'll go over how to make healthy living a part of your library's mission and therefore part of your identity. We'll also look at how libraries get to this point through strategic planning, memoranda of understanding, and external funding (i.e. grants).

BikeKDL at the Kent District Library

This story was submitted by Calli Crow, volunteer coordinator at the Kent District Library. Calli is a great example of the new type of library staff being hired to support and sustain healthy living in libraries. We're hiring people with backgrounds in bicycling, parks, nutrition, public health, social work, and more, as part of our commitment to long-term support for healthy living.

Kent District Library is an award-winning system that continually pushes the envelope in the areas of innovation, customer service, and what today's library can offer communities beyond books. Full disclosure: I'm not a librarian, but I am a library geek from way back. With my background in nonprofit and community organizing, I'm so proud to be KDL's volunteer coordinator and bike ninja.

I started at KDL in January 2016, fresh from a year working as a paid employee in bicycle advocacy with Greater Grand Rapids Bicycle Coalition. The timing for me and KDL couldn't have been better, as the KDL Cruisers

Bicycle Check-Out Program was slated to start that very spring. All the pieces just came together. In addition to the development and administrative skills I was hired for, I was able to provide much-needed expertise on bicycle safety for our new bicycle program and plenty of connections to the bicycle community to generate more partnerships for mutual support.

One of my first priorities was to sign KDL up to participate in Grand Rapids Active Commute Week. It's an area-wide event that urges folks to choose alternative transportation options to reduce traffic congestion and increase health and wellness. I dug out my pom-poms and started recruiting my coworkers to be supporters and champions, and what do you know? We won the award for Most Trips Logged for a Large Organization, beating long-time winner Calvin College! And then we did it again, in 2018 and in 2019. KDL's sponsorship of and strong participation in Active Commute Week have helped boost awareness and increase overall community participation. Thanks in large part to the City of Grand Rapids and Mobile GR, 2019 was a record-breaking year for getting people out of their single-occupancy vehicles to Walk, Roll, + Ride instead.

From there we formed BikeKDL, an internal committee with the mission to support bicycle initiates and programs and to serve as a social club for team-building activities like employee group rides to breweries and ice cream shops. One of BikeKDL's first agenda items was to apply for the League of American Bicyclists Bicycle Friendly Business designation for our Service and Meeting Center (KDL headquarters) in Comstock Park. We achieved Bronze status in 2016 and the Silver in 2019 for providing employees and visitors access to free bicycles; close proximity to safe riding on the White Pine Trail State Park; end-of-trip amenities like bike racks, lockers, and showers; KDL's White Pine Trail Public Rest Stop and Fixit Station; and for demonstrating support for bicycle education and advocacy in our community.

The KDL Cruisers program and our leadership's subsequent support of bicycle safety and education have had a decidedly positive impact in our

To sustain this energy, the Kent District Library strategically planned for its new BikeKDL campaign, signaling to itself and to the community that support for bicycling would be a long-term priority of the library. For more photographs from this initiative, visit the book's online supplement at http://letsmovelibraries.org/healthy-living-at-the-library. Reprinted with permission from Calli Crow.

community and have even helped some of our patrons make positive life-style changes. One of my favorite impact stories is about a couple from the Krause Memorial Branch in Rockford, Michigan. They had never ridden the trails before but, inspired by their experience with KDL Cruisers, they decided to purchase their own bicycles and adopt a new healthy hobby.

Bicycles can be great fun for recreation rides and exercise, but let's not forget their role as transportation. One of the biggest barriers to accessing resources in underserved communities is lack of transportation. Bikeable, walkable communities, adequate public transit, and fully funded libraries are the recipe for equitable communities that prioritize access. The library as a trusted institution can lead the way to healthy, equitable communities. It can all start with bicycles!

Strategic Planning for Healthy Living

Some libraries have begun making healthy living part of their strategic plans. Let's take a trip to Niagara Falls, New York, to see what it looks like. The library's 2018–2023 Strategic Plan includes the general **goal** of providing "lifelong learning opportunities for residents of all ages," which includes the more specific **objective** of supporting "learning with information sharing on health, wellness" which in turn includes concrete **actions** the library will take, including "1. Identify 4 topics and ask community experts from local businesses, colleges/universities/high schools to present workshops in this program. (Recruit retired staff who are well-liked, well-known)," and "2. Create an outreach effort/marketing campaign for offerings for the 4 additional health and wellness classes covering topics of nutrition, health, exercise, the arts, etc. for branding purposes that includes social media, press releases, website announcements, and targeted advertising on Facebook" (Niagara Falls Public Library 2018).

The focus on healthy living in the Niagara Falls Public Library strategic plan did not emerge out of thin air. It came from librarians asking their community what they wanted at the library. The strategic plan states:

When asked to comment on which of the items the residents themselves were most interested in, the top 10 answers fell in the following categories:

1. Local History Department
2. Health, Wellness, Yoga, Nutrition programs (Niagara Falls Public Library 2018)

The point here is that if you're *not* asking about healthy living in your community needs assessment, this need may go unrecognized! As we all know, unfortunately, many have antiquated, stereotypical ideas of what libraries provide. We need to get this conversation started by *making sure our community knows we're ready to support healthy living*.

Nearly identical community needs assessments followed by making healthy living a part of library strategic plans played out in La Crosse, Wisconsin; Salt Lake City, Utah; West Point, Iowa; and in Santa Clarita, California (Lenstra 2018f; and see chapter 12).

The strategic planning process of the Salt Lake City Public Library (2018) illustrates how an urban library embraces healthy living. This library has made such a strong embrace of this trend that the cover of its 2018 "Strategic Roadmap" features a photograph of one of their hugely successful Rooftop Yoga at Main Library programs. The plan itself frames "healthy together" as one of eight strategic goals for the library. This goal focuses on "supporting pathways to a healthy community—specifically physical, mental, and emotional health—and facilitating solutions to our city's health concerns: The City Library will embrace its role in fostering health and wellness as a foundation to learning, full participation in society, and quality of life" (Salt Lake City Public Library 2018).

I love this language! Here we see a library embracing its role in fostering health and wellness as a foundation to (1) learning, (2) full participation in society, and (3) quality of life. Without healthy living, nothing else is possible. This is the perfect way to think about healthy living in your strategic plan.

Each of these two plans have lessons that you can use in your library. The Niagara Falls plan does a great job of breaking down broad goals into more specific objectives, and each of these has tangible action plans. The Salt Lake City plan, in contrast, does a great job at articulating why the library is embracing healthy living at the library in the context of the overall mission of the library (learning, civic participation, and quality of life).

Your strategic planning process could also reference the urgency that undergirds these programs. Since 2011 the Oklahoma Department of Libraries has made health literacy a cornerstone of its strategic plan. Its most recent plan (2018–2022) states that the library's health literacy "program represents a partnership between the Oklahoma State Library, library and literacy programs, and their community partners." The **Audiences** section of the plan then states that these programs are targeted at "[A]dults and families at risk due to a lack of understanding and/or information about healthy diets and lifestyle choices. Specifically targeted audiences are adult learners, non-English speakers, and other at-risk populations" (Oklahoma Department of Libraries 2018, 20). The **Processes** used to achieve this goal with these audiences are supporting "libraries and community-based literacy organizations by providing resources, continuing education, and ongoing technical assistance to grantees" (Oklahoma Department of Libraries 2018). Here is a third approach to planning for healthy living programming. In this model, you focus on the audiences to be reached and the processes you will use to reach them. Unsurprisingly, as in the other two plans, the processes center around forming and sustaining community partnerships.

Get Written into Another Organization's Strategic Plan

You know things are really going well if your library is included in the strategic plans of your collaborators. That is what has been happening in mostly rural Jackson County, North Carolina (pop. 40,271). For nearly a decade, the library has been framed as an integral component of the Jackson County Health Department (2019) Strategic Plan: Healthy Carolinians of Jackson County. The health department's plan frames libraries as vital venues for educational programs focused on helping local residents meet physical activity and nutrition recommendations. Being part of this plan has led the public health department (and others) to offer a variety of free programs at the public library, and assistant county librarian Jessica Philyaw now goes to two monthly subcommittee meetings organized by the Department of Public Health: Injury and Substance Abuse Prevention and Healthy Eating and Physical Activity.

Thus far, this partnership has focused on programs for children and teens, but the library hopes to expand it to adults in the future. In any case, by becoming involved in the health department's strategic planning process, the library staff decided to participate in the health department's Get Fit Challenge that takes place every fall. I'm thrilled to report that the library team won in 2013, proving once again that library staff who care about healthy living are library staff who care about healthy living programs.

How Do I Make Healthy Living Part of My Strategic Planning Process?

You've tested the waters, offered a few programs, and formed some relationships. At this point, it is good to take a step back and consider the big picture: What's your vision for how your library will support healthy living in your community? Every community is unique. Every library is unique. So no two libraries will have the same vision. Below are some fill-in-the-blank statements to get you started.

These questions can help you consider what might be new, different, or enhanced as a result of healthy living programs being available at your library. In other words, how might your community *change* as a result of what your library is uniquely able to offer? You don't need to have a specific partner or activity in mind to consider this; the bigger question is simply, What long-term vision does this programming support?

Jot down some high-level vision statements in the items below. While all elements of your vision may not be explicitly addressed in one specific program, these statements may serve as reference points for program priorities or future goals. If you've done some programs already and have collected some data, use that to inform your vision. If not, you may want to fill out this sheet with some of your trusted partners, especially any that may already be experts on your community's health needs.

1. As a result of healthy living programming, library patrons will
2. As a result of healthy living programming, my library will
3. As a result of healthy living programming, our partners will
4. As a result of healthy living programming, I personally will

Thinking about a desired vision often raises more questions than it answers. What additional thoughts, questions, concerns or priorities come to mind as you answer these questions? Identifying these early can help you refine your vision, along with input from others.

Memorandum of Understanding

After strategic planning, the next tool you have in your arsenal is memoranda of understanding. Building long-term partnerships takes time and energy. To really make them work, you'll want to set aside time to plan and evaluate with your partners how things are going. In simple terms, a memorandum of understanding lays out exactly who the partners are, the purpose of the partnership, what is within the scope of the partnership, and who is responsible for what. The memorandum should be signed by someone with authority from the two partnering institutions.

You'll also want to revisit the document with your partners at least annually, to check to see how things have been going and to revise the agreement appropriately. The perfect example of this process appears in the long-term relationship between the Chicago Public Library and the Museum of Science and Industry. They've worked together on summer programming since 1988! The partnership initially focused on getting kids exposed to nature in a project called NatureConnections. It has since expanded and evolved, with the current iteration, as of 2019, called ScienceConnections.

According to the librarians, the memorandum of understanding with the museum is revised annually: "This evaluation and preparation have been an essential part of the process as we continue to refine our programmatic offerings, deepen our mutual understanding of each other's institution, and set overarching goals" (McChesney and Wunar 2017, 28). By writing down with your partner what you *think* the partnership will entail, you will be ready to evaluate what *actually* happened and revise the agreement accordingly.

A memorandum of understanding is not a contract; it is a good-faith agreement entered into by two (or more) different organizations. It sets the stage for the work to follow but doesn't dictate it. It also gets you and your partners strategically planning together, which can pave the way for program expansion. As the Chicago librarians have said, "By nurturing the relationship, a strong collaboration can present new opportunities for both organizations [including] fund-raising implications. In Chicago, we did not base our partnerships on the requirement of new financial resources. . . . However, as we began to see signs of success, each organization shared information about the impact of our partnership with funders. We soon realized that we had mutual funders who were willing to consider not only their support for each institution, but also were interested in expanding their investments to support the work of the partnership. We have broadened our collaboration to now include the development of joint grant proposals that are intended to sustain the work of the partnership for the foreseeable future" (McChesney and Wunar 2017, 30).

What I love about this quote is that it directly addresses a concern I often hear from librarians who tell me they *don't* partner more intensively with other organizations because they fear that if they get too involved with what are all too often unnecessarily seen as competing organizations, the library's slice of the pie will diminish. In fact, in almost all cases, the opposite occurs. The value communities ascribe to libraries only increases the more interconnected we are with everything else going on in our communities. The trick, I think, is communicating that message. And memoranda of understanding can help with that process, as they lay out in black and white what the library brings to the table, showing that the library is a vital contributor to community health goals. Furthermore, by taking a driving seat in drafting these documents, you show your partners that you are administratively savvy—a bonus!

Grants and Other External Funding

To wrap up this book, let's consider how you can sustain and grow your long-range vision through funding. There's no point beating around the bush: innovation takes money. Now is a good time to focus on how to get the assets you need to support healthy living at your library for the long term. While some health literacy programming can be implemented with little or no external funding, your efforts to sustain and expand programming to align with your strategic priorities can benefit from extra funding.

To get started, you will want to brainstorm potential funding sources, such as:

- Hospitals and hospital foundations
- American Red Cross

- Local businesses, including sports retailers and fitness centers or gyms
- Library Friends and foundations
- Local health department
- Local, regional, or state family foundations
- Local USDA-related Extension Service
- Area agencies on aging
- National Network of Libraries of Medicine, which offers funding for projects that improve access to health information, increase engagement with research and data, expand professional knowledge, and support outreach that, in turn, promotes awareness and use of NLM resources in local communities
- State health literacy coalitions and initiatives via the Centers for Disease Control and Prevention: https://www.cdc.gov/healthliteracy/statedata/index.html
- The Library Grants blog for health-related opportunities: http://librarygrants.blogspot.com
- The Foundation Center's Visualizing Funding for Libraries directory: https://libraries.foundationcenter.org
- Your state library and their public library consultant, to see if LSTA funding may be available to support your programming

Make the Case for Money

I think sometimes the process of asking for funding can be mystifying. Really, what this process actually entails is good communication skills, that is, being able to craft a convincing message that adheres to the expectations of the funders, or in other words, knowing how to pitch a message to the desired audience. WebJunction's *Health Happens in Libraries Communications Guide* includes key messages and strategies for library staff to target communications to multiple stakeholders about the important role of libraries in supporting community health. Learn more at https://www.webjunction.org/content/dam/WebJunction/Documents/webJunction/2015-04/communications-guide.pdf.

The best communication plan empowers your partners (and your patrons and your supporters) to communicate on your behalf. We can see this in action in the small town of Bucyrus, Ohio (pop. 12,362), where since 2010, children's librarian Barbara Scott and community partners have gotten young children and their caregivers moving and grooving at the library.

The project started in 2010 through a partnership with the Ohio Department of Health. The program started as "Tots, Tales, and Tunes" and focused on increasing physical and musical literacy through dancing and singing. In 2013 the library turned to the United Way of Crawford County to sustain the program after the initial infusion of cash from the health department ended.

Since then, every year the United Way has provided the library with the funds it needs to offer the program, including supplies and other materials. And every year the program has grown more popular. It wouldn't be a big exaggeration to say that nearly every four-year-old in the town has participated! Thanks to the United Way, the library most recently purchased a set of stability ball drums, for some cardio drumming at the library.

The United Way has also made their support of this program a key aspect of its operations, including it on their fund drives, with their website asking, "What matters more? A $5 cup of coffee? Or 4 children attend music class in Crawford County" (Lenstra, Scherrer, and Scott, 2018).

Final Considerations for Fund-Raising

Some key considerations to keep in mind when asking or applying for funding include:

1. What are the stated **impacts** that local foundations or funding bodies are **seeking?**
2. What **case** can you make to **demonstrate** why your library is the perfect partner for **their** efforts?

Before you reach out or start writing, you should have the answers to these questions clear in your head. Now is not the time to succumb to that old bugaboo, impostor syndrome. You may not think you have a lot to offer, but you do! You represent one of the most beloved, trusted institutions on the planet. Now is the time to leverage that reputation to make the case that the library can (and in many cases already does) positively impact community health. If you've already offered some programs and have collected some assessment data, make sure to include that! Also include stories and photographs. Use whatever you have available to make your case.

Your messaging with current or potential funders should reference the value of partnering with the public library and the leveraged impact of cross-sector collaborations. This last point is especially relevant when communicating with health funders—make the connection that health, particularly preventive and public health, happens *everywhere* in communities, including in libraries (see chapter 1). Likewise, if the funder is interested in addressing the health outcomes of a particular demographic, consider the community members most in need of accessible, culturally relevant health programs. Do members of this community already frequent the library? Make sure to mention that. In every case, illustrate how the library is a strong, trusted, and uniquely impactful place to provide these programs.

Exercises

1. What long-term community partnerships could you develop to build and maintain the momentum begun through specific healthy living programs?
2. How could you make healthy living a part of your library's strategic plan?
3. What could you do to ensure that your community needs assessment includes needs related to healthy living? (If you're not making health a part of this conversation, this need may go unrecognized!)

Appendix A

Waiver of Liability

The following two general examples of a waiver of liability form capture the essence of the type of form you may wish to have patrons sign before engaging in healthy eating and active living (HEAL) programs at your library. A few important points: You want your form to explicitly state the *activity* in which patrons will be engaging as well as the *venue*. And it is important to state that although waivers do offer a layer of protection, they are *not* totally infallible. As discussed in chapter 8, some risk is inevitable; in fact, some risk is **always** inevitable. The safest thing we could do would be to never open the doors of our libraries.

The first example is what I call a complete form, one that exhaustively waives all liabilities (even those far beyond the pale of reality, such as death).

The second example is what I call a streamlined form, which I have seen some libraries use when the perceived risks are minimal.

Versions of both forms are and have been used by actual libraries for years! Use these as starting points to structure conversations in your library team, and for more examples visit http://letsmovelibraries.org/resources.

WAIVER AND RELEASE—You acknowledge that your attendance or use of [ACTIVITY] programs offered by [NAME OF LIBRARY AND PARTNERS] of the [NAME OF CITY/COUNTY/UNIVERSITY/SCHOOL], including without limitation to your participation in any programs or activities, and your use of the [NAME OF LIBRARY'S] equipment and facilities could cause injury to you. In consideration of your participation in the programs, you hereby assume all risks of injury that may result from or arise out of your attendance at or use of the library or its equipment, activities, or facilities, and you agree, on behalf of yourself and your heirs, executors, administrators, and assigns, to fully and forever release and discharge [NAME OF LIBRARY AND PARTNERS] and both entities' affiliates and their respective officers, directors, employees, agents, successors and assigns, and each of them (collectively the "Releasees") from any and all claims, damages, rights of action, or causes of action, present or future, known or unknown, anticipated or unanticipated, resulting from or arising out of your attendance at or use of the library or its equipment, activities, or facilities, including without limitation to any claims, damages, demands, rights of action, or causes of action resulting from or arising out of the negligence of the Releasees. Further, you hereby agree to waive any and all such claims, damages, demands, rights of action, or causes of action. Further, you hereby agree to release and discharge the Releasees from any and all liability for any loss or theft of, or damage to, personal property. You acknowledge that you have carefully read this waiver and release and fully understand that it is a waiver and release of liability.

You understand and are aware that [ACTIVITY], including the use of [COOKING OR EXERCISE] equipment, is a potentially hazardous activity. You also understand that [COOKING OR EXERCISE] activities involve the risk of injury and even death and that you are voluntarily participating in these activities and using equipment and machinery with knowledge of the dangers involved. You hereby agree to expressly assume and accept any and all risks of injury or death.

It is recommended that you consult your physician before enrolling in this or any [COOKING OR EXERCISE] program.

NAME:
SIGNATURE:
DATE:

Streamlined Form

I am fully aware that participation in [NAME OF LIBRARY] programs is voluntary, and I assume the risks associated with the [COOKING OR EXERCISE ACTIVITY] in which I am participating. I further certify that I have no medical, physical conditions, or allergies that would restrict my participation in this [COOKING OR EXERCISE ACTIVITY].

I hereby agree to release and hold harmless [NAME OF LIBRARY, LOCATION OF LIBRARY], its officers, employees, volunteers, partners, committees, and boards, from and against any and all liability, loss, damages, claims, or actions (including costs and attorneys' fees) for bodily injury and/or property damage from acts occurring due to "negligence" or "fault" of the library or its staff, to the extent permissible by law.

DATE:

Printed Name	Signature

Appendix B

Memorandum of Understanding

This agreement outlines a partnership between [LIBRARY] and [PARTNER] to [BRIEF SUMMARY OF FOCUS OF PARTNERSHIP, WITH ACTIVITIES UNDERTAKEN].

Program Purpose [NAME OF LIBRARY]
[Summarize purpose of program from library POV]

Program Purpose [NAME OF PARTNER]
[Summarize purpose of program from partner POV]

Locations and Logistics
[NAME OF LIBRARY] will: [LIST]
[NAME OF PARTNER] will: [LIST]

Media and Community Relations
[NAME OF LIBRARY] will: [LIST]
[NAME OF PARTNER] will: [LIST]

[NAME OF LIBRARY]:
SIGNATURE OF AUTHORIZED AGENT:
DATE:

[NAME OF PARTNER]:
SIGNATURE OF AUTHORIZED AGENT:
DATE:

References

Aiken, Julian, Femi Cadmus, and Fred Shapiro. 2012. "Not Your Parents' Law Library: A Tale of Two Academic Law Libraries." *Green Bag* 16 (1): 13–22.

Akron-Summit County Public Library. 2019. "Mind, Body & Sole: A Universe of Stories!" Accessed July 9, 2019. https://akronlibrary.org/images/Events/MBS/2019_Mind _Body_and_Sole_Flyer.pdf.

Albright, Meagan, Kevin Delecki, and Sarah Hinkle. 2009. "The Evolution of Early Literacy." *Children & Libraries* 7 (1): 13.

Aldrich, Rebekkah Smith. 2018. *Sustainable Thinking: Ensuring Your Library's Future in an Uncertain World*. Chicago: ALA Editions.

Allen, Melyssa. 2017. "Library Resources for De-Stressing During Finals." Meredith College, April 25, 2017. Accessed December 23, 2019. https://www.meredith.edu/news /library-resources-for-de-stressing-during-finals.

American Library Association. 2017. "National Impact of Library Public Programs Assessment Proposal." Institute of Museum and Library Services, January 13, 2017. Accessed December 23, 2019. https://www.imls.gov/sites/default/files/grants/lg-96-17-0048-17 /proposals/lg-96-17-0048-17-full-proposal-documents.pdf.

American Library Association. 2018. "From Awareness to Funding: Voter Perceptions and Support of Public Libraries in 2018." OCLC, March 2018. Accessed December 23, 2019. https://www.oclc.org/research/awareness-to-funding-2018.html.

American Public Health Association. 2019. "Most-Read Public Health News Stories of the Year, 2018." *Nation's Health*. Accessed December 23, 2019. http://thenationshealth .aphapublications.org/content/most-read-public-health-news-stories-year-2018.

Arlington Public Library. 2012. "Bikes, Buildings and Broccoli: Integrating Arlington County's Smart Growth and Fresh AIRE Principles into Who We Are and All We Do." Urban Libraries Council. Accessed December 24, 2019. https://www.urbanlibraries .org/innovations/bikes-buildings-and-broccoli-integrating-arlington-countys-smart -growth-and-fresh-aire-principles-into-who-we-are-and-all-we-do.

Ashby, Cary. 2018. "New StoryWalk 'Win-Win Situation' for City, Library, Families." *Norwalk Reflector*, Updated May 6, 2018. Accessed December 23, 2019. http://www .norwalkreflector.com/Local/2018/05/06/New-StoryWalk-win-win-situation-for-city -library-families.

Banks, Carrie Scott, and Cindy Mediavilla. 2019. *Libraries and Gardens: Growing Together*. Chicago: ALA Editions.

Bass Library (@Bass Library). 2018. "RECHARGE Tonight with a Free ZUMBA Class at Yale Library!" Twitter, December 10, 2018. Accessed December 23, 2019. https://twitter.com/BassLibrary/status/1072231286390120448.

Beckman, Sarah. 2018. "Clive Library Debuts New Veggie Exchange." We Are Iowa, July 18, 2018. Accessed December 23, 2019. https://www.weareiowa.com/news/local-news/clive-library-debuts-new-veggie-exchange.

Bei Yi, Seow. 2018. "Community Facilities under One Roof at New Bedok Lifestyle Hub." *The Straits Times*, February 4, 2018. Accessed December 24, 2019. https://www.straitstimes.com/singapore/community-facilities-under-one-roof-at-new-bedok-lifestyle-hub.

Bellingham Public Library. 2017. "SkillShare." Accessed July 9, 2019. https://www.bellinghampubliclibrary.org/skillshare.

Binghamton.com. 2018. "Your Home Public Library Promotes Health Initiative." December 4, 2018. Accessed December 23, 2019. https://www.binghamtonhomepage.com/news/local-news/your-home-public-library-promotes-health-initiative.

Birmingham Public Library. 2019. "Bend & Stretch." Accessed December 24, 2019. http://www.bplonline.org/calendar/?trumbaEmbed=view%3Devent%26eventid%3D131503533.

Blue Hill Public Library. 2018. "'How to Enjoy Winter' at Blue Hill Library." *Bangor Daily News*, December 12, 2018. Accessed December 23, 2019. https://bangordailynews.com/bdn-maine/event/2018/12/12/how-to-enjoy-winter-at-blue-hill-library.

Bonala, Joy. 2019. "Lowcountry's largest YMCA opening Saturday in Cane Bay." The Gazette (Summerville, South Carolina), April 22, 2019. Accessed December 24, 2019. https://www.ourgazette.com/news/lowcountry-s-largest-ymca-opening-saturday-in-cane-bay/article_90e4c466-64ec-11e9-b8e3-ef0f5f7b3d82.html.

Brantley, Ashley. 2017. "Library Partners with Community Organizations to Provide Free Health and Wellness Activities." Better Tennessee, April 21, 2017. Accessed December 23, 2019. https://bettertennessee.com/library-partners-to-provide-community-free-health-activities.

Brantley, Terra. 2018. "Healthy Haley Elementary Is Positively Fort Wayne." WANE.com, October 23, 2018. Accessed December 23, 2019. https://www.wane.com/news/positively-fort-wayne/healthy-haley-elementary-is-positively-fort-wayne/1475417858.

Braveman, Paula, Elaine Arkin, Tracy Orleans, Dwayne Proctor, and Alonzo Plough. 2017. *What Is Health Equity? And What Difference Does a Definition Make?* Princeton, NJ: Robert Wood Johnson Foundation. Accessed December 23, 2019. https://www.rwjf.org/en/library/research/2017/05/what-is-health-equity-.html.

Broward County Library. 2018. "BCLFit Wellness Centers." Urban Libraries Council. Accessed December 24, 2019. https://www.urbanlibraries.org/innovations/bclfit-wellness-centers.

Burlingame Public Library. 2018. "Get Jazzed about Healthy Living: Open House Extravaganza." Burlingame Public Library. Accessed July 9, 2019. https://burlingame.libcal.com/event/4336368.

Carlson, Scott. 2009. "Is It a Library? A Student Center? The Athenaeum Opens at Goucher College." *Chronicle of Higher Education*, September 14, 2009. Accessed December 23, 2019. https://www.chronicle.com/article/Is-It-a-Library-A-Student/48360.

Carson, Jenn. 2016. "Library Walking and Running Clubs." *Programming Librarian* (blog), June 3, 2016. Accessed December 23, 2019. http://www.programminglibrarian.org/blog/library-walking-and-running-clubs.

Celano, Donna C., Jillian J. Knapczyk, and Susan B. Neuman. 2018. "Public Libraries Harness the Power of Play." *YC Young Children* 73 (3): 68–74.

ChangeLab Solutions. "Healthy Neighborhoods: Shared Use." 2019. Accessed July 9, 2019. https://www.changelabsolutions.org/healthy-neighborhoods/shared-use.

Chatfield, Jim. 2018. "Plant Lovers' Almanac: Winter Workshops to Motivate the Restless Gardener." *Akron Beacon Journal*, January 11, 2018. Accessed December 23, 2019. https://www.ohio.com/akron/lifestyle/plant-lovers-almanac-winter-workshops-to-motivate-the-restless-gardener.

Christensen, Tom. 2016. "Turning Enthusiasm into Exercise with Adaptive Zumba." San Diego County News Center. Accessed July 9, 2019. https://www.countynewscenter.com/turning-enthusiasm-exercise-adaptive-zumba.

City of London (Ontario). 2018. "Grand Opening Celebration of Bostwick Community Centre, YMCA and Library." City of London Newsroom. Accessed December 24, 2019. http://www.london.ca/newsroom/Pages/Bostwick-Community-Centre,-YMCA-and--Library-Grand-Opening.aspx.

Crandon Public Library. 2015. "Iron Chef—Healthy Fruits & Vegetables Edition." Health Happens in Libraries. Accessed July 9, 2019. https://www.webjunction.org/content/dam/WebJunction/Documents/webJunction/2015-09/healthy-foods-competition-heats-up-at-crandon.pdf.

CSLP Child and Community Well Being Committee, and Heather West. 2019. "Libraries and Summer Food." Collaborative Summer Library Program, April 2019. Accessed December 23, 2019. https://www.cslpreads.org/libraries-and-summer-food/.

Cunningham, Courtney M. 2012. "The Athenaeum: A Modern Model for Academic Library Design." Master's Final Project, University of North Carolina at Chapel Hill, April 2012. Accessed December 23, 2019. https://cdr.lib.unc.edu/record/uuid:a6af61da-a840-428c-a8bd-2d9c1cd6aacd.

Daily, Laura. 2018. "Kayaks, Ukuleles, Neckties: The Weird and Useful Things You Can Check Out from Local Libraries." *Washington Post*, October 30, 2018. Accessed December 23, 2019. https://www.washingtonpost.com/lifestyle/home/kayaks-ukuleles-neckties-the-weird-and-useful-things-you-can-check-out-from-local-libraries/2018/10/29/82731d80-d7a5-11e8-a10f-b51546b10756_story.html.

Darville, Sarah. 2018. "'Everything Is Different Now': Stoneman Douglas Librarian Reflects One Month after Shooting." Chalkbeat, March 19, 2018. https://www.chalkbeat.org/posts/us/2018/03/19/everything-is-different-now-stoneman-douglas-librarian-reflects-one-month-after-shooting.

Davies, David W. 1974. *Public Libraries as Culture and Social Centers: The Origin of the Concept*. Metuchen, NJ: Scarecrow Press.

Day, Cassandra. 2018. "Inventive Book Talks at Middletown's Russell Library Lead Readers to Walks Downtown and More." *Middletown Press*, August 20, 2018. Accessed December 23, 2019. https://www.middletownpress.com/middletown/article/Inventive-book-talks-at-Middletown-s-Russell-13169719.php.

DeClercq, Caitlin P., and Galen Cranz. 2014. "Moving beyond Seating-Centered Learning Environments: Opportunities and Challenges Identified in a POE of a Campus Library." *Journal of Academic Librarianship* 40 (6): 574–84.

Delaney, Robin. 2019. "Geri-Fit Begins at West Point Library." *Daily Democrat (Ford Madison, Iowa)*, January 14, 2019. Accessed December 24, 2019. http://www.mississippi valleypublishing.com/daily_democrat/geri-fit-begins-at-wp-library/article _34d68986-184b-11e9-ab66-e3d7d2347241.html.

Derenthal, Samantha. 2018. "Ballyfermot Library. Unique Dance Programme." Echo, November 22, 2018. Accessed December 23, 2019. http://www.echo.ie/show/article /ballyfermot-library-unique-dance-programme.

Deschenes, Jordan. 2018. "Taunton Middle School Library Adds Stationary Bikes for Energetic Readers." *Taunton Daily Gazette*, January 10, 2018. Accessed December 23, 2019. http://www.tauntongazette.com/news/20180110/taunton-middle-school-library-adds -stationary-bikes-for-energetic-readers.

Dewe, Michael. 2016. *Planning Public Library Buildings: Concepts and Issues for the Librarian*. London: Routledge.

Droege, Thomas A. 1995. "Congregations as Communities of Health and Healing." *Interpretation* 49 (2): 117–29.

Duckworth, Angela. 2018. *Grit: The Power of Passion and Perseverance*. New York: Scribner.

East Tennessee State University. 2018. "Bike Share and Yoga Mats Available at the Medical Library." Accessed December 23, 2019. https://www.etsu.edu/news/medical_library /bikesandyoga18.aspx.

Eberle, Michelle. 2018. "Bringing Mindfulness to the Academic Library." *Community Engagement* (blog), Massachusetts Library System, July 23, 2018. Accessed December 23, 2019. https://www.masslibsystem.org/blog/2018/07/23/bringing-mindfulness-to-the -academic-library.

Eberle, Michelle. 2018. "Medway Public Library's Summer Lunch Program." *Community Engagement* (blog), Massachusetts Library System, May 14, 2018. Accessed December 28, 2019. https://www.masslibsystem.org/blog/2018/05/14/medway-public-librarys -summer-lunch-program/.

Engeszer, Robert J., William Olmstadt, Jan Daley, Monique Norfolk, Kara Krekeler, Monica Rogers, Graham Colditz, et al. 2016. "Evolution of an Academic–Public Library Partnership." *Journal of the Medical Library Association: JMLA* 104 (1): 62–66.

Ewan, Lara. 2018. "A Movable Feast: Libraries Use Mobile Kitchens to Teach Food Literacy." *American Libraries*, September 4, 2018. Accessed December 23, 2019. https:// americanlibrariesmagazine.org/2018/09/04/movable-feast-library-mobile-kitchens.

Fargo Public Library. 2016. "Flashback Fitness at the Dr. James Carlson Library." Facebook. Accessed July 9, 2019. https://www.facebook.com/events/1724566314482878.

Ferguson, Anne. 2017. "The StoryWalk® Project: Frequently Asked Questions—March, 2017 Update." Accessed July 9, 2019. https://docs.wixstatic.com/ugd/0f622b_c05909 b9e8a548f3ba89b7f261f57b21.pdf.

Ferraro, Julie A. 2018. "Decades of Square Dancing Continues at Cove Library." *Cove Herald*, March 2, 2018. Accessed December 23, 2019. http://kdhnews.com/copperas_cove _herald/community/decades-of-square-dancing-continues-at-cove-library/article _24f4edea-1d93-11e8-a8f0-8389290d9d06.html.

Finney, Mike. 2019. "Hot Fun in the Summertime: Dover Parks & Rec Set for Busy Season." *Delaware State News*, May 28, 2019. Accessed December 23, 2019. https://delawarestatenews.net/news/hot-fun-in-the-summertime-dover-parks-rec-set-for-busy-season.

Flaherty, Mary Grace. 2018. *Promoting Individual and Community Health at the Library*. Chicago: ALA Editions.

Flaherty, Mary Grace, and David Miller. 2016. "Rural Public Libraries as Community Change Agents: Opportunities for Health Promotion." *Journal of Education for Library and Information Science* 57 (2): 143–50.

Fletcher, Mary C. 2019. *The Creative Edge: Inspiring Art Explorations in Libraries and Beyond*. Santa Barbara, CA: ABC-CLIO.

Flowers, Sarah. 2017. *Crash Course in Young Adult Services*. Santa Barbara, CA: Libraries Unlimited.

Free Library of Philadelphia. 2017. "Culinary Literacy: A Toolkit for Public Libraries." Accessed July 9, 2019. https://libwww.freelibrary.org/assets/pdf/programs/culinary/free-library-culinary-literacy-toolkit.pdf.

Fresno County Public Library. 2011. "Fit for Life at the Library." Urban Libraries Council: Wellness, Safety and Sustainability Innovations. Accessed July 9, 2019. https://www.urbanlibraries.org/innovations/fit-for-life-at-the-library.

Fritz, Anita. 2019. "Literacy Project Students Write, Choose Poems for Food Poetry Walk." *Greenfield Recorder*, June 13, 2019. Accessed December 23, 2019. https://www.recorder.com/Food-poetry-downtown-26192347.

Gail Borden Public Library. 2017. "LitClub: The Walking Book Club." LitLovers. Accessed July 9, 2019. http://www.litlovers.com/featured-clubs/walking.

Galston, Colbe, Barb White, and Kari May. 2014. "Engaged, Embedded, and Enriched Creative Community Connections." Colorado State Library In-Session Webinar Series. Accessed July 9, 2019. https://cslinsession.cvlsites.org/past/engaged-embedded-and-enriched-creative-community-connections.

Gercken, Tammie. 2018. "Story-Walk to Add Educational Element to Burke Greenway." *News Herald*, June 27, 2018. Accessed December 23, 2019. https://www.morganton.com/news/local/story-walk-to-add-educational-element-to-burke-greenway/article_0c64e170-7a33-11e8-ac27-1f0dfad6f804.html.

Gercken, Tammie. 2019. "Libraries Provide Wide Range of Activities for Adults." *News Herald*, April 25, 2019. Accessed December 23, 2019. https://www.morganton.com/news/libraries-provide-wide-range-of-activities-for-adults/article_bdc7bb66-678d-11e9-b8bf-4b2463345774.html.

Getaneh, Mary. 2018. "Construction on Track for Sprawling New YMCA in Calgary's Deep Southeast." *The Star* (Calgary), September 14, 2018. Accessed December 23, 2019. https://www.thestar.com/calgary/2018/09/14/construction-on-track-for-sprawling-new-ymca-in-calgarys-deep-southeast.html.

Glum, Julia. 2019. "200 Random Things Libraries Will Let You Check Out for Free: From Instant Pots to Skulls." *Money*, May 16, 2019. Accessed December 23, 2019. http://money.com/money/5644765/library-of-things-check-out-free.

Goulding, Anne. 2009. "Engaging with Community Engagement: Public Libraries and Citizen Involvement." *New Library World* 110 (1–2): 37–51.

Grabarek, Kristin, and Mary R. Lanni. 2019. *Early Learning through Play: Library Programming for Diverse Communities*. Santa Barbara, CA: ABC-CLIO.

Haggard, Nancy, and Danielle Henson. 2011. "Reaching Forward: Walking Book Club." Accessed July 9, 2019. https://www.slideshare.net/gailborden/reaching-forward-walking -book-club.

Halpern, Sue. 2019. "In Praise of Public Libraries." *New York Review of Books*, April 18, 2019. Accessed December 23, 2019. https://www.nybooks.com/articles/2019/04/18/in -praise-of-public-libraries.

Hampton Public Library. 2015. "Community Members Move and Groove at Hampton Public Library." Health Happens in Libraries. Accessed July 9, 2019. https://www .webjunction.org/content/dam/WebJunction/Documents/webJunction/2015-09 /community-members-move-and-groove-at-hampton-public-library.pdf.

Herring, Steve. 2013. "Former Librarian Works to Advance National Conversation about Women and Ag." *Goldsboro News-Argus*, October 7, 2013. Accessed December 23, 2019. https://web.archive.org/web/20140226223638/https:/www.newsargus.com/news /archives/2013/10/07/former_librarian_works_to_advance_national_conversation _about_women_and_ag.

Hill, Ashley. 2016. "Bike & Read." DonorsChoose.org. October 28, 2016. Accessed December 23, 2019. https://www.donorschoose.org/project/bike-read/2302036.

Hill, James. 2017. "Book-a-Bike: Increasing Access to Physical Activity with a Library Card." In *Audio Recorders to Zucchini Seeds: Building a Library of Things*, edited by Mark Robison and Lindley Shedd, 43–51. Santa Barbara, CA: Libraries Unlimited.

Hinchliffe, Lisa Janicke, and Melissa Autumn Wong. 2010. "From Services-Centered to Student-Centered: A 'Wellness Wheel' Approach to Developing the Library as an Integrative Learning Commons." *College & Undergraduate Libraries* 17 (2–3): 213–24. https:// doi.org/10.1080/10691316.2010.490772.

Hincks, Kelly. 2018. "Code to Move: Mixing Coding with Brain Breaks." Knowledge Quest. October 10, 2018. Accessed December 24, 2019. https://knowledgequest.aasl.org/code -to-move-mixing-coding-with-brain-breaks/.

Holmes, Paula. 2016. *Curiosity Creates: Innovative Library Programming for Children*. Chicago: The Association for Library Service to Children. Accessed December 23, 2019. http://www.ala.org/alsc/sites/ala.org.alsc/files/content/awardsgrants/minigrants /ALSC_Curiosity_Creates_Best_Practices_Final.pdf.

Horrigan, John B. 2015. "Libraries at the Crossroads." Pew Research Center. September 15, 2018. Accessed December 24, 2019. https://www.pewresearch.org/internet/2015/09 /15/libraries-at-the-crossroads/.

Houston Public Library. 2014. "Healthy L.I.F.E." Urban Libraries Council. Accessed December 24, 2019. https://www.urbanlibraries.org/innovations-old/2014-innovations /health-wellness-and-safety/healthy-l-i-f-e.

Jackson County Department of Public Health. 2019. "Healthy Carolinians of Jackson County." Accessed July 9, 2019. http://health.jacksonnc.org/healthy-carolinians.

Jaffe, Ina. 2017. "Xbox Bowling for Seniors? Visit Your Local Library." NPR, July 4, 2017. Accessed December 23, 2019. https://www.npr.org/2017/07/04/534431175/xbox -bowling-for-seniors-visit-your-local-library.

Janney, Cristina. 2019. "Library Launches Babynauts, Early Literacy Programs." Hays Post (Kansas), June 3, 2019. Accessed June 4, 2019. https://www.hayspost.com/2019/06/03/library-launches-babynauts-early-literacy-programs/.

Jordan, Mary W. 2013. "Public Library Gardens. Playing a Role in Ecologically Sustainable Communities." In *Public libraries and Resilient Cities*, edited by Michael Dudley, 101–110. Chicago: ALA Editions.

Kansas City Public Library. 2013. "A Health and Wellness Desert." Urban Libraries Council. Accessed December 24, 2019. https://www.urbanlibraries.org/innovations-old/2013-innovations/health-wellness-safety/a-health-and-wellness-desert.

Kaplan, Allison. 2014. "Get Up and Move! Why Movement Is Part of Early Literacy Skills Development." University of Wisconsin Madison Webinar Series. Accessed July 9, 2019. http://ics.webcast.uwex.edu/Mediasite6/Play/742415b55a104bb7a9cfb5542de850d41d.

Kimmelman, Arlen. 2017. "Booking on a Bike." Presentation at the New Jersey Library Association Conference, Atlantic City, NJ, April 25, 2017. Accessed December 23, 2019. https://docs.google.com/presentation/d/1S-Hl2QMUYMUD3rzeDzbU7z12z0399wC2m9k-S8PycGc/edit#slide=id.p4.

Klinenberg, Eric. 2018. *Palaces for the People: How Social Infrastructure Can Help Fight Inequality, Polarization, and the Decline of Civic Life*. New York City: Penguin Random House.

Lenstra, Noah. 2017. "Movement-Based Programs in US and Canadian Public Libraries: Evidence of Impacts from an Exploratory Survey." *Evidence Based Library and Information Practice* 12 (4): 214–32.

Lenstra, Noah. 2018a. "Bike Check-Out: Coming Soon to a Library Near You?" *Public Libraries Online*, March 10, 2018. Accessed December 23, 2019. http://publiclibrariesonline.org/2018/03/bike-check-out-coming-soon-to-a-library-near-you.

Lenstra, Noah. 2018b. "The Cooperative Extension System: Your Library's Go-To Partner for Gardening, Nutrition, and Healthy Living Programming." *Programming Librarian* (blog), September 13, 2018. Accessed December 23, 2019. http://www.programminglibrarian.org/blog/cooperative-extension-system-your-library%E2%80%99s-go-partner-gardening-nutrition-and-healthy-living.

Lenstra, Noah. 2018c. "December 2018 Newsletter." Let's Move in Libraries. Accessed July 9, 2019. http://letsmovelibraries.org/newsletter-december-2018.

Lenstra, Noah. 2018d. "Don't Do It All Yourself: Creating Health Fairs through Partnerships." *Programming Librarian* (blog), March 20, 2018. Accessed December 23, 2019. http://programminglibrarian.org/blog/don%E2%80%99t-do-it-all-yourself-creating-health-fairs-through-partnerships.

Lenstra, Noah. 2018e. "The Experiences of Public Library Staff Developing Programs with Physical Activities: An Exploratory Study in North Carolina." *Library Quarterly* 88 (2): 142–59.

Lenstra, Noah. 2018f. "Health and Wellness at the library." *Public Libraries Online*, April 12, 2018. Accessed December 23, 2019. http://publiclibrariesonline.org/2018/04/health-and-wellness-at-the-library.

Lenstra, Noah. 2018g. "Health and Wellness Programming: Collaborating with Local Businesses." *Programming Librarian* (blog), August 2, 2018. Accessed December 23,

2019. http://programminglibrarian.org/blog/health-and-wellness-programming-colla borating-local-businesses.

Lenstra, Noah. 2018h. "'I Didn't Expect to See That at the Library': Fun Palace Engages Community." *Public Libraries Online*, September 4, 2018. Accessed December 23, 2019. http://publiclibrariesonline.org/2018/09/i-didnt-expect-to-see-that-at-the-library -fun-palace-engages-community.

Lenstra, Noah. 2018i. "Let's Move! Fitness Programming in Public Libraries." *Public Library Quarterly* 37 (1): 61–80.

Lenstra, Noah. 2018j. "Partnering with Academic Institutions for Health and Wellness Programming." *Programming Librarian* (blog), December 19, 2018. Accessed December 23, 2019. http://www.programminglibrarian.org/blog/partnering-academic -institutions-health-and-wellness-programming.

Lenstra, Noah. 2018k. "The Role of Public Librarians in Supporting Physical Activity." In *Challenging the "Jacks of All Trades but Masters of None" Librarian Syndrome*, edited by George J. Fowler and Samantha Schmehl Hines, 185–205. Bingley, UK: Emerald Publishing Limited.

Lenstra, Noah. 2019a. "4 Ways to Play with the YMCA." *Programming Librarian* (blog), May 17, 2019. Accessed December 23, 2019. http://programminglibrarian.org/blog/4 -ways-play-ymca.

Lenstra, Noah. 2019b. "Go4Life in Libraries Report—Spring 2019." Let's Move in Libraries. Accessed December 23, 2019. http://letsmovelibraries.org/go4life-in-libraries.

Lenstra, Noah. 2019c. "Health and Wellness: Worthy of Full-Time Programming." *Programming Librarian* (blog), April 25, 2019. Accessed December 23, 2019. http://programminglibrarian.org/blog/health-and-wellness-worthy-full-time -programming.

Lenstra, Noah. 2019d. "Scouts Can Help Make Your StoryWalk® Grow." *Programming Librarian* (blog), June 19, 2019. Accessed December 23, 2019. http://programminglibrarian .org/blog/scouts-can-help-make-your-storywalk%C2%AE-grow.

Lenstra, Noah. 2019e. "Thinking Outside of the Stacks: The Growth of Nature Smart Libraries." Children & Nature Network, June 20, 2019. Accessed December 23, 2019. https:// www.childrenandnature.org/2019/06/20/thinking-outside-of-the-stacks-the-growth -of-nature-smart-libraries.

Lenstra, Noah, and Jenny Carlos. 2019. "Public Libraries and Walkable Neighborhoods." *International Journal of Environmental Research and Public Health* 16 (10): 1780.

Lenstra, Noah, and Christine D'Arpa. 2019. "Food Justice in the Public Library: Information, Resources, and Meals." *International Journal of Information, Diversity, & Inclusion* 3 (3): 1–24.

Lenstra, Noah, Katie Scherrer, and Barbara Scott. 2018. "Movin' and Groovin' at the Library." Presentation at the Association for Library Services to Children's Institute, Cincinnati, Ohio, September 27–29, 2018. Accessed December 23, 2019. http://letsmovelibraries .org/movin-and-groovin-in-the-library.

Lesneski, Traci. 2017. "Get Moving: Library Design." *Library Journal*, September 26, 2017. Accessed December 23, 2019. https://www.libraryjournal.com/?detailStory=get -moving-library-design.

Lorain Public Library System. 2019. "Lorain Bike Share." Accessed July 9, 2019. https://www.lorainpubliclibrary.org/blog?action=show&id=579.

Luo, Lili. 2018. "Health Information Programming in Public Libraries: A Content Analysis." *Public Library Quarterly* 37 (3): 233–47.

Maize Unified School District 266. 2018. "Read and Ride Program Celebrates Technology, Reading, and Exercise." Accessed December 23, 2019. https://www.usd266.com/site/default.aspx?PageType=3&DomainID=8&ModuleInstanceID=3374&ViewID=6446EE88-D30C-497E-9316-3F8874B3E108&RenderLoc=0&FlexDataID=7551&PageID=9.

Maryland Today Staff. 2018. "Unlikely Library Loans: Students Needing Study Break Can Borrow Sports Equipment." *Maryland Today*, December 7, 2018. Accessed December 23, 2019. https://today.umd.edu/articles/unlikely-library-loans-748bf068-cf9d-4f05-8e00-f546a8c6d3b6.

Matos, Nefertiti. 2018. "Accessible Personal Fitness: Tips, Tech, and Resources." *Barrier-Free Library* (blog), New York Public Library. April 3, 2018. Accessed December 23, 2019. https://www.nypl.org/blog/2018/04/03/accessible-personal-fitness-disabilities-tips-tech.

McChesney, Elizabeth M., and Bryan W. Wunar. 2017. *Summer Matters: Making All Learning Count.* Chicago: ALA Editions.

McNeil, Heather. 2012. *Read, Rhyme, and Romp: Early Literacy Skills and Activities for Librarians, Teachers, and Parents.* Santa Barbara, CA: ABC-CLIO.

Meyers-Martin, Coleen, and Laurie Borchard. 2015. "The Finals Stretch: Exams Week Library Outreach Surveyed," *Reference Services Review* 43 (4): 510–32.

Miller, Carolyn E., and Anita Chandra. 2018. "Measuring Progress toward a Culture of Health . . . at the Library." *Health Affairs.* https://doi.org/10.1377/hblog20181119.551788.

Monaghan, Elizabeth Michaelson. 2016. "The Library Is In." *Library Journal*, October 6, 2016, 28–31. Accessed December 23, 2019. https://www.libraryjournal.com/?detailStory=the-library-is-in.

Moore, Phyllis. 2018. "Library Garden Plows Ahead." *Goldsboro News-Argus*, October 30, 2018. Accessed October 31, 2018. https://www.newsargus.com/news/library-garden-plows-ahead/article_d85058af-309a-50b3-91fa-61cb64a4dc7e.html.

Morgan, Elizabeth. 2019. "Library District to Review Upcoming Contract." *Clearwater Tribune*, April 17, 2019. Accessed December 23, 2019. https://www.clearwatertribune.com/news/top_stories/library-district-to-review-upcoming-contract/article_c95eedc2-6130-11e9-9aaf-5f831e2508ab.html.

Morris, Liz. 2016. "Community Health Program Worksheet." OCLC/WebJunction. Accessed July 9, 2019. https://www.webjunction.org/documents/webjunction/community-health-program-worksheet.html.

Mulholland, Jessica. 2011. "Libraries Now Offering Books and Workouts." Governing, March 2011. https://www.governing.com/topics/health-human-services/Libraries-Now-Offering-Books-and-Workouts.html.

Nashville Public Library. 2019. "Be Well at NPL." Accessed July 11, 2019. https://library.nashville.org/event/be-well-npl.

Nashville Public Library Foundation. 2018. "Libraries Transform: 2017–2018 Annual Report." Accessed July 11, 2019. https://www.paperturn-view.com/nplf/npl?pid=NDI42131 (site discontinued).

National Association of Counties. 2019. "Fighting Food Insecurity and the Summer Slide." NACo Achievement Award Search. Accessed December 23, 2019. https://explorer.naco.org/cf_naco/cffiles_web/awards/Award_program.cfm?SEARCHID=108461.

National Center for Chronic Disease Prevention and Health Promotion (NCCDPHP), Centers for Disease Control and Prevention. 2019. "Division of Nutrition, Physical Activity, and Obesity at a Glance." Accessed July 9, 2019. https://www.cdc.gov/chronicdisease/resources/publications/aag/dnpao.htm.

National Center for Complementary and Integrative Health. 2019. "About NCCIH." Accessed July 9, 2019. https://nccih.nih.gov/about.

Neil, Emily. 2018. "Fresh Produce Market a Breath of Fresh Air for North Philly Community." *Al Día*, May 7, 2018. Accessed December 23, 2019. https://aldianews.com/articles/culture/health/fresh-produce-market-breath-fresh-air-north-philly-community/52552.

Niagara Falls Public Library. 2018. "Niagara Falls Public Library Strategic Plan, 2018–2023." Accessed July 9, 2019. http://www.niagarafallspubliclib.org/FINAL-NFPL-sp-2018-smaller.pdf.

Nicholson, Gilbert. 2017. "Gadsden City High School Program a Tasty Success." Alabama News Center, December 5, 2017. https://alabamanewscenter.com/2017/12/05/gadsden-city-high-school-program-a-tasty-success.

Nicholson, Scott. 2010. *Everyone Plays at the Library: Creating Great Gaming Experiences for All Ages*. Medford, NJ: Information Today.

North Carolina Division of Public Health. 2011. "Faithful Families Eating Smart and Moving More." Accessed December 24, 2019. http://eatsmartmovemoresc.org/pdf/2011SummitPresentations/Faith/FFESMM-Guide-FINAL.pdf.

Oklahoma Department of Libraries. 2018. "Library Services and Technology Act Five-Year Plan, 2018–2022." Accessed July 9, 2019. https://libraries.ok.gov/LSTA/LSTA.Plan.2018-2022.pdf.

Pateman, John, and Ken Williment. 2016. *Developing Community-Led Public Libraries: Evidence from the UK and Canada*. London: Routledge.

Payerchin, Richard. 2019. "Sidewalks, Bike Lanes on Project List for Lorain." *Morning Journal*, June 18, 2019. Accessed December 23, 2019. https://www.morningjournal.com/news/lorain-county/sidewalks-bike-lanes-on-project-list-for-lorain/article_039816a6-9144-11e9-a6c8-d782d21fa58e.html.

Pendleton Community Library. 2019. "Read 'n' Feed." Accessed July 9, 2019. https://www.pendleton.lib.in.us/get-involved/read-and-feed.

Philbin, Morgan M., Caroline M. Parker, Mary Grace Flaherty, and Jennifer S. Hirsch. 2019. "Public Libraries: A Community-Level Resource to Advance Population Health." *Journal of Community Health* 44 (1): 192–99. https://doi.org/10.1007/s10900-018-0547-4.

Phillips, Roberta, Sallie Hambright-Belue, and Constantina Green. 2018. "Fresh Food, Fresh Thinking: An Innovative Approach to Youth Development and Learning in Rural Communities." Public Library Association webinar. Accessed July 9, 2019. http://www.ala.org/pla/education/onlinelearning/webinars/ondemand/fresh.

Plagman, Emily. 2019. "Measuring the Success of Health Programs and Services." Public Library Association webinar, May 29, 2019. Accessed December 23, 2019. http://www .ala.org/pla/education/onlinelearning/webinars/ondemand/measuringhealth.

Poland, Katie. 2018. "Read and Ride in the Library." DonorsChoose.org, March 1, 2018. Accessed December 23, 2019. https://www.donorschoose.org/project/read-and-ride -in-the-library/3105343.

Prato, Stephanie. 2014. "Music and Movement at the Library." *Association for Library Services to Children Blog*, Accessed July 9, 2019. http://www.alsc.ala.org/blog/2014/11/music -and-movement-at-the-library.

Public Library Association, a Division of the American Library Association. 2016. "PLA Focus Groups: 2016 PLA Conference: Part B: Health." Unpublished manuscript in the author's possession.

Purcell Register. 2019. "Play Street Program a Hit: Program's Numbers Far Exceed Expectations." *Purcell Register*, July 11, 2019. Accessed December 23, 2019. http://www .purcellregister.com/news/play-street-program-a-hit/article_af527c7a-a337-11e9 -bca9-ebb7858dc38f.html.

Quatrella, Laura, and Barbara Blosveren. 1994. "Sweat and Self-Esteem: A Public Library Supports Young Women." *Wilson Library Bulletin* 68 (7): 34–36, 139.

Richmond, Andy. 2012. "Running and Reading at Rye Public Library." *Granite State Libraries* 48 (3): 12.

Robert Wood Johnson Foundation. 2017. "Fun and Fitness in a Library Parking Lot." Accessed July 9, 2019. https://www.youtube.com/watch?v=ES5tQCRCyeI.

Robotham, John S., and Lydia LaFleur. 1976. *Library Programs: How to Select, Plan and Produce Them*. Metuchen, NJ: Scarecrow Press.

Roth, Elizabeth. 2018. "Be Well at NPL: Let's Move in Libraries Webinar." Accessed July 11, 2019. https://www.youtube.com/watch?v=UkRIdDyBxdk.

Rubenstein, Ellen L. 2012. "From Social Hygiene to Consumer Health: Libraries, Health Information, and the American Public from the Late Nineteenth Century to the 1980s." *Library & Information History* 28 (3): 202–19.

Salt Lake City Public Library. 2018. "Strategic Roadmap." Accessed July 9, 2019. http://www .slcpl.org/files/board/strategicroadmap032618.pdf.

Salt Lake County Library Services. 2014. Sustainability Initiative. Urban Libraries Council. Accessed December 24, 2019. https://www.urbanlibraries.org/innovations-old/2014 -innovations/sustainability/sustainability-initiative.

San Antonio Public Library. 2012. "Building a Teen Nutrition Program." Urban Libraries Council. https://www.urbanlibraries.org/innovations/building-a-teen-nutrition-program.

San Francisco Public Library. 2016. "Biblio Bistro." Urban Libraries Council. Accessed December 24, 2019. https://www.urbanlibraries.org/innovations/biblio-bistro.

San Francisco Public Library. 2019. "Summer Stride 2019." Accessed July 9, 2019. https:// sfpl.org/?pg=2001098901.

Santa Clarita Library. 2017. "Needs Assessment for the Saugus Library Center." Accessed July 9, 2019. http://www.santaclaritalibrary.com/about/saugus-library-center/needs -assessment-for-the-saugus-library-center.

Scherrer, Katie. 2017. *Stories, Songs, and Stretches! Creating Playful Storytimes with Yoga and Movement*. Chicago: American Library Association.

Scott-Martin, Donna. 2018. "3D, Tactile Storybook Walk, Now @ Laurel Branch Courtyard." Prince George's County Memorial Library System, May 7, 2018. Accessed December 23, 2019. https://ww1.pgcmls.info/website/2690.

Slapnik, Jill. 2018. "Active Learning 2: Read and Ride to Retain Info." DonorsChoose.org, March 31, 2018. Accessed December 23, 2019. https://www.donorschoose.org/project/active-learning-2-read-and-ride-to-ret/3184837.

Snape, Robert. 1995. *Leisure and the Rise of the Public Library*. London: Library Association Publishing.

State Library of Ohio. 2019. "State Library of Ohio vs Childhood Hunger!" June 21, 2019. Accessed December 23, 2019. http://www.teamvittles.org/11-news/24-state-library-of-ohio-vs-childhood-hunger.

Stauffer, Suzanne M. 2016. "Supplanting the Saloon Evil and Other Loafing Habits: Utah's Library-Gymnasium Movement, 1907–1912." *Library Quarterly* 86 (4): 434–48.

Stewart, Jennifer. 2019. "Library Walk ON: Build Healthier and Happier Communities with Reading." Princh, January 30, 2019. Accessed December 23, 2019. https://princh.com/library-walk-on-build-healthier-and-happier-communities-with-reading/#.XSUCOZNKi8o.

Swiech, Paul. 2015. "Walking Book Club Provides Spine for Library's Fitness Program." The Pantagraph, November 20, 2015. Accessed December 23, 2019. https://www.pantagraph.com/lifestyles/health-med-fit/walking-book-club-provides-spine-for-library-s-fitness-program/article_8ad2cae9-e344-53d8-ab9d-318e68684c10.html.

Taylor, Jermaine. 2014. "Stationary Bikes Join Books in Virginia School Library." *School Library Journal*, February 17, 2014. Accessed December 23, 2019. https://web.archive.org/web/20150318050353/http://www.slj.com/2014/02/buildings/stationary-bikes-join-books-in-virginia-school-library.

Team Vittles. 2018. "Feed the Whole Child: Un-Limiting Approaches to Filling Children's Heads, Bellies, and Hearts." Accessed July 9, 2019. http://www.teamvittles.org/images/PPT/ALSC.pptx.

Thompson, Anna. 2015. "NHHS Receives Bikes So Students Can 'Read and Ride.'" WECT-6 News. November 18, 2015. Accessed December 23, 2019. http://www.wect.com/story/30544021/nhhs-receives-bikes-so-students-can-read-and-ride.

Thompson, John. 2018. "Storybook Trail Has Successful Debut Despite Snow." *Johnson City Press*, December 5, 2018. Accessed December 23, 2019. https://www.johnsoncitypress.com/Education/2018/12/05/Storybook-Trail-has-successful-debut-despite-snow-and-wind.

Toner, Valerie. 2018. "Lunch & Literacy: A Library's Tale of Curbing Summer Hunger." Alliance for a Healthier Generation, June 7, 2018. Accessed December 23, 2019. https://www.healthiergeneration.org/articles/lunch-literacy-a-librarys-tale-of-curbing-summer-hunger.

Trapp Davis, Jeffrey. 2017. *The Collection All Around: Sharing Our Cities, Towns, and Natural Places*. Chicago: ALA Editions.

United States Department of Agriculture. 2019. "What Is MyPlate?" Accessed July 9, 2019. https://www.choosemyplate.gov/WhatIsMyPlate.

United States Department of Health and Human Services. 2010. "Let's Move Faith and Communities: Toolkit for Faith-Based & Neighborhood Organizations." Accessed July 9, 2019. https://www.hhs.gov/sites/default/files/lets_move_toolkit.pdf.

United States Department of Health and Human Services. 2018. "Move Your Way." Accessed July 9, 2019. https://health.gov/moveyourway.

University of Colorado, Children, Youth and Environments Center for Community Engagement. 2011. "Benefits of Gardening for Children." Fact Sheet 3, October 2011. Accessed December 23, 2019. https://www.colorado.edu/cedar/sites/default/files/attached-files/Gardening_factsheet_2011.pdf.

Vaughan, Todd. 2016. "Little Free Pantry Helps Families in Need: The Library Accepts Donations of Food and Household Items." *Sylvan Lake News*, September 27, 2016. Accessed December 23, 2019. https://www.sylvanlakenews.com/news/little-free-pantry-helps-families-in-need.

Vian, Jourdan. 2019. "La Crosse Residents Looking for Flexibility out of Combined Senior Center, Library Project." *La Crosse Tribune*, May 15, 2019. Accessed December 23, 2019. https://lacrossetribune.com/news/local/la-crosse-residents-looking-for-flexibility-out-of-combined-senior/article_1d565b86-0dd5-56e6-86b6-cc2ddd891395.html.

Vilelle, Luke. 2017. "Uniquely Lendable Collections." *Virginia Libraries* 62, no. 1. Accessed December 23, 2019. http://www.ejournals.ejournals.vtlibraries.net/valib/article/view/1577.

Wallis, Lori. 2016. "Reading + Peddling = Smarter, More Active Kids." DonorsChoose.org. August 22, 2016. Accessed December 23, 2019. https://www.donorschoose.org/project/reading-peddling-smarter-more-activ/2145647.

Warwick Valley Central School District. 2018. "Warwick's First StoryWalk Installation Features Student Artwork." August 13, 2018. Accessed December 23, 2019. https://www.warwickvalleyschools.com/warwicks-first-storywalk-installation-features-student-artwork.

Weekes, Lisa, and Barbara Longair. 2016. "Physical Literacy in the Library at Lethbridge Public Library." *BCLA Connect*, January 31, 2016. Accessed December 23, 2019. https://bclaconnect.ca/perspectives/2016/01/31/physical-literacy-in-the-library.

Whiteman, Eliza D., Roxanne Dupuis, Anna U. Morgan, Bernadette D'Alonzo, Caleb Epstein, Heather Klusaritz, and Carolyn C. Cannuscio. 2018. "Peer Reviewed: Public Libraries as Partners for Health." Preventing Chronic Disease 15. https://doi.org/10.5888%2Fpcd15.170392.

Wiegand, Wayne A. 2017. "Falling Short of Their Profession's Needs: Education and Research in Library and Information Studies." *Journal of Education for Library and Information Science* 58 (1): 39–43.

Wisconsin Library Association. Youth Services Section. 2017. "Dance! Dance! Dance!" *Youth Services Shout-Out: YSS Blog.* Accessed July 9, 2019. http://yssevents.blogspot.com/2017/01/dance-dance-dance.html.

World Health Organization. 2018a. "More Active People for a Healthier World: The Global Action Plan on Physical Activity 2018–2030." Accessed July 9, 2019. https://www.who.int/ncds/prevention/physical-activity/gappa.

World Health Organization. 2018b. "WHO Launches ACTIVE: A Toolkit for Countries to Increase Physical Activity and Reduce Noncommunicable Diseases." October 17, 2018. Accessed December 23, 2019. https://www.who.int/ncds/prevention/physical-activity/active-toolkit/en.

World Health Organization. 2019. "Noncommunicable Diseases and Their Risk Factors." Accessed July 9, 2019. https://www.who.int/ncds/prevention/en.

Yu-Yuk Jung, Deborah. 2015. "Learning through Movement: Applying Exercise Education and Movement Activities in a Library Setting." Charlotte Teachers Institute. Accessed July 9, 2019. http://charlotteteachers.org/wp-content/uploads/2016/01/DJung_unit _11-22-15.pdf.

Zaker, Jessica. 2014. "'I've Never Been So Sweaty in a Library': Programs That Pop." *Library Journal*, January 10, 2014. Accessed December 23, 2019. https://www.libraryjournal .com/?detailStory=ive-never-been-so-sweaty-in-a-library-programs-that-pop.

Index

About the Author

Noah Lenstra directs the Let's Move in Libraries initiative at the University of North Carolina–Greensboro, where he is a faculty member in library and information studies. He has served on the Public Library Association's Health Literacy National Advisory Board, and his research on healthy physical activity promotion in public libraries has been published in *Library Quarterly*, *Evidence Based Library and Information Practice*, and the *Journal of Library Administration*, among others. He blogs for *Public Libraries Online* and the *Programming Librarian*. He's always up for trying a new form of physical activity!

CPSIA information can be obtained
at www.ICGtesting.com
Printed in the USA
BVHW040611311020
592253BV00020B/161